D1430023

QUICK & EASY
COOKING

KNACK™

QUICK & EASY
COOKING

A Step-by-Step Guide to Meals in Minutes

LINDA JOHNSON LARSEN

PHOTOGRAPHS BY LIESA COLE

Guilford, Connecticut
An imprint of The Globe Pequot Press

Copyright © 2009 by Morris Book Publishing, LLC

Editor-in-Chief: Maureen Graney
Editor: Katie Benoit
Cover Design: Paul Beatrice, Bret Kerr
Text Design: Paul Beatrice
Layout: Kevin Mak
Cover photos by Liesa Cole
All interior photos by Liesa Cole with the exception of p. 1 (right): Bret
Kerr/Globe Pequot Press; p. 17 (right): Edward Hardam/shutterstock;
p. 18 (right): Courtesy of Oneida Ltd, photo by James Demarest; p. 22
(left): Courtesy of Polder; p. 22 (right): Courtesy of www.brookstone
.com; p. 27 (right): © Joe Gough | Dreamstime.com; p. 28 (right):
MalibuBooks/shutterstock; p. 30 (right): Robert Pernell/shutterstock;
p. 31 (left): jocicalek/shutterstock; p. 34 (right): George Peters/
istockphoto; p. 69 (left): Debi Harbin; p. 152-53: Debi Harbin

Library of Congress Cataloging-in-Publication Data is available on file.

ISBN 978-1-59921-513-6

The following manufacturers/names appearing in *Knack Quick & Easy
Cooking* are trademarks:
Boboli®, Crock-Pot®, eBay®, Prepara® Trio Tri-Blade Peeler, Silpat®,
Tabasco®

Printed in China

10 9 8 7 6 5 4 3 2 1

To my dear husband Doug, as always

Acknowledgments

Thanks go to my agent Barb Doyen, my editors Katie Benoit and Maureen Graney, and especially to my family who has always supported me.

~Linda Johnson Larsen

I would like to thank my talented, tireless, and good-humored accomplices: Specifically, thank you to Anthony Rodio for his photo assistance and digital tech expertise (not to mention his role as "supreme taster"). Thanks to my favorite culinary craftsmen, Jonathon Schnoer and Christophe Nicolet., as well as the incomparable Chatham Hellmers for the styling, propping, and entertainment she provided. Linda, these recipes really are delicious and so deceptively simple to prepare! Thank you, Maureen, and all the wonderful people at Globe Pequot for including us on such a satisfying project!

~Liesa Cole, photographer (Omni Studio)

CONTENTS

INTRODUCTION

Quick and easy cooking is all the rage these days, epitomized in 30-minute meals and five-ingredient recipes. But there's more to quick cooking than short cooking times and tiny ingredient lists. You must have an organized kitchen, understand cooking concepts, and be proficient in several kitchen skills.

The first thing you need to learn is how to read a recipe. If this is your first foray into the kitchen, read through some simple recipes and make sure that you understand all the terms and directions. You have to read and understand every recipe completely before you can begin.

There are lots of large cookbooks that define cooking terms, or you can look for information on the Internet. Never assume that you know what a term means; if you're unsure, look it up. Start by making some simple recipes, preferably those that can be completed in a short amount of time, with a short ingredient list, and with little or no cooking. Once you're comfortable using basic kitchen tools and working with food, you can proceed.

Then you'll need to organize your kitchen. Any kitchen can be made more efficient by knowing exactly what you have on hand and where it's stored. Every utensil, pot, pan, spice jar, and can of tomatoes should have a "home" in your kitchen. And when it's used and washed, it should be put away in that home. If you have to stop and search for a tool or an ingredient, you're wasting valuable time in the kitchen.

Your kitchen consists of a refrigerator, freezer, pantry or shelf space, appliances, and countertop. Take a good, hard look at the kitchen and see if there are some things you can change. Most kitchens benefit from adding a table or portable butcherblock counter to increase your work space. Each appliance should have landing space nearby to hold pots, pans, and bowls. You can't move your appliances, but you can reassign equipment to different spaces around the kitchen, making each item more accessible to the appliance it's used with.

Food safety is the next lesson. If your food isn't wholesome and safe, it doesn't matter how good it tastes or how perfectly it's cooked. You must follow these rules for best results. Always wash your hands before and after handling food. And wash your hands and utensils again with hot soapy water after you've handled perishable foods that need cooking before serving: raw beef, pork, chicken, seafood, and eggs.

Never let cooked perishable food stand out of refrigeration longer than two hours, or one hour if the ambient room temperature is above 90 degrees F. Those same perishable foods should be refrigerated promptly after cooking if they aren't going to be served immediately.

Never partially cook meat and refrigerate or freeze it. That will put it through the danger zone of 40 degrees F to 140 degrees F too many times. Always completely cook meat if you plan on holding it for later consumption or freezing it for later use. Meats and eggs have to be cooked to specific internal temperatures. Cook steak to 140 degrees F, pork to 155 degrees F, ground meat to 165 degrees F, and chicken to 170 degrees F. Cook seafood until it flakes with a fork, and cook eggs until the yolks are firm. The exception to the egg rule is if you use pasteurized eggs; they can be cooked until the white is firm and the yolk soft.

Finally, keep cooked and uncooked foods separate. Never place cooked meat on the same platter used to hold the uncooked food. And be sure to wrap raw meats well and don't let their juices drip onto foods like fruits or vegetables.

There are many appliances that will help you cook food quickly and easily. When you buy a new appliance, whether it's a dual contact indoor grill or an immersion blender, be sure that you read the manufacturer's instruction booklet from front to back before you use it.

The booklet has lots of safety information, and there are usually some easy recipes that will get you started using that appliance.

Now that you have an organized kitchen arranged for maximum efficiency, and you understand the basics of cooking and food safety, it's time to concentrate on filling the pantry, freezer, and fridge. Everyone should have basic items like oil, flour, salt, pepper, butter, eggs, milk, and canned and frozen fruits and vegetables. The items you choose beyond that will depend on the recipes you make.

Salads and simple side dishes are probably the easiest foods to make. Salads, which are just combined and tossed with a dressing, can be an entire meal. Following these easy recipes will give you a lot of confidence. And a side dish, like roasted potatoes or scalloped corn, is perfect for accompanying a rotisserie chicken from the deli or one of those marinated salmon fillets you just bake and eat.

If your family loves beef, start by cooking simple beef recipes. Marinated and grilled or broiled steak, beef stir-fries, and casseroles are good recipes to choose. A meat pasta sauce, served over linguine or penne, and a classic meatloaf are easy to make too.

For chicken lovers, look for recipes using baked, pan-fried, or broiled boneless, skinless chicken breasts. This cut of poultry is the easiest to work with, it cooks very quickly, and it's adaptable to many cuisines and flavors. For seafood lovers, boneless fish fillets are the easiest to handle and cook. This type of fish cooks very quickly and is so mild you can use it in almost any recipe. Fish soups, grilled fish, and broiled fish are the fastest quick-cooking seafood recipes. And for pork lovers, look for simple recipes that use pork tenderloin and pork chops. Both of these cuts of meat cook quickly, are easy to work with, and again pair well with almost any ethnic cuisine flavors.

Once you've become comfortable making the basic recipes for each different cut of meat and the different categories of recipes, you can start having fun. Create your own recipes using your favorite flavors and foods.

For instance, once you've mastered broiling fish fillets with a simple mustard glaze, make your own glaze using Tex-Mex ingredients like chili powder, serrano peppers, and salsa. Or add a Spanish flair by using paprika, ground almonds, some chopped olives, and a lemon sour cream glaze.

When you are comfortable making a basic recipe, it's time to branch out! Use the same type of food, proportions, and cooking times as in the original recipe but add your own touch. Use your family's favorite ingredients, or change the seasonings, spices, and herbs to the ones you like best. Substitute mushrooms and green bell peppers for cherry tomatoes and zucchini in a chicken quiche, or add some jalapeño peppers and spicy salsa to a salad for some extra zing.

When you create a recipe that you and your family love, be sure to write it down. It's hard to recreate a successful recipe from memory, even if it's very simple. Keep notes as you work and your cooking skills will get better and better as your repertoire increases.

Now let's get started cooking! The initial work and preparation to transform your kitchen into a quick and easy kitchen seems daunting, but once you've accomplished that, you'll be able to get an excellent and delicious dinner on the table in about 30 minutes, start to finish.

THE QUICK AND EASY KITCHEN

An organized workspace, from a work triangle to pantry shelves, is key to quick cooking

A well-stocked and organized pantry, fridge, and freezer are key to quick and easy cooking. With a good supply of food on hand in an organized space to make tried-and-true recipes, you'll be able to whip up great breakfasts, lunches, snacks, and dinners at a moment's notice.

Even if you have a less than desirable kitchen, you can arrange the work space and equipment to help you prepare food quickly and efficiently. You can add a small portable table for more work space, clear paths between appliances, and set up mini work stations. A large kitchen can be broken down into several preparation areas so more than one person can comfortably work in the space.

Workspace Options

- Add a portable butcher block table to the center or edge of your kitchen.

- Be sure there is counter space next to the fridge, stove, pantry, and sink.

- Clear any unnecessary items from the counters.

- If you don't use an appliance every day, it should be in a drawer or cupboard.

- Sort through drawers and cupboards. Throw away food older than 6 months.

- Store or give away utensils or equipment you have not used in a year.

- Under-cabinet racks can hold cookbooks, wine glasses, and utensils.

- Know where everything is in your kitchen.

Work Triangle

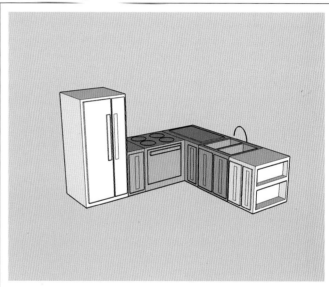

- In the traditional work triangle, the sink, stove, and fridge make up the 3 points.

- The distance between the points of the triangle should be 4 to 9 feet. Any closer, and there isn't enough counter space. Any longer, and cooking will be tiring.

- That's a good arrangement, but some larger kitchens may have 2 or even 3 work triangles.

- An island can break up several triangles so more than one cook can perform tasks in comfort.

It's important to keep the counters free of clutter; if you find that your counters are used for everything from homework to bill paying, find other areas of the house for those tasks and keep the counters free for cooking.

Keep the kitchen, refrigerator, freezer, and pantry clean and well organized. Everything, from foil to canned beans, should have a "home"; then you can find what you need. And make sure that every utensil, piece of equipment, food item, and tool is returned to its home after it is used and cleaned.

Shopping and Organizing Tips

- Shopping efficiently not only can save you money, but saves time. Make a list every time you go shopping, stick to it, and use coupons whenever possible.

- Shop at off-hours, make sure you know the layout of the grocery store, and plan your list according to that layout.

- Try not to take children with you when shopping. Use coupons as much as possible, and come straight home from the store.

- Your pantry should be organized by food category. Make sure you can see all the food; use risers for a better view.

Organized Fridge and Freezer

- Clean out the refrigerator once a week, so you know what foods need to be used and replenished.

- Remove everything, check the use-by dates, throw away old food, and clean the shelves with soapy water.

- Clean your freezer every 3–4 months. For most energy efficiency, the freezer should be full.

- A notebook placed next to the freezer will help you remember what's inside, what you should use by certain dates, and what you need to replenish.

FRIDGE STAPLES

These staples are used in almost every recipe

Many of the ingredients used in these recipes must be stored in the refrigerator after opening. Most have use-by dates or best-if-used-by dates stamped onto the package.

If they do not, write the date you purchased the item on the label using a waterproof pen. Most staples like salad dressings, mayonnaise, and cheeses should be used within one to two months of opening.

Fresh fruits and vegetables can be stored only for a few days until they lose quality or start to wilt or develop soft spots.

Meats should be used or frozen within one to three days; seafood sooner, pork, chicken and beef a bit later. And dairy products have sell-by dates. You can use these one week past the sell-by date; no longer.

Organize your refrigerator by using the shelves to group the

Refrigerator Staples

- Milk
- Orange and other juices
- Eggs
- Butter
- Cheeses
- Salad dressings
- Ketchup and mustard
- Mayonnaise
- Soy sauce and teriyaki sauce
- Pickles and olives
- Cream cheese and butter spreads
- Sour cream and yogurt

Dairy Products

- It is very important to follow the use-by dates on dairy products. Throw away any product past its date.

- Keep dairy products in the body of the refrigerator, not the door (except for butter and milk), because the door area is warmer.

- Think about using the drawers to hold these products, which can be stored for longer periods of time.

- Keep milk, cream, buttermilk, yogurt, and cheeses tightly wrapped or sealed, because they can easily pick up stray refrigerator odors.

food. Keep all dairy products on the top shelf, use the second shelf for salad dressings and cheeses, and the third and fourth shelves for the perishable products you buy and use frequently. The door is a good place to store ketchup, mustard, pickles, and olives. Oddly enough, the door, which usually has those cute little indentations to hold eggs, is not the place to store them; it's too warm. Keep eggs in their original carton in the body of the fridge. A notepad with a magnetic back and attached pencil should be on your refrigerator to keep track of foods you need to add to your shopping list.

GREEN ● LIGHT

The temperature of your refrigerator must stay just below 40 degrees F. This is the cut-off point where bacteria start to grow. To be sure your refrigerator is safe, purchase a refrigerator thermometer. Hang it on the front of the middle shelf, toward the side, so you can see it every time you open the fridge.

Condiments

- Even condiments like soy sauce, hoisin sauce, ketchup, and mustard eventually need to be replaced.

- If there is no use-by date on the label, write down the date of purchase and use them within 6 months.

- Read labels carefully. Many condiments instruct you to store them in the refrigerator once opened; others do not.

- In the door, arrange the bottles by height, placing the taller products at the back. It's easier to see what you have at a glance.

Eggs and Butter

- Keep eggs in their carton, even if your door has those cute little hollows for holding eggs. The jostling from opening and closing the door is too much.

- If you buy pasteurized eggs for food safety reasons, remember they have very short expiration ranges.

- Pasteurized eggs are only good for a few days after purchase, so buy only what you need at one time.

- Butter lasts for a long time as long as it is well wrapped. Keep it in the butter shelf in the door.

PANTRY STAPLES

A well-stocked pantry helps you make delicious meals at very short notice

The pantry can act as a mini grocery store when it's complete and well stocked. Once you have the staples, buy the fun foods that you use to add flavor and character to your dishes.

Flour, sugar, vinegar, shortening, pastas, and rice are all basic pantry staples. Depending on what you cook and bake, other staples can include canned fruits and vegetables, special seasonings like stir-fry sauces and spice blends, and pasta and cooking sauces.

Have fun and expand your repertoire by buying flavored oils and vinegars, unusual pastas, lots of dried herbs and spices, and exotic canned produce. Take some time every month to

Pantry Staples

- White and whole-wheat flours and cornstarch
- Sugar, brown sugar, honey
- Baking powder, soda, yeast
- Oils, shortening, and vinegars
- Pasta variety
- White, brown, wild, and basmati rice
- Potatoes and onions
- Canned tomato products
- Canned vegetables
- Canned fruits
- Foil, plastic wrap, waxed paper

Organizing Pantry Staples

- Just as you do in the refrigerator, organize your pantry according to food categories.

- On one shelf, keep baking staples like flour, sugar, brown sugar, baking powder, spices, and extracts. Decant dry ingredients into tightly sealed containers.

- On another shelf, store pasta, grains, and rice along with canned fruits and vegetables, juices, and soda.

- And on the other shelves, store measuring equipment, mixing bowls, baking and cake pans, and foil.

go through the aisles at your grocery store and look for new products you may want to try.

Clean out your pantry once every month or two. Remove all items, reorganize if necessary, wash down the shelves, and replace food. Take the time to look at all of the expiration and "best if used by" dates on the products. Use foods close to the dates, or give them to a food shelf if you know you won't use them. Never give expired products away for someone else to use; just toss it. Use wire risers, if necessary, so you can see all the way to the back of the pantry.

ZOOM

Little critters like moths, fruit flies, and other pests love munching on foods like flour, pasta, and rice, and spilled foods like honey and juices. You can buy food-safe traps that will get rid of these pests. Make sure you only purchase traps labeled food-safe. Keep them in your pantry just to make sure your food stays uncontaminated.

Storing Pasta

- Dried pasta keeps well for a long time at room temperature. Have a good selection of different shapes and sizes on hand.

- You can decant the pasta into glass or plastic containers with a tight seal. This is also decorative!

- If you do decant the pasta, be sure to make a note of the cooking time in a small notebook kept on the pasta shelf.

- For problems with pantry pests, there are many food-safe traps you can buy.

Canned Vegetables and Fruits

- A good stash of canned tomato products, plus pasta, can let you make a meal in minutes.

- Canned diced tomatoes, tomato juice, paste, and sauce, and flavored tomato products belong on your pantry shelves.

- Canned vegetables are also important staples. Look for flavored vegetables, like corn with peppers and artichokes packed in a spicy marinade, for double duty.

- Canned fruits add interest to salads and can be the basis for quick and simple desserts.

FREEZER STAPLES

Your freezer can become your own in-house store, with delicious meal starters

A stand-alone freezer is a real luxury and the perfect aid for quick and easy cooking. But with just the freezer attached to your refrigerator, you can stock a great selection of foods that will help you get food on the table in a flash.

Any freezer has to be well organized. You have to know what's in the freezer. No packages of mystery meat are al-

lowed! Wrap and label everything in the freezer, and keep a notebook with a running tab of what the appliance contains. When you use a food from the freezer, cross it out on the running tab. If it's a staple, make a note of it on your grocery list so you can replace it.

You can freeze almost anything as long as it's prepared

Freezer Staples

- Frozen meats
- Puff pastry and phyllo dough
- Bread dough and rolls
- Ice cream
- Frozen mixed and single vegetables
- Frozen fruits and fruit combos
- Frozen chicken breasts and thighs
- Frozen pizza and pizza crust
- Fish and fish sticks
- Shrimp and scallops
- Frozen stock and broth

Frozen Meat

- Meat freezes very well. You should have a good supply of meats, including beef, pork, chicken, and fish in your freezer.

- Well-wrapped meats should be labeled using a grease pencil or waterproof marker. Use meats within 6 months.

- To thaw meat, let it stand in the refrigerator overnight, or if you're going to cook it immediately, use the microwave. Never thaw meats at room temperature.

- You can cook some meats from frozen, especially commercially prepared products. Follow label directions.

and wrapped properly. Be sure to use freezer wrap, paper, or freezer bags; ordinary wraps and foils aren't thick enough to protect the food from the harsh freezer environment.

Just as with the pantry, you must mark and label every food that goes into your freezer. Use a grease pencil. As a general rule, use the food within one year.

Stock your freezer with purchased and homemade foods for your own in-house mini grocery store. Keep in mind that a freezer thermometer is an essential tool. Your freezer should always be at 0 degrees Fahrenheit or lower.

RED ● LIGHT

Never freeze meats in their original packaging. Freezer burn is the number one cause of spoiled meats in this appliance. It is caused by dehydration. The freezer is a very dry place. Improperly wrapped foods will dry out. Remove meat from the original package and wrap in freezer paper, bags, or plastic wrap.

Freezer Tips

- Every freezer is more efficient and freezes food more evenly when it's full. But don't pack food tightly.

- There should be about an inch of airspace around each package so the cold air can circulate.

- Most foods should be thawed in the refrigerator, but some, like breads, can safely thaw at room temperature.

- You can refreeze some foods, like phyllo dough or food that has been thoroughly cooked. Food thawed in the refrigerator can be refrozen, but can lose quality.

Freezing Homemade Foods

- When you add homemade foods to the freezer, they should already be cool.

- You want foods to get quickly out of the danger zone of 40 degrees F to 140 degrees F.

- Refrigerate hot foods or place them in an ice water bath so they cool quickly, then wrap well and freeze.

- If you lose power, don't open the freezer. The food should stay frozen for 24 hours. If it still has ice crystals, it is safe to eat.

SHOP FOR FRESH FOODS

Shop for fresh foods a few times a week to supplement pantry items

Once you have a good stock of food on hand in the pantry, fridge, and freezer, it's time to shop for fresh foods. Shop once or twice a week for these products. Be sure to store certain foods in the refrigerator immediately and wrap according to the needs of that food.

When you shop for perishable foods, plan your trip so you return home immediately. Refrigerate these foods within two hours; one hour in the summer.

Designate a special shelf or spot in your refrigerator and pantry for these fresh foods. Since waste is the biggest food budget-buster, you need to know what you have on hand and use it or freeze it while the food retains quality. Be sure to look through this shelf every day and rotate foods so you use the older foods first, before they lose quality.

Since the refrigerator is very dry, unwrapped fresh foods will quickly dry out, shrivel, or otherwise spoil. More delicate

Fresh Foods

- Strawberries, raspberries, blackberries
- Baby carrots, mushrooms, celery
- Bell peppers, zucchini, and summer squash
- Greens and lettuces
- Ground beef and stew meats
- Chicken breasts and thighs
- Peaches and plums
- Watermelon and cantaloupe
- Tomatoes
- Fresh herbs
- Apples and pears

Fresh Meats

- Fresh meats are very perishable; they should last about 2 to 3 days in your refrigerator. Freeze them after that time.

- Read your refrigerator manual to discover the coldest part of the appliance, then store fresh meats there.

- Some meats have expiration dates that tell you to use or freeze by that time. If not, mark the date of purchase on the meats.

- Use the meat within 3 days of that date, including marinating time. And always marinate meat in the fridge.

foods can also absorb flavors of other foods. It's a good idea to keep everything in your fridge wrapped in good quality bags or wrap.

Meats should always be refrigerated. Leafy greens, and tender fruits and vegetables should be refrigerated too. Others, like apples, pears, and bananas, store best at room temperature. Don't refrigerate tomatoes, potatoes, or onions. The chill changes cell structures, reducing quality and altering flavor in these foods.

ZOOM

Green storage bags claim that they keep produce from becoming too ripe. Independent tests have shown that the bags do help, but the food usually doesn't stay fresh as long as claimed. The best way to prevent waste is to keep an eye on the food and use it at its peak.

Fresh Fruit

- Fresh fruit should be refrigerated, unless it isn't quite ripe. Most fruits ripen well at room temperature.

- Berries are very perishable, should be stored in the refrigerator, and should never be washed until you're ready to use them.

- If you like to bite into a cold, crisp apple or juicy pear, refrigerate the fruit for a few hours before eating.

- Keep fresh fruit well wrapped. The refrigerator is a very dry place, and delicate fruit can shrivel easily.

Fresh Vegetables

- Fresh vegetables that are high in water content, including bell peppers, summer squash, and celery, should be well wrapped.

- Refrigerator drawers have special controls that help regulate temperature and humidity, perfect for fresh produce.

- Be sure to use the produce in those drawers every day. Examine the food for any sign of decay, and keep the drawers impeccably clean.

- Read your manual to learn how to use the temperature and moisture controls in the drawers.

VALUE-ADDED FOODS

Foods that combine more than one ingredient save steps in preparation and cooking

One of the best ways to eliminate time in cooking is to use foods that replace two or more steps. Premade pasta sauces, marinades, salad dressings, and mixes save time in the kitchen.

Be sure to choose value-added foods carefully. Read labels and pick the products that are closest to fresh, with as few artificial ingredients as possible. And look for low-fat and low-sodium versions of these improved products. You may be able to find organic varieties of these foods, or those with enhanced vitamin or mineral content.

Value-added foods for the pantry include marinades, salad dressings, baking mixes, cooking sauces, and flavored vinegars.

Value-Added Foods

- Tortellini and ravioli
- Basil and tomato pestos
- Prepared fruits and veggies
- Marinated meats
- Marinades and salad dressings
- Cake, cookie, and pudding mixes
- Premade pie crusts
- Frozen pasta and vegetable combos
- Pasta and stir-fry sauces
- Alfredo sauce and gravy
- Seasoned canned vegetables

Frozen Pastas

- Frozen pastas include tortellini, ravioli, and pierogies. These foods can be made into a meal with a simple butter sauce.

- Cook the pasta according to package directions. These types of pasta usually just need to be defrosted, so don't overcook them.

- These products are delicious additions to soups and salads, and can be used instead of lasagna noodles for a fast stovetop version.

- Think about substituting value-added pastas for plain pastas in recipes for a nice change of pace.

10

Freezer value-added foods include frozen pastas and pasta/vegetable combinations, fruits, and prepared meats.

And within the past decade, grocery stores have added lots of refrigerator value-added foods, from prepared carrot sticks and fruit combinations to stir-fry blends and salad mixes.

With a good supply of these foods on hand, you'll be able to whip up a pasta dinner or meal on the grill in minutes without having to set food out the door. When you find a product that you like and use, always pick up a can or package or two at the grocery store so you're prepared.

•••••••••••••• GREEN ● LIGHT ••••••••••••••

There are always new value-added foods coming into the market. Take some time each month to look through the canned food, frozen food, and shelf-stable aisles of the supermarket. Try these new foods and add them to your regular shopping list if you and your family like them. Be sure that the value that is added works for you and does save time.

Prepared Pasta Sauce

- The greatest advances in prepared sauces have been in the pasta sauce department. Pesto, Alfredo sauces, and tomato sauces are essentials.

- Bottled gravies and sauces can be high in sodium, so read labels carefully and choose wisely.

- These sauces are great straight out of the jar, or you can add your own twist with herbs, spices, or liqueurs.

- Combine these sauces with prepared vegetables and value-added pastas to save time and serve delicious meals quickly.

Dessert Products

- Desserts can be made in a flash using value-added products like premade pie crusts, whipped topping, and flavored chocolate chips.

- These products do have expiration dates, so follow them closely. Store according to package directions.

- You can make your own value-added products and freeze for later use. Good choices include cookie dough, pie crusts, and bread dough.

- Store a variety of dessert products, from tubs of frosting to tartlet shells to pie crusts and pudding mixes.

POTS AND PANS
Sturdy, well-made pots and pans in a variety of sizes will help you cook most foods

A quality, heavy duty set of pots and pans is essential for quick and easy cooking. You don't need to buy a complete set; buy individual pieces to suit the way you cook.

Look for stainless steel, anodized aluminum, heatproof glass, or cast iron equipment that is solidly made. You may spend more for a good set of pots and pans, but they will last for a lifetime. It's a good idea to look for pots and pans that are ovenproof. That means the handles can be placed in the oven or under the broiler without danger of melting.

Always lift and handle equipment before you buy it. Make sure that the pots and pans feel good in your hand; that the weight is evenly balanced, and that they aren't too heavy.

Cookware Set

- A cookware set should include one 10-inch skillet, one 8-inch sauté pan, one 3-quart and one 2-quart saucepan, a 9-quart stockpot, and an 8-inch skillet.

- Vary this collection depending on your cooking needs. Look for 18/10-gauge steel.

- If you cook pasta, buy a pasta or steamer insert for the stockpot to easily drain cooked pasta and vegetables.

- All of these pots should have sturdy, close-fitting lids and solid, well-attached handles.

Wok and Steamer

- A wok is a good addition to your collection. Its sloped sides help you keep the food moving when you stir-fry.

- A wok should have a sturdy handle that doesn't conduct heat so you can hold it while you cook. Do not purchase nonstick woks because they can scratch easily.

- A steamer addition makes cooking vegetables and fish very easy. Collapsible steamers take up less storage space.

- Separate steamers, especially when made of bamboo, also present beautifully at the table.

Some pans can get very heavy; especially cast iron.

Saucepans are about 4–5 inches deep and they have straight sides. A skillet has a low, straight side and large bottom. Frying pans have sloped or flared sides. And sauté pans have sides in between skillets and saucepans.

Some manufacturers combine different sizes of pots and pans into sets. If you find one that includes the pans you need, at a good price, buy it. You can always add more pans in the future.

ZOOM

What type of cookware should you buy? It depends on what you cook. Glass can break, but it goes from oven to microwave to table. Stainless is sturdy and dishwasher-safe. Cast iron will last a lifetime, but it can be heavy, and anodized aluminum is sturdy but expensive. Lift and examine the pots and pans before you buy to make sure they are comfortable.

ESSENTIAL EQUIPMENT

Ovenproof Glass Cookware

- Glass cookware can be used on the stovetop, in the oven, in the microwave, and even the freezer.

- Ovenproof pots and pans are made of tempered glass. This material conducts heat unevenly so isn't the best choice if you do lots of pan-frying.

- Porcelain-coated steel or aluminum can chip or crack fairly easily so must be handled gently.

- Sets are priced lower than the individual pieces. Price isn't always an indicator of value. Cheaper sets can be quite sturdy.

Broiler Pans and Cookie Sheets

You'll find yourself reaching for one pan more than others. Buy at least 2 of them so you always have one on hand.

- Broiler pans and cookie sheets are used for more than broiling food and baking cookies. Look for sturdy stainless steel equipment.

- You can bake meatballs and meatloaf on a broiler pan so fat melts away from the meat.

- Cookie sheets can be used to flash freeze food and hold foods going out to the grill. Purchase some cookie sheets with sides and some without.

- Buy half-sheet and full-sheet cookie sheets for baking different batches of cookies, brownies, and cakes.

UTENSILS

Utensils from spatulas to knife sets assist in food preparation

Sturdy utensils are like extensions of your hands. They have to be comfortable and easy to use and must be sturdy. Hold them in your hand before you buy. A good quality utensil will last for many years; you don't want to buy something flimsy. There's nothing more frustrating than stirring a thick frosting and having the handle snap off the spatula.

Essential equipment includes heatproof spatulas, wooden spoons, measuring cups and spoons, a set of wire whisks, some sieves with handles, ladles, and metal or plastic spatulas for removing cookies from the pan and turning meat on the grill.

Take some time and browse through a kitchenware store or a well-equipped grocery store. There are lots of specialty utensils that you may want to buy if it will make your cooking

Spatulas for Scraping

- There are 2 kinds of spatulas: the ones with a slight curve to the bowl that are used for scraping, and stiff, flat spatulas used for lifting.

- Silicone spatulas are the newest addition to the spatula family. These utensils are heatproof and durable.

- You should have at least 2 silicone spatulas in your utensil drawer.

- Offset spatulas are great for frosting cakes and cookies. There is a slight bend to the blade that keeps your fingers away from the frosting.

Measuring Cups

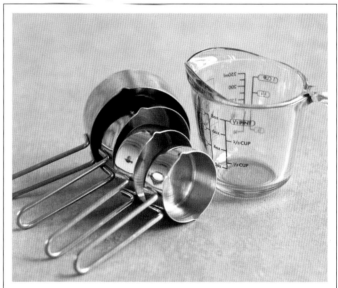

- Always have at least 2 sets of measuring cups and spoons. Then as you use them, drop them into soapy water or the dishwasher.

- You'll need measuring cups and spoons for dry and liquid measuring. For dry ingredients, the cups are straight-sided with a handle.

- For wet ingredients, the cup is made of tempered glass with the measurements marked on the side.

- There's a new type of glass measuring cup that lets you measure by looking straight down into the cup.

chores easier. Not everyone needs a shrimp deveiner or an egg slicer, but if you do, don't feel guilty about buying one.

You may want to keep these utensils in a decorative ceramic or stoneware pot sitting on the countertop for easy access. That way it's easy to see what you have on hand while you're busy cooking.

Wire Whisks

- Wire whisks are essential for making lump-free sauces, gravies, and puddings.

- This utensil can also get into the corners of the pan so sauces, gravies, and puddings don't burn.

- Large whisks shouldn't be too big or they can become unwieldy. Look for whisks about 8 inches long.

- Small whisks can be very handy when making a small amount of sauce. If you have an old hand mixer that breaks, save the whisk beaters.

Spatulas for Lifting

- There are several types of spatulas used for lifting and moving food. Metal, plastic, and silicone spatulas are all available.

- You can find different sizes and shapes of these spatulas for every need. Fish spatulas are very wide and shallow.

- Round spatulas work well for transferring cookies to cooling racks and flipping eggs, while square spatulas flip sandwiches.

- Very long and sturdy spatulas are good choices for turning large meats when grilling and roasting.

HIGH-TECH PREP EQUIPMENT

From immersion blenders for pureeing to electronic timers, these tools are like kitchen assistants

There are many wonderful appliances that truly do cut down on food preparation time. Mixers, blenders, and food processors make quick work of chopped fruit, shredded cheese, and julienned vegetables.

A scale is handy if you do a lot of baking, since weighing ingredients is more accurate than measuring. And the newer blenders are very powerful machines, with special actions that make the appliance very efficient.

As with pots, pans, and utensils, the sturdier and more well-made the equipment you buy, the longer it will last. Heavy duty food processors, blenders, and mixers are serious appliances. Study online recommendations before you buy.

Food Processors

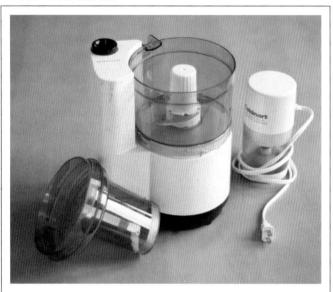

- If you prepare large quantities of food, a full size food processor is probably for you.

- But if you only make small quantities, think about a mini food processor. This smaller appliance can be very versatile.

- Be very careful of the food processor blades because they are razor sharp. Choose a processor that has dishwasher-safe blades and attachments.

- Regularly clean the food processor casing and inspect the cord before each use for safety reasons.

Blenders

- Blenders can do everything from mix drinks and smoothies to chop vegetables and liquefy soups.

- The newest blenders have large motors and specially shaped blades to move the food around.

- "Wave action" technology moves the food from the top to bottom, so stopping to scrape down the sides is a thing of the past.

- Immersion blenders are portable, and can be used to puree soups directly in the pot on the stove or in the slow cooker.

The appliances you buy will depend on the food you make. If you use lots of shredded vegetables and grated cheese in your cooking, a food processor will come in handy. If you make lots of soups, an immersion blender is a good choice.

Small versions of larger appliances may be just what you need. A mini food processor, for instance, can be just as powerful as a full-size processor, but is less expensive, takes up less counter space, and is easier to clean.

Read through the manufacturer's instruction booklet completely before using the equipment.

Mixers

- Stand mixers and hand mixers are both useful. If you make lots of breads and cookies, consider investing in a stand mixer.

- With a stand mixer and several bowls and mixing paddles, you can quickly make several batches of dough.

- Hand mixers are more powerful than ever. They can't knead dough, but can easily mix cake and cookie batters.

- Hand mixers work well for almost every kitchen need, and are much less costly.

Scales

- A scale, whether manual or digital, will help in measuring and helps control portion sizes.

- When baking, measuring ingredients by weight is the most accurate way and will give you the best results.

- High-tech scales can have nutritional content of the food you are weighing programmed into them.

- You can add up to 1,000 foods to the programs in these dietary computer scales. You can also record food intake and keep track of total calories.

LOW-TECH PREP EQUIPMENT

Utensils from mandolines to knife sets assist in food preparation

Low-tech prep equipment includes tools and utensils that don't use electricity and usually only have one purpose. Many have been around for years. Some of these utensils have been updated with the latest materials, but they have always been an essential part of the quick and easy kitchen.

Buy the best quality preparation equipment you can afford. A good knife set is essential to a good kitchen experience; and they have to be kept sharp. Tools like basting brushes, graters, microplanes, and mandolines make food preparation easy. And when you have an easy time in the kitchen, you'll be encouraged you to spend more time there.

You can find this equipment in grocery stores, in kitchenware shops, at hardware stores, and online. You can find apple corers, swivel-bladed vegetable peelers, and other tools in many styles and levels of quality.

Store the equipment in drawers separated by type. But it's

Knives

- Whether you buy knives individually or in sets, there are certain basic knives every kitchen needs.

- A chef's knife, 2 paring knives of different sizes, a utility knife, a bread knife, scissors, and a sharpening steel are essentials.

- Purchase other knives, like boning knives, as you need them. A knife block keeps them stored safely.

- Be sure that any knife set you buy is heavy duty, with a full tang, or steel blade, running the length of the knife.

Mandoline

- A mandoline, or slicing tool, can speed preparation and allow you to make fancy cuts.

- You can julienne vegetables or cut potatoes into chips or waffle slices with a mandoline. The mandoline should have good safety features.

- The price ranges for this tool are very wide. You can find a mandoline for under $40, and some retail for $200.

- Read reviews online to find the best tool for you. Then make sure you understand how to use it before you start.

not a good idea to store knives in drawers because it's too easy to cut yourself reaching for one.

Then take care of your equipment. Clean using hot soapy water, and dry each item thoroughly after each use. If the tool is dishwasher-safe, that's the best way to clean it. Be sure to follow the manufacturer's instructions for cleaning and storage. Your tools should last a lifetime with proper care.

Cheese Graters

- Cheese graters are excellent tools, whether you're shredding 2 cups for a pizza or just a small amount for a garnish.

- Have several different sizes of graters in your kitchen drawers. Box graters can also serve as measuring tools, while microplane graters are good for garnishing.

- Buy microplane graters in hardware stores and kitchen stores. Use for grating nutmeg and zesting citrus fruit.

- Be careful with your fingers when using graters. Work slowly, and discard the last bit of food.

Silicone Tools

- There are many kitchen tools made of silicone. This material stands up well to high heat and cleans beautifully.

- Silicone basting brushes are great for basting foods on the grill. They are dishwasher safe and easy to clean.

- Silicone pot holders and mitts can stand up to very high heat, protecting your hands from pans and hot food.

- Most good quality silicone products, like spatulas and brushes, have steel handles or steel cores.

TIME-SAVING COOKING DEVICES

Equipment from rice cookers to food processors makes quick work of food prep

Small appliances make quick and easy cooking very simple. A rice cooker makes rice perfectly while you are stir-frying the chicken and vegetables. A toaster oven can keep food warm or make perfect grilled bread while you are tossing the salad. And a microwave oven is great for prepping food and making complete meals.

Many of these appliances have multiple uses. A toaster oven can make toast as well as bake small batches of cookies and cakes, and can broil garlic bread to perfection. A rice cooker can be used to cook other foods; the Internet has lots of recipes.

A dual-contact grill can be equipped with different plates to cook everything from a grilled panini to pancakes.

Dual Contact Indoor Grill

- Dual contact indoor grills are countertop appliances that cook food on both sides at the same time.

- George Foreman is one common brand of this type of indoor grill.

- The large versions of these grills can cook enough food for 4–6 people at once. Grease and fat drain off, so the food is healthy too.

- The food cooked on these grills has grilled flavor without the hassle of dealing with charcoal or gas in an outdoor grill.

Toaster Oven

- Toaster ovens do more than toast. You can bake small batches of cookies and rolls, small cakes, and everything from meatloaf to sandwiches.

- Look for toaster ovens with varied settings so you can toast, broil, and bake.

- Cleaning the ovens is fairly easy. Most come with a crumb tray that pulls out, and some are dishwasher safe.

- The price range for these ovens is $40 to $300. The expensive ovens have features like convection cooking.

When you're looking for a small appliance, it's helpful to read reviews online or in consumer magazines. Compare products in the store to see which one has the features you want.

Always fill out warranty cards, and keep the purchase information, together with the instruction and care booklets, in a drawer or cupboard. Even these things should have a "home."

Be sure that you understand how these appliances function and read the safety precautions before you start using them. With care, these appliances, which aren't inexpensive, can last for years.

Rice Cooker

- A rice cooker can do more than just cook plain rice! You can cook rice pudding, macaroni and cheese, potatoes, and main dishes.

- Look for a rice cooker with the largest capacity you can afford. The capacity is the amount of raw rice it holds.

- You can brown foods, cook, and hold them on warm in a rice cooker.

- The easiest way to use the cooker is to cook rice, but add other ingredients, like spices, herbs, and vegetables.

Microwave Oven

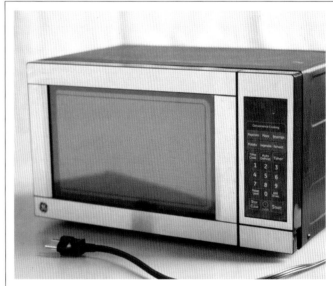

- The microwave oven hasn't transformed the kitchen as much as first thought. Most people still use it as a prep tool.

- Microwave ovens cook by making molecules vibrate, creating heat in the food. The waves the oven uses are radio waves, and are not radioactive.

- Follow cooking, covering, stirring, venting, and standing times to the letter for best results.

TIME-SAVING GADGETS

You can have fun in the kitchen with these cool gadgets

These gadgets make cooking easier and more fun. One of the best ways to save money and make cooking more efficient is to try new ways to keep track of your food.

You can go digital with many kitchen tasks, including checking the temperature of food, writing a shopping list, and writing a shopping list. Special green bags are useful for extending the shelf life of produce. And that saves time be-

cause you won't have to run to the store to buy an ingredient that has gone bad.

The types of gadgets you'll need vary depending on the type of food you cook. If you love Italian food, a garlic press and a fancy corkscrew will make mealtime easier. For Tex-Mex and Mexican cuisine, a tortilla press would be important, as would a mortar and pestle for grinding spices.

Multi-Use Timer

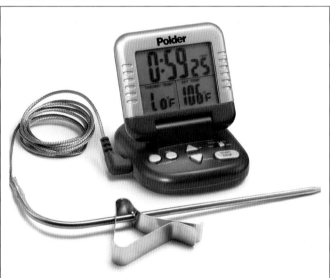

- A multi-use timer is very useful when you're cooking more than one item. It can be programmed to emit different sounds for each time.

- Some timers can be set to vibrate, or will illuminate when the time is up.

- Pick a timer that's small enough so you can slip it into an apron pocket.

- Some timers come with thermometers, so you can place food in the oven, set the final temp, and the timer will beep when that temp is reached.

Digital Shopping List

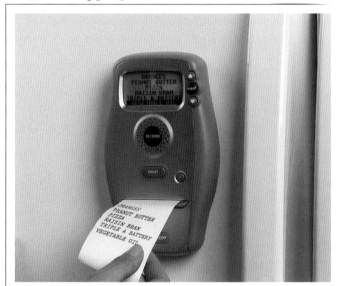

- Digital shopping lists are very convenient. You simply talk into the machine, telling it what you want to buy.

- The machine remembers your list, and can print it out with a touch of a button.

- Voice recognition software allows the transfer of words

into a printed list. You pre-record your voice so the machine recognizes it.

- The gadget can even organize items on your list according to the layout of the store, making shopping more efficient.

Timers are a basic kitchen essential; you should have at least two. Multi-use timers will help you keep track of several dishes cooking at once.

Other fun toys include corn on the cob butter appliers, heated ice cream scoops, bun warmers, snow cone and ice cream makers, chocolate fountains, kitchen goggles, cheese slicers, and Silpat cooking mats. There's a gadget for every need, including needs you didn't know you had!

ZOOM

Depending on what you cook, you may want other kitchen gadgets including a Y-shaped potato peeler, which follows the curves of fruits and vegetables, a garlic press, which easily crushes garlic with little effort, and a melon baller, which can be used to core apples or pears as well as make melon balls.

Meat Thermometer

- The final temperature of meat has to be accurate so it's not undercooked or overcooked.

- There are 2 types of meat thermometers you need in your kitchen.

- One is a thermometer that comes with a timer. You set

the final temp, insert the probe, then bake or grill the food. When the temp is reached, the timer beeps.

- The other type is an instant-read thermometer, used for testing the temperature of meats.

Green Bags

- Food waste is one of the biggest budget-busters. But did you know that there are bags that will extend the life of produce?

- These little bags are reusable. They work by removing ethylene gas, which is a gas that fruit emits while it opens.

- The bags don't keep food fresh and in superior condition as long as the package states, but they will extend the food's life by a few days.

- To reuse, just wash the bags and let dry.

STIR-FRYING

Learn the basics of stir-frying, one of the quickest cooking methods on the planet

Stir-frying is a method of quickly cooking food. The skillet or wok is heated until very hot, then a small amount of oil is added. The food, cut into small pieces, cooks very fast and is kept moving by a stirring action, thus the name.

Stir-frying was originally developed as a cooking style to preserve precious wood. Since the food cooks so quickly, less fuel can be used.

This method of cooking helps preserve nutrients and color in vegetables. A sauce, sometimes a marinade used to tenderize the meat, is usually added during the last few minutes to blend the ingredients and add flavor.

Stir-frying isn't difficult; it just takes a bit of practice to make

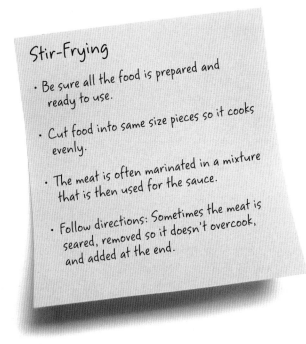

Stir-Frying

- Be sure all the food is prepared and ready to use.

- Cut food into same size pieces so it cooks evenly.

- The meat is often marinated in a mixture that is then used for the sauce.

- Follow directions: Sometimes the meat is seared, removed so it doesn't overcook, and added at the end.

Wok on Stovetop

- Preheat the wok on the stovetop before you add the oil and the rest of the ingredients.

- A nonstick wok isn't necessary. If you preheat it and add the oil, then let the oil get hot before adding the food, the food won't stick.

- If you're adding eggs, as in stir-fried rice, make a well in the center of the food and add egg; cook until done.

- Do not interrupt the cooking when stir-frying, or the food will overcook.

sure that you turn all the food evenly. After a minute or two, you will fall naturally into a pattern.

You don't need a wok to stir-fry. A large, heavy skillet with sloping sides is a good substitute. If you have a gas range, a wok stand will help keep the wok stable as you cook.

Most of the meat and vegetables can be prepared ahead of time and quickly cooked just before serving. for prepared stir-fry veggies for an even quicker dinner.

Stir-fried food is usually served over rice. Cook that in your rice cooker to make serving these healthy meals easy.

Stir-Frying in Wok

- The food has to be kept moving as it cooks. You can use a metal spatula or a silicone rubber spatula.

- Use your dominant hand to stir the food, and your non-dominant hand to hold the wok as the food cooks.

- Have all of the food lined up by the stove, in the order it will be added to the wok.

- The whole cooking process should be done in about 6–8 minutes.

Stir-Frying in Skillet

- Add the vegetables to the skillet in the order of cooking time. Add the longer-cooking vegetables, like carrots and potatoes, first.

- Then add more tender vegetables. The harder vegetables continue to cook while the soft vegetables become crisp-tender.

- If you add a sauce at the end of the cooking time, be sure to stir it so the seasonings and cornstarch are blended.

- This type of dish should be served immediately, while the ingredients are still hot.

COOKING METHODS

PAN-FRYING

There are rules to learn about pan-frying to create juicy and delicious meats

Pan-frying, which is also known as sautéing, is a quick cooking method that uses the stovetop or an electric skillet.

A small amount of fat is placed in the skillet, and then the food is added and quickly cooked. This method produces pan drippings, which can be used to make a sauce to finish the dish.

It's important to preheat the pan and get the fat hot before adding the food. If the fat is too cold, the food will steam instead of fry and it will absorb some of the oil. If the oil is too hot, the food can burn.

You must know the smoke point of the oil you use. This is the temperature at which the oil begins to break down and

Pan-Frying 101

- You can use a nonstick or regular skillet. Heat the oil in the pan until a drop of water sizzles.

- Add food and don't move it until it releases easily. Then carefully turn and continue.

- Coat meat in flour or breadcrumbs to thicken the sauce and protect the meat from the heat.

- Pan-fried meats are sometimes finished in the oven, especially if they are thicker than ½ inch.

Pan-Frying Bacon

- Bacon and other breakfast meats are good candidates for pan-frying.

- When you pan-fry meats, you must let the meat cook until it releases easily. If you force the meat, it will tear.

- When the meat is done on one side, it will release eas-

ily. Bacon should be turned often so it cooks evenly.

- Other meats only need to be turned once. Cook until the outside is golden brown. You can check doneness with a meat thermometer.

smokes. When the oil reaches this temperature, byproducts can add an unpleasant taste to food.

Regular olive oil can be used for pan-frying since its smoke point is around 420 degrees F, but extra-virgin olive oil can have a lower smoke point. Since the temperature of the pan is around 350 to 400 degrees F, any oil with a smoke point above 420 degrees F will work well.

The skillet or frying pan you use has to be heavy, with a thick bottom so it transfers heat to the food evenly.

Cooking Pancakes

- Pancakes are the perfect breakfast food to cook in a pan. They cook in minutes.

- Use a mix or make your own from scratch; it's easy. Lightly grease the skillet and add batter in ¼-cup amounts.

- Let the pancakes cook, undisturbed, until the edges start to look dry and bubbles form on the surface and just begin to pop.

- Carefully shimmy a spatula under the pancake and turn, using your wrist to flip. Cook for 2-3 minutes on second side.

Pan-Frying Steak

- Steaks, especially thinner, tender steaks like hanger and flat iron steaks, are good candidates for pan-frying.

- To make a sauce, remove the meat and place on a warmed platter; cover to keep warm. You can also place the meat in a 300 degree F oven.

- Add beef broth, seasonings, and herbs to the pan and stir to release pan drippings.

- Swirl in a bit of butter and pour the sauce over the meat; serve immediately.

COOKING METHODS

BROILING

Broiling is an underused quick cooking method that produces delicious results

Broiling is a dry heat cooking method similar to grilling. The food is placed 4–6 inches from the hot upper burners in the oven, and is cooked quickly. The food browns easily and caramelizes well, giving lots of flavor.

You can broil everything from chicken paillards to fish steaks, from bell peppers to frittatas. All you need is an oven, and ovenproof pans that will withstand the high heat.

If you don't have ovenproof pans, you can wrap a double layer of heavy-duty foil around the handle of the pan and it can be used under the broiler.

There are two keys to broiling; the placement of the food and the cooking time. Don't step away from the food even for a mo-

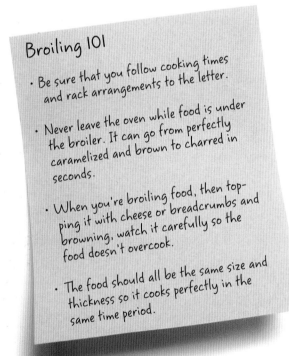

Broiling 101

• Be sure that you follow cooking times and rack arrangements to the letter.

• Never leave the oven while food is under the broiler. It can go from perfectly caramelized and brown to charred in seconds.

• When you're broiling food, then topping it with cheese or breadcrumbs and browning, watch it carefully so the food doesn't overcook.

• The food should all be the same size and thickness so it cooks perfectly in the same time period.

Preheating Gas Broiler

• In some older or antique ovens, the gas broiler may be a drawer in the top of the stove.

• Follow the manufacturer's directions for your broiler; they are different for every oven.

• Always use an oven mitt, not a hot pad, to add and remove the broiler pan to protect your hands and arms from the intense heat.

• You can cover the rack with foil for easy cleanup, but be sure to cut slashes in the foil so the grease can drain.

KNACK QUICK & EASY COOKING

28

ment, because it can go from beautifully browned to burned. Use the oven racks to place the food according to the recipe.

On most ovens, the oven door has to be open for the broiler to be at its highest heat. Arrange the rack below the broiler according to the manufacturer's directions, and keep a close eye on the food as it cooks.

Some ovens have a variable broil feature, but most broil at just one temperature: high. Broil steaks, hamburgers, chicken breasts, pork chops, fish fillets, cake toppings, and bread or cheese crusts on casseroles for a crunchy caramelized finish.

Broiling is a low-fat form of cooking. Trim excess fat from foods and use marinades that are low fat.

Broiling Racks

- Broiling racks are specially made to withstand the high heat of the broiler, and to drain off fat.

- The pan is usually in 2 parts: a rack or top with slots cut into it, and a bottom pan with sides to hold grease.

- Never use the parts of a broiler pan separately in the oven. You can use the top or bottom to hold uncooked food.

- You can sometimes find replacement broiler racks on eBay if you broil a lot.

Carefully Place Food

- Some foods need to be flipped or turned when under the broiler; others will cook through perfectly from the intense heat.

- Use a spatula or tongs, not a fork, to turn the food so it doesn't lose juice.

- If the food you are broiling has been marinated, drain the marinade from the food to avoid flare-ups and grease fires.

- Always have a fire extinguisher or box of baking soda or salt nearby when using this intense heat, to extinguish fires.

GRILLING

Grilling, whether indoors or out, is one of the best quick cooking methods

You can grill indoors or out, depending on the weather and the equipment you have. Outdoor grilling is an event in itself, requiring equipment and utensils peculiar to that cooking art.

There are two basic types of outdoor grills: gas and charcoal. Gas grills are more expensive and simpler to use; you just push a button and wait for the grill to heat. Charcoal grills require more finesse; you must light the fire and maintain it throughout the cooking process.

As always, be sure to read and follow manufacturer's instructions for using a grill, whether it's charcoal, gas, or a dual contact indoor grill. There are also grill pans with ridges that fit onto your stovetop to mimic the effect of the outdoor grill.

Grilling 101

- Foods that should be directly grilled are sturdy and fairly large, like steaks or pork chops.

- If you think a food will fall through the grill grate, use a grill mat or a grill basket to hold the food.

- You can also wrap food in heavy duty foil and grill it. The food won't have a smoky flavor, but will be juicy.

- Thread food on skewers to keep it together on the grill. Use soaked bamboo skewers or metal skewers.

Stovetop Grill

- For stovetop grills, make sure that you have the vent fan turned on. Grilling naturally creates a lot of smoke.

- Look at the Web site of your stove's manufacturer to see if they have a grill pan made for your stove.

- You can place a stovetop grill pan on almost any stovetop, but there will be hot and cold areas.

- Let the stovetop grill cool completely before you remove it from the stove and clean it.

A grill must always be preheated before the food is added. It takes about thirty minutes for charcoal to reach the proper cooking temperature, but gas grills and stovetop grills preheat in ten minutes.

Never leave a hot grill unattended. Keep kids and pets away from the cooking area. And also think about food safety. Perishable foods must be refrigerated after two hours; one hour if the ambient temperature is over 80 degrees F. Separate cooked and uncooked foods, and wash hands and equipment in hot soapy water before and after cooking.

Dual-Contact Indoor Grill

- Indoor grills are a great addition to any kitchen. They cook quickly and fat drains away, lowering the fat content of your food.

- Look for the largest grill you can afford so you can cook an entire meal at once.

- The grill should have a floating hinge so it will accommodate thicker foods.

- These grills have to be preheated before the food is added. You should hear a sizzling sound when you place the food on the grill.

Grill Marks

- Grill marks are beautiful and add a lot of flavor to the food. You can make crosshatch marks with this method.

- Place the food at a 45-degree angle to the grate and let it cook until the food releases.

- Lift the food completely off the grill, then turn it 90 degrees, and place it down, on the same side.

- Lift the food off when it releases and repeat on the other side.

MICROWAVING

Your microwave is more than a butter melter, so use it to its fullest capacity

The microwave can do more than just pop popcorn, melt butter, and defrost foods; you can cook an entire meal in this appliance. It just takes a bit of attention and following a few rules.

There are several types of microwave ovens. You can buy very basic models that are low wattage, but remember that it can be difficult to cook in those appliances. And high-end microwave ovens, which are usually mounted over an oven, can have 1200 watts, with lights and vent fans. Whichever type of oven you buy, be sure that you understand how to use it before you start cooking.

Most microwave ovens have about 600–800 watts of power, and that's the range that recipes are developed for. If your mi-

Microwaving 101

- Start with microwave-safe cooking dishes. The correct pots and pans are marked as microwave-safe.

- Also use microwave-safe plastic wrap and paper towels. Vent by peeling back one corner of the plastic wrap.

- Dense foods like meatloaf, pork chops, or chicken breasts, take some time to microwave. The energy needs a few minutes to move through the food.

- Check the final temperature with an instant-read meat thermometer after standing time. If it's not correct, microwave for 1-minute intervals.

Microwave-Safe Containers

- Not all glass is microwave-safe. To determine if a container is microwave-safe, fill it with water.

- Microwave on high power for 1 minute, then let stand for 1 minute.

- If the container is hot but the water isn't, you shouldn't use it in the microwave oven.

- Never use glass or ceramic dishes with metallic trim or decorations. You'll know if the dish isn't meant for the microwave; there may be sparks or arcing in the appliance.

crowave is more or less powerful, reduce or increase the cooking time by 30–40 percent, then write down the changes on the recipe. With some experimentation, you'll be able to accurately estimate cooking times.

Microwave recipes are written with venting, stirring, rotating, and standing times included; follow all of them to the letter for best results.

Foods don't brown in the microwave oven, but you can compensate for that fact by searing food in a pan or under the broiler, or using browning agents like colorings and spices.

Standing Time

- Standing time is an important part of microwave cooking. The food stands on a solid surface after cooking.

- This allows heat to move throughout the food, finishing cooking and eliminating hot and cold spots.

- The food has to stand on a solid surface, not a wire rack, or heat will escape from the top and bottom, cooling the food.

- Test the food with an instant-read thermometer after standing time to make sure it's at the correct temp.

Microwave a Quiche

- Yes, you can cook a quiche in the microwave oven. This is where you can use a browning trick.

- Brush the crust with soy sauce, or other sauce like hoisin, teriyaki, or Worcestershire to add color. Spices like curry powder or smoked paprika also add color.

- Microwave the pie crust first before adding filling to prevent a soggy bottom crust.

- Standing time is very important when cooking main dishes in the microwave, so don't skimp on it.

SLOW COOKING

Slow cookers do all of the work after just a little bit of food preparation

The slow cooker (commonly known by the brand name Crock-Pot) doesn't cook food quickly, but it does all the work for you once the food is added.

There are slow cookers to meet every need: from 1 or 2-cup minis perfect for appetizer dips, to 7- or 8-quart behemoths that will cook an entire turkey or roast to perfection. You should have several in different sizes for the most ease and efficiency.

There's really no trick to using a slow cooker. Add the food, usually in a precise order, then turn it on and get on with the rest of your life. Some recipes call for stirring or adding food toward the end of cooking time; be sure that you read the

Slow Cooking 101

- It's important to add food to the slow cooker in a certain order. Foods that take longer to cook go on the bottom.

- You can add tender fruits and vegetables along with pasta to the slow cooker at the end of cooking time.

- Some foods, like rice, wild rice, barley, and legumes, must be on the bottom so they are covered with liquid.

- Cheaper cuts of meat like pork shoulder or beef chuck become tender when cooked in the slow cooker.

Small Slow Cooker

- Small slow cookers are perfect for appetizer dips and condiments. They cook just like their larger counterparts.

- Some recipes require stirring times. Don't stir more than the recipe requires or the slow cooker will lose too much heat.

- Every time the lid is lifted, you must cook the food for 20–30 minutes longer.

- You can make batches of preserves or condiments in the slow cooker and freeze them for gifts or later use.

entire recipe before leaving the slow cooker to its work.

Newer slow cookers, of the last four to five years, cook hotter than the slow cookers of the twentieth century. With recipes written in that era, you should reduce the cooking time so food doesn't overcook or burn. Newer recipes are written with the hotter temps in mind, but still you should check the food for doneness at the earliest time.

Foods that cook best in the slow cooker include soups and stews, roasts, casseroles, and side dishes. You can also cook sandwich fillings, ingredients for salads, and some desserts.

Large Slow Cooker

- Add ingredients in order as the recipe directs. Some foods need to be covered with liquid to cook evenly.

- It may seem surprising, but hard vegetables take longer to cook than meats, so onions and potatoes go on the bottom.

- You can brown meats before adding them to the slow cooker. This will add flavor and color to the dish.

- Remember that no evaporation takes place when using the slow cooker, so use 1/3 less liquid when converting recipes.

Stirring Food

- Some recipes need to be stirred during the cooking time. Do this quickly so not much heat escapes.

- Dry beans and legumes should be soaked for 18–24 hours before cooking in the slow cooker.

- To thicken soups, chilis, or stews, combine 2 tablespoons cornstarch with 1/3 cup liquid in a small bowl.

- Stir into the slow cooker at the end of cooking time; cook for 20–30 minutes on high until thickened.

DIPS

Creamy dips are the perfect appetizer served with crudités and crackers

An appetizer can be a great tool for the host or hostess. With ingredients for an appetizer or two in your pantry, fridge, and freezer, you can be ready to entertain at a moment's notice.

These foods also keep your guests occupied while you put the finishing touches on dinner. They are also great appetite prompters, and can set the tone for the evening.

Dips are the easiest type of appetizer. All you really need is some sour cream and a package of onion dip, but these recipes can be a lot more interesting than that.

And the foods you serve to dip in the dip can be varied and inventive, from baby vegetables to gourmet crackers and exotic fruits. *Yield: 6 servings*

Ingredients

1 (8-ounce) package cream cheese

⅓ cup low-fat sour cream

¼ cup mayonnaise

1 tablespoon lemon juice

⅓ cup freshly grated Parmesan cheese

2 tablespoons chopped fresh basil

2 tablespoons fresh thyme leaves

2 tablespoons minced celery leaves

Creamy Herb Dip

- Place cream cheese in microwave-safe bowl. Microwave on 50 percent power for 1 minute, then remove and let stand.

- Beat cream cheese with electric mixer until very smooth. Gradually beat in sour cream, mayonnaise, and lemon juice until smooth.

- Add cheese, basil, thyme, and celery and beat well. Cover and refrigerate for 4–5 hours to blend flavors.

- When ready to serve, let dip stand at room temperature for 20 minutes before serving with toasted French bread, breadsticks, apple slices, and baby carrots.

Buffalo Dip

In large saucepan, combine 2 (8-ounce) packages of cream cheese with 1½ cups ranch dressing, 3 tablespoons Tabasco sauce, ½ cup crumbled blue cheese, and 1 cup shredded Swiss cheese. Cook and stir until dip is melted and smooth. Serve with celery sticks, baby carrots, and cooked chicken fingers.

Enchilada Dip

Soften 2 (8-ounce) packages of light cream cheese in the microwave oven for 1 minute on 50 percent power. Drain 1 (14-ounce) can diced tomatoes and add the liquid gradually to the cream cheese, beating until smooth. Stir in tomatoes, 1 chopped red onion, 2 cloves garlic, 1 tablespoon chili powder, and ½ teaspoon dried oregano.

Chop Herbs

- It's easy to chop fresh herbs using a chef's knife. First, rinse the herbs well and shake off excess water.

- Then pull or cut the leaves from the stems. Gather the leaves in a tight bundle and cut, rocking the blade across.

- Then fluff up the pile and continue cutting with the knife, changing direction to produce even, small pieces.

- Parsley, basil, and sage should be cut from the stem, while rosemary, oregano, and thyme leaves need to be pulled off by hand.

Soften Cream Cheese

- You can soften cream cheese by just letting it stand at room temperature for an hour or two.

- Another way to soften is to place the cream cheese on a microwave-safe plate and microwave on 50 percent power for 1 minute.

- When combining cream cheese with other ingredients, beat the cream cheese well and gradually add liquids so no lumps form.

- Cream cheese dips will harden when chilled; let stand at room temperature for 15–20 minutes before serving.

APPETIZERS

ETHNIC DIPS

You can add an ethnic spin to dips with these easy recipes

Dips can span the world from Buffalo, New York, to Greece to Japan. Once you have a basic dip base that you like, change it by varying the herbs, spices, and condiments you add.

Classic ethnic dips include fruit and vegetable salsas, mixtures with different types of cheeses and yogurt, and dips using legumes and grains.

The typical flavors for different cuisines are easy to find. Tex-Mex flavors include chile peppers, onion, and tomato. From

Greece, lemon, yogurt, olives, and tomatoes are common. Spanish dips include almonds and oregano, while Asian dips would use soy sauce, hoisin sauce, five-spice powder, lemongrass, and citrus juices. Mix and match these flavors to create your own special dip recipes. *Yield: 8 servings*

Ingredients

1 (8-ounce) package cream cheese

1½ cups Greek yogurt

½ cup chopped oil-packed sun-dried tomatoes

1 (8-ounce) container refrigerated hummus

1 cucumber, peeled and chopped

2 tomatoes, chopped

½ cup chopped kalamata olives

⅓ cup crumbled feta cheese

3 tablespoons toasted sesame seeds

Layered Greek Dip

- Soften cream cheese in microwave oven. Beat until smooth, and then gradually beat in yogurt until smooth.

- Stir in the sun-dried tomatoes. Spread in even layer on serving platter.

- Stir the hummus and spread over cream cheese

layer, leaving a small border of cream cheese exposed.

- Cover and refrigerate up to 24 hours. When ready to serve, prepare cucumber, tomatoes, and olives and sprinkle over dip. Top with feta and sesame seeds and serve.

• • • • RECIPE VARIATION • • • •

Creamy Sesame Dip: Use 1 cup Greek yogurt or 1 cup drained plain yogurt. Combine in small bowl with 2 tablespoons soy sauce, ½ teaspoon five-spice powder, ⅛ teaspoon cayenne pepper, 2 teaspoons sesame oil, and ⅓ cup toasted sesame seeds. Mix well and chill for 1–2 hours before serving.

Prepare Vegetables

Assemble Dip

APPETIZERS

- The cucumber should be peeled and seeded. To seed, cut peeled cucumber in half lengthwise. Use a spoon to scoop out the seeds, then chop.

- The oil-packed sun-dried tomatoes are ready to use. Just drain them on paper towel and cut into small pieces.

- Because the tomatoes are so strongly flavored, the dip will be better balanced if they are finely chopped.

- You can vary this recipe by adding green bell peppers, red onion, or chopped zucchini.

- Make sure that you leave some of the yogurt mixture showing when you layer the hummus on top.

- To toast sesame seeds, place them in a dry skillet over medium heat. Toast, shaking the pan frequently, until the seeds are fragrant.

- Let the seeds cool completely before adding them to the dip.

- Serve this dip with toasted pita chips. Cut pita breads into wedges, brush with olive oil, sprinkle with salt, and bake at 400 degrees F for 10 minutes.

SPREADS

A spread or two, some knives, and hearty bread make appetizers a breeze

Spreads are just thick appetizer dips that you can spread on everything from toasted French bread to breadsticks to tiny bagels, crackers, or apple slices.

Use your prettiest platters for serving appetizer spreads. Layered spreads are fun to make, too, and are very beautiful. Think about investing in some small knives with decorative handles to make it easy for your guests to use the spread.

For best results, the ingredients should be at the same temperature. You want the base of the spread to be as smooth as possible. Then you can add ingredients like chopped nuts, herbs, spices, minced onion and garlic, shredded or grated cheese, or chutneys and preserves. *Yield: 8 servings*

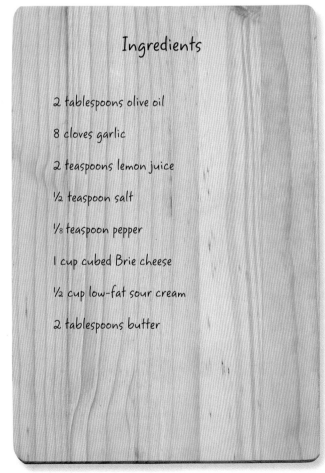

Ingredients

2 tablespoons olive oil

8 cloves garlic

2 teaspoons lemon juice

½ teaspoon salt

⅛ teaspoon pepper

1 cup cubed Brie cheese

½ cup low-fat sour cream

2 tablespoons butter

Roasted Garlic Herb Spread

- Place oil in small pan over medium heat. Add garlic cloves; cook, watching carefully, until cloves turn brown.

- You can also roast the whole head, cut in half, in a 350 degree F oven for 1 hour until soft.

- Remove from oil and let cool, then squeeze garlic from peel. Combine garlic with lemon juice, salt, and pepper.

- In food processor, combine garlic mixture with remaining ingredients; process until smooth. Cover and chill for 2–3 hours before serving.

Roasted Garlic Spread
Roast 1 head of garlic as the recipe directs, cool, and remove cloves. Combine in food processor with 1 1(5-ounce) jar of drained roasted red peppers, 3 table-spoons lemon juice, ½ cup sour cream, and ½ cup crumbled goat cheese. Process until smooth, then chill for 2–4 hours.

Spicy Shrimp Spread
Thaw 8 ounces of cooked frozen shrimp. Place in food processor along with 1 (8-ounce) package of softened cream cheese, ½ cup cocktail sauce, 3 tablespoons orange juice, ½ teaspoon salt, ¼ teaspoon cayenne pepper, and 2 teaspoons chili powder. Process until almost smooth. Chill before serving.

Roast Garlic

Remove Flesh from Skins

- Garlic, that pungent and fiery vegetable, becomes unbelievably sweet and mild when roasted or toasted.

- It's easy to roast 6–7 heads of garlic all at once, then remove the sweet meat from the skins and freeze.

- Then when you need it, just remove the amount you need, defrost in the micro-wave, and proceed with the recipe.

- You can toast garlic in oil on the stovetop for 7–9 minutes until brown. Discard the oil and let the cloves cool.

- Removing the garlic from the skins is a messy process, but it's not difficult.

- Just try to get all of the tender roasted flesh out of the skins. Discard the skins when you're done.

- You can serve the roasted garlic heads all by them-selves, as a side dish to meat or as an appetizer.

- Let your guests remove the cloves from the heads and spread them directly on toasted bread or grilled steak.

APPETIZERS

41

KABOBS

Kabobs, grilled or not, are the perfect little appetizer for a cookout

Kabobs don't have to be meal-sized. Tiny kabobs are one of the best and most elegant quick and easy appetizers.

They can be made of meat and fruit, or meat and vegetables, or all vegetables, or fruit and cheese. Marinades, salad dressing, and simple oil mixtures can be brushed on these little treats while they're being grilled.

Bamboo skewers are the easiest choice to make these little kabobs because they don't cook long on the grill. Bamboo is easier to handle, too, since the skewers cool off in seconds.

Soak the skewers in water for at least thirty minutes so they don't burn to a crisp in the high heat. The skewers can be 4–8 inches in length. *Yield: 12 servings*

Ingredients

1 (15-ounce) can pineapple chunks

¼ cup barbecue sauce

¼ cup pineapple preserves

1 tablespoon chopped fresh mint leaves

2 cloves garlic, minced

½ teaspoon salt

⅛ teaspoon pepper

1½ pounds large raw shrimp, shelled

2 nectarines, cut into wedges

16 mango-seasoned skewers

Fruit Shrimp Kabobs

- Drain pineapple chunks, reserving ¼ cup juice. Pat the pineapple dry and place in medium bowl.

- In small bowl, combine barbecue sauce, preserves, mint, reserved juice, garlic, salt, and pepper.

- Thread shrimp, pineapple, and nectarines on skewers, nestling the fruit in the curve of each shrimp. Brush with sauce; chill 1 hour.

- Grill kabobs, turning and frequently brushing with sauce, until done, about 4–6 minutes total. Discard remaining sauce. Serve kabobs immediately.

Asian Chicken Kabobs

In medium bowl, combine ¼ cup soy sauce, 2 tablespoons brown sugar, 2 tablespoons olive oil, 2 minced garlic cloves, and ½ teaspoon ginger. Add 3 boneless chicken thighs cut into 1-inch pieces, 2 green onions, sliced, and 2 cups small mushrooms; chill 2 hours. Thread on skewers; grill for 9–12 minutes, turning once, until done.

Almond Salmon Kabobs

Combine 3 tablespoons each honey mustard, vegetable oil, and lemon juice in bowl; mix well. Add 1 salmon steak, cubed, and 1 cup small mushrooms. Marinate 2 hours in fridge. Thread on skewers, grill for 8–10 minutes; roll in chopped toasted almonds to coat.

Prepare Shrimp

Skewer Food

- Large shrimp are needed in this recipe because they will cook through in the same time as the other ingredients.

- If the shrimp still have the shells and tail on, remove the shells by cutting down the back of the shrimp.

- If you see a dark, thin vein running down the back of the shrimp, cut along it and rinse to remove.

- You can leave the tails on for a pretty appearance, or remove them for easier eating.

- Mango-seasoned skewers are made by Callison's and can be found online and in specialty shops.

- The seasoned skewers help flavor the food from the inside out. If you can't find them, use regular bamboo skewers.

- The fruit nestled into the curve of the shrimp helps shield them from the heat so they don't overcook; plus, it looks pretty.

- You could make this recipe into a main dish by using metal skewers and adding more food per skewer.

APPETIZERS

PIZZAS

Mini pizzas aren't just for kids; these sophisticated recipes are elegant, too

Mini pizzas are an excellent appetizer. Once you know how to make and bake or grill the base, you can make these appetizers out of practically anything. For these tiny pizzas, you can use pizza dough cut out with biscuit cutters, little tortillas, or mini pita breads. Other choices for the crust include cracker bread, cocktail breads, and crackers.

With these small appetizers, you can splurge on more expensive ingredients, like exotic mushrooms, authentic ethnic cheeses, and out of season fruits and vegetables.

To grill pizzas, place the dough on a grill mat. Grill until one side is crisp, then turn, top, and grill until the second side is crisp and the toppings are blended. *Yield: 8–10 servings*

Ingredients

2 tablespoons butter

1 tablespoon olive oil

2 onions, chopped

2 cloves garlic, minced

1 teaspoon sugar

½ teaspoon salt

⅛ teaspoon pepper

1 (14-ounce) can refrigerated pizza dough

2 tablespoons cornmeal

2 plum tomatoes, chopped

½ cup shredded Grùyere cheese

½ cup crumbled blue cheese

Onion and Blue Cheese Pizza

- In large pan, melt butter with olive oil over medium heat. Add onion and garlic; cook and stir until translucent and very tender.

- After about 8–10 minutes, sprinkle with sugar, salt, and pepper; remove from heat.

- Preheat oven to 425 degrees

F. Roll out pizza dough on cornmeal to ¼-inch thickness. Cut into 3-inch rounds. Place rounds on Silpat liner on cookie sheet.

- Top with onion mixture, tomatoes, and cheeses. Bake pizzas for 8–11 minutes or until crust is golden and cheese melts.

Mini Grilled Greek Pizzas

Cook 1 chopped onion and 2 cloves garlic in 2 tablespoons olive oil. Remove from heat and add ½ cup chopped kalamata olives. Divide among 12 tiny pita breads; top with ⅓ cup minced sun-dried tomatoes, ½ cup crumbled feta cheese, and 2 tablespoons Romano cheese. Grill pizzas on grill mat over medium heat for 6–8 minutes.

Tex-Mex Mini Pizzas

Top 12 4-inch tortillas with 1 cup of salsa, then 1 cup cooked crumbled pork sausage, 1 cup cooked and drained black beans, and 1 cup shredded Pepper Jack cheese over the salsa. Bake the pizzas at 425 degrees F for 8–12 minutes until tortillas are crisp and cheese melts and browns.

Caramelize Onions

Cut Pizza Dough

- The onions are cooked for a long time so they caramelize. The mixture will turn light brown; stir constantly so the onions don't burn.

- That means the sugars and proteins in the onion break down and combine to form new compounds.

- These new compounds are very flavorful. The onion and garlic become sweet and nutty tasting.

- You can make the onion mixture ahead of time and freeze it. Thaw in the microwave at 30 percent power for 2 minutes.

- Anything you'd put on a big pizza can be added to a mini pizza. Use your imagination!

- Refrigerated pizza dough can be used for the base, or you can make your own dough, use frozen bread dough, or crescent rolls.

- Place the biscuit cutter right next to the round you just cut out so you waste very little of the dough.

- If you don't have a biscuit cutter, use a large drinking glass or cut a circle out of cardboard.

APPETIZERS

QUESADILLAS

Quesadillas don't have to be Tex-Mex; try Greek or French varieties

Quesadillas are thin sandwiches, usually grilled or pan-fried, that are made of a small amount of filling between two tortillas. These quick and easy sandwiches are simple to serve and eat, and they are very versatile.

You can cook quesadillas on a dual contact indoor grill, on the outdoor grill, or in any pan or skillet. Cheese is always used to help hold the tortillas and filling together.

It's important to not overfill the quesadillas, or the filling will just drop out as they are being eaten. Choose highly flavored filling ingredients because of the proportion of filling to bread.

Have fun with your quesadilla creations, and be sure to write down the winners so you'll be able to reproduce them. *Yield: 8–10 servings*

Ingredients

1 red bell pepper, chopped

1 (8-ounce) can crushed pineapple, drained

2 green onions, chopped

2 tablespoons lemon juice

1 tablespoon olive oil

½ teaspoon salt

⅛ teaspoon pepper

8 (10-inch) flour tortillas

1 (8-ounce) package cream cheese

6 ounces smoked salmon

1 cup cubed Brie cheese

½ cup crumbled Roquefort cheese

2 tablespoons butter

Creamy Salmon Brie Quesadillas

- In small bowl, combine red pepper, pineapple, green onion, lemon juice, olive oil, salt, and pepper; mix and refrigerate.

- Place tortillas on work surface. Spread 4 of them with the cream cheese. Divide salmon, Brie, and Roquefort cheeses on top.

- Top with remaining 4 tortillas and press gently. Heat butter in large pan.

- Cook quesadillas on both sides, turning once, for 4–5 minutes or until cheese melts. Cut into wedges and serve with red pepper mixture.

~ VARIATIONS ~

Tex-Mex Quesadillas
Spread 6 large corn tortillas with 1 cup refried beans. Top with 1 cup browned spicy chorizo sausage, ½ cup thawed frozen corn, 1 cup shredded Pepper Jack cheese, and ½ cup shredded sharp cheddar cheese. Top with 6 tortillas, then broil 6 inches from heat for 4 minutes. Turn and broil for 4–5 minutes longer. Serve with salsa.

Green Chicken Quesadillas
Spread 6 flour tortillas with 1 (8-ounce) package softened cream cheese. Add 1 cup chopped cooked chicken, 1 cup green salsa, and 1 chopped green bell pepper. Top with 1½ cups shredded Monterey Jack cheese. Top with remaining tortillas, brush with oil, and grill, turning once, for 7–9 minutes until cheese is melted.

Prepare Filling

- Each tortilla should hold about ½ to ¾ cup of filling. Chop the filling ingredients so they are about the same size.

- Cheese is an essential part of the quesadilla. You could use lower fat cheeses, but nonfat do not melt as well.

- Mix the ingredients gently but thoroughly so each bite of the quesadilla has all of the ingredients.

- Serve the finished quesadillas with a dip: Salsa, ranch dressing, or a dip from this chapter would be delicious.

Grill Quesadillas

- The easiest way to cook quesadillas is on a nonstick skillet. You can cook them in a dry pan, or you can brush or spray them with oil or butter.

- Use a spatula to press down on the quesadillas as they cook to help hold them together.

- A large, round spatula will hold the quesadilla and turn it easily.

- When it's browned on both sides and the cheese is melted, let stand for 3–4 minutes, then cut into quarters.

SIMPLE EGGS

The perfect fried egg is a work of art if you follow a few simple rules

A fried egg seems like an easy food to cook, but there are quite a few rules to follow. Whether you like your eggs simply fried or over easy or hard, follow these directions.

Eggs are best when cooked over low or medium-low heat. Unless you're using pasteurized eggs, the eggs have to be cooked until the yolk is firm. The easiest way to accomplish this is to flip the egg when the whites are firm.

You can also cook the yolk by spooning some of the butter over the egg while it is cooking. With the heat low, you can cover the pan; the steam will help cook the yolk. Just don't overcook the eggs, or they will be rubbery. *Yield: 2 servings*

Ingredients

2 tablespoons butter

4 eggs

½ teaspoon sea salt

⅛ teaspoon white pepper

Classic Fried Eggs

- Heat a nonstick skillet over low heat for 3 minutes. Add butter to skillet; let melt.

- Break eggs into a shallow saucer one at a time, and slip into a shallow bowl, making sure that yolks stay intact.

- Add eggs, carefully and all at once, to the skillet.

- Sprinkle with salt and pepper. Cover and let cook for 3 minutes.

- Uncover and spoon some of the butter over each egg. At this point you can flip them if you'd like. Cover and cook for 30 seconds longer until yolks are set, then serve immediately.

Pasteurized eggs are eggs that have been heat treated while still in the shell. The eggs are heated at 130 degrees F for several minutes. This kills bacteria but doesn't coagulate the egg. Pasteurized eggs have very specific expiration dates, so be sure to follow them to the letter.

• • • • RECIPE VARIATION • • • •

Cheesy Eggs Over Hard: Melt 3 tablespoons butter in a skillet over low heat. Break 4 eggs into a saucer and slip into the butter. Sprinkle with ½ teaspoon salt, ⅛ teaspoon white pepper, and ¼ cup finely grated Parmesan cheese. Cover and cook for 3-4 minutes until whites are firm. Flip the eggs, cover, and cook for 2–3 minutes until the yolks are no longer runny.

Break Eggs Individually

- Most people break eggs by tapping them on the side of the bowl.

- But this method results in broken egg yolks and can force the shell into the egg.

- The best way to crack an egg is to tap it quickly but firmly on the counter. This will break the shell but keeps the yolk intact.

- Break each egg, one at a time, into a saucer, then combine them in a bowl and slip into the pan, so if one yolk breaks, it doesn't ruin the whole pan.

Cook Eggs

- Be sure that the butter is melted and slightly foamy before you add the eggs to the pan.

- Let the eggs set for a few minutes, then gently shake the pan to make sure the eggs aren't sticking.

- As the eggs firm, continue shaking them gently. If you are going to flip the eggs, use a large, round spatula.

- Gently slip the spatula under each egg, or all of them if the spatula is large enough, and flip using your wrist.

SCRAMBLED EGGS

Light and fluffy scrambled eggs are a delicious and healthy breakfast food

Scrambled eggs are the easiest eggs to make, but everyone has eaten dry, hard eggs. You can serve creamy, flavorful, moist eggs in minutes with these simple hints.

Adding air is the secret to fluffy scrambled eggs. Beat the eggs well, turning the mixture with a whisk to incorporate as much air as possible.

Once the eggs start to set on the bottom, it's time to move them around. Using a heatproof spatula, gently push the eggs around the pan, scraping the cooked eggs from the bottom and letting the uncooked mixture flow underneath.

Serve your scrambled eggs immediately. They shouldn't have to wait any longer than an omelette. *Yield: 4 servings*

Ingredients

2 tablespoons butter

8 eggs

2 tablespoons sour cream

1 tablespoon skim milk

½ teaspoon salt

⅛ teaspoon white pepper

2 tablespoons chopped fresh parsley

Creamy Scrambled Eggs

- Melt butter in large non-stick skillet over medium heat. Meanwhile, combine eggs, sour cream, milk, salt, and pepper in medium bowl.

- Beat eggs with wire whisk or eggbeater for 2 minutes until light and foamy. Add to butter in pan.

- Cook eggs over medium heat, moving a heatproof spatula through the eggs occasionally. When the eggs start to set, turn them over as you move them.

- When eggs are set but still moist, sprinkle with parsley and turn out onto serving plate. Serve immediately.

It's worth your while to search out free-range organic eggs, especially if you're cooking these for a special occasion. The yolk will be a deep orange color, the white very thick, and the flavor very rich, nutty, and smooth. You can find free-range eggs at food co-ops and at farmers' markets.

• • • • RECIPE VARIATION • • • •

Scrambled Eggs with Cheese: Combine all ingredients, except omit parsley. Cook as directed, turning the eggs as they begin to set. When eggs are almost done, add 1 cup grated Gouda cheese; cover and remove from heat. Let stand 3 minutes, then serve.

Beat Eggs with Milk

- You can use an eggbeater or a wire whisk to beat the eggs. Never beat or season the eggs ahead of time, or they will be watery.

- The eggs should be cold, just out of the refrigerator, for best results.

- You can add everything from water to heavy cream to eggs. Use about 1 tablespoons of addition for each egg.

- Water or low-fat milk makes eggs fluffy, and sour cream or cream makes them creamy.

Cook Eggs

- Scrambled eggs have to be moved pretty constantly once they have started to cook.

- Scrape the bottom and let the uncooked egg flow onto the pan. The cooked egg will pile up in "curds."

- You can make scrambled eggs ahead of time; just cook until barely done, then top with a bottled Alfredo sauce.

- Refrigerate the eggs for 24 hours. To reheat, stir to blend and bake for 15–20 minutes at 400 degrees F.

OMELETTES

Omelettes aren't difficult to make with these tips and tricks

A light, fluffy omelette is one of French cuisine's best contributions to the world of cooking. They aren't difficult to make with just a few tips.

Unlike fried or scrambled eggs, omelettes are cooked over high heat so the eggs set quickly, trapping the air beaten into them.

Omelettes should be made one at a time, unless you're making an oven omelette, which is sturdier than pan omelettes.

The pan has to be hot, and the bottom coated with melted butter before you add the eggs. As the eggs start to set, lift up the edges to let uncooked egg flow underneath.

Then top with fillings, fold one half over the other, slide onto a plate, and eat! *Yield: 2 servings*

Ingredients

2 tablespoons butter

4 eggs

1 tablespoon water

½ teaspoon salt

⅛ teaspoon white pepper

⅓ cup minced Brie cheese

2 teaspoons fresh thyme leaves

Brie French Omelette

- Have all ingredients ready before you start. Heat butter in a nonstick omelette pan over medium-high heat.

- Beat eggs with water, salt, and pepper until foamy. Add to butter in pan and swirl the mixture in the pan.

- Let cook for 1 minute, then swirl the pan again. Gently lift the edges of egg mixture and let uncooked egg flow underneath.

- When eggs are almost set, sprinkle with Brie and thyme. Cook for 1 minute, then slide half of omelette onto plate and flip other half on top. Serve immediately.

~ VARIATIONS ~

Spinach Gouda Omelette

Melt 2 tablespoons butter. Add 1 chopped onion and ½ cup sliced mushrooms; cook until tender. Add 1 cup fresh baby spinach leaves and cook until wilted. Add 5 eggs beaten with 2 tablespoons milk, ½ teaspoon salt, and ⅛ teaspoon pepper. Cook until moist, then top with 1 cup shredded Gouda cheese. Fold over and serve.

Baked Bacon Omelette

Preheat oven to 350 degrees F. Cook 4 slices of bacon until crisp; drain and crumble. Beat 9 eggs with ⅓ cup milk, 1 tablespoon Dijon mustard, ½ teaspoon salt, and ⅛ teaspoon pepper. Add bacon, and ½ cup each shredded Havarti and Colby cheeses. Pour into greased 9-inch casserole dish. Bake for 40–50 minutes until set.

Prepare Filling

- The filling ingredients must be completely cooked if you're using onions or meats.

- Or you can cook the food in the omelette pan, spread in an even layer, then add the eggs and cook as directed.

- Be sure to chop all of the filling ingredients to about the same size so nothing stands out and the omelette is easy to eat.

- A nonstick skillet is the best choice for omelettes. The finished omelette should slide right out of the pan.

Finish the Omelette

- Add the filling when the omelette is set and there is no more runny egg, but the top is very moist and shiny.

- Don't overfill an omelette. You want to be able to taste the egg as well as the cheeses and meats in the filling.

- Omelettes have to be served the second they are made. They will start to deflate almost immediately.

- That means you have to stand at the stove making each omelette individually, but it's worth it.

FRITTATAS

A frittata is like a sturdy omelette and can be seasoned so many ways

A frittata is the perfect last minute dish for a late supper or brunch. Frittatas are delicious and easy to make. They are a sturdier version of an omelette and aren't as finicky to make.

One of the best things about them is they can be served warm or cold. Because the eggs are cooked for a longer period of time over lower heat and it's cooked on both sides,

the frittata can be cut into wedges to serve.

Use any meat, cheese, or vegetable to fill your frittata. This recipe is a great way to use up leftover pasta, meats, and breadcrumbs. You can use more filling than in an omelette because you use more eggs. *Yield: 4 servings*

Ingredients

2 links chorizo sausage, chopped

2 tablespoons olive oil

1 onion, chopped

2 cups shredded frozen potatoes

8 eggs, beaten

½ teaspoon salt

⅛ teaspoon pepper

½ teaspoon dried oregano

⅓ cup shredded manchego cheese

Spanish Frittata

- In large nonstick saucepan, cook sausage over medium heat until crisp. Remove; drain on paper towels.

- Drain saucepan; add olive oil. Cook onion and potatoes until tender.

- Mix remaining ingredients. Add to pan with chorizo.

Cook lifting to let uncooked mixture flow to bottom, until set.

- Preheat broiler. Sprinkle frittata with cheese and place pan under broiler; cook until top is lightly browned and set. Cut into wedges to serve.

54

Mini Frittatas

Spray 48 mini muffin tins with nonstick baking spray; set aside. Cook 1 chopped onion in a tablespoon of butter. In a medium bowl, beat 8 eggs with ⅓ cup cream, salt, and pepper, and ⅓ cup grated Romano cheese. Add onion and divide among muffin tins. Bake at 375 degrees F for 9–11 minutes.

Breadcrumb Frittata

Melt 2 tablespoons butter and add 1 cup breadcrumbs with 2 cloves minced garlic; cook until crumbs are toasted. Beat 8 eggs with ½ cup milk, salt, pepper, and ⅓ cup chopped parsley. Melt 2 tablespoons butter in pan and add egg mixture; cook until partially set. Add breadcrumbs and 1 cup shredded Swiss cheese. Broil until brown.

Cook Until Set

Finish under the Broiler

- The filling can be cooked before you add the eggs, or you can cook the eggs until partially set, then add the filling.

- Be sure to continually move the eggs in the pan, letting the uncooked egg flow underneath the cooked parts.

- A heatproof silicone spatula is the best tool for this job, since it won't scratch a nonstick pan.

- A frittata is always cooked on both sides. You can flip the frittata, or broil the top.

- To flip the frittata, turn it onto a cookie sheet, then slide back into the pan.

- Watch the frittata carefully when it's under the broiler. You may need to turn it a bit so it browns evenly.

- Serve the frittata immediately, or let cool for 10 minutes, then chill in the refrigerator.

- Frittatas are delicious cold, or you can warm them in the microwave at 50 percent power for 1–2 minutes until hot.

EGGS

EGG CASSEROLES

Egg, sausages, fruits, and vegetables combine in tasty casseroles

Casseroles are a great choice for breakfast. Whether you choose a strata, which is bread layered with ingredients and baked in an egg custard, or a casserole with potatoes and bacon, these easy recipes are perfect.

Because they usually should be made ahead of time, egg casseroles are a great asset for entertaining. You just pull the casserole out of the fridge, bake, and you're ready to eat!

You can also make these recipes and bake them immediately. They only take about 20 minutes to put together.

Think about your favorite flavor combinations when creating your own breakfast casseroles. Ham and potatoes, sausage with cracked wheat bread, and leftover roast beef with spinach and cheese are all great ideas. *Yield: 8 servings*

Ingredients

2 tablespoons butter

1 tablespoon olive oil

1 onion, chopped

3 cups shredded hash brown potatoes, thawed

2 cups frozen vegetarian sausage crumbles, thawed

1 cup chopped tomatoes, drained

1 cup shredded sharp cheddar cheese

10 eggs

1 cup milk

1 tablespoon flour

½ teaspoon salt

⅛ teaspoon pepper

¼ cup grated Parmesan cheese

Egg Potato Casserole

- In large skillet, heat butter and olive oil in large skillet. Cook onion until tender, about 6–7 minutes.

- Spray a 3-quart casserole dish with nonstick cooking spray. Layer potatoes, onion, crumbles, tomatoes, and cheddar cheese.

- Beat eggs, milk, flour, salt, and pepper until smooth. Pour into casserole; top with Parmesan.

- Now you can cover and refrigerate up to 12 hours. Preheat oven to 375 degrees F. Bake casserole for 30–40 minutes until set and turning brown.

There are many types of frozen potatoes you can use in a breakfast casserole. Southern style hash browns are cubed potatoes, sometimes mixed with chopped peppers. Regular hash browns are made from grated or shredded potatoes. And French fries and potato wedges can also be used in these recipes.

•••• RECIPE VARIATION ••••

Croissant Egg Bake: Cut 4 large croissants; place bottoms in greased casserole. Add 1 cup shredded Swiss cheese. Cook 1 chopped onion and 2 cloves garlic in 2 tablespoons butter; spoon over croissants; add tops. Beat 6 eggs with 1 cup milk, salt, pepper, and 1 dried thyme; pour over croissants; add ¼ cup Parmesan. Chill overnight; bake at 350 degrees F 30 minutes.

Layer Ingredients

- It's important to drain frozen and thawed ingredients very well before layering in the casserole.

- If you don't, the finished casserole will have too much liquid, which will dilute the eggs. The casserole will be runny and won't cut nicely into squares.

- You can substitute just about any ingredients for the layered ingredients in this recipe.

- All of the foods, like onions, garlic, bell peppers, raw potatoes, and meat should be cooked before layering in these casseroles.

Add Egg to Casserole

- Beat the egg mixture until well combined, but don't overbeat or the casserole will be tough.

- Pour the egg mixture slowly over the ingredients in the baking dish, allowing it to soak into the ingredients.

- You may need to push the bread and other ingredients down into the casserole a few times until the egg is absorbed.

- Cover the casserole tightly when it's in the refrigerator so it doesn't absorb flavors from other foods.

CREPES

Make crepes like a French chef, then fill them with wonderful healthy fillings

Crepes seem fancy and intimidating, but they are actually quite easy to make. The secret is all in the wrist. Once you've learned how to add batter to the pan and swirl it around, a crepe will take about two minutes to make.

Once made, you can freeze crepes, each separated by foil or waxed paper, then thaw and fill with anything you'd like.

Thaw crepes by letting them stand at room temperature for about thirty minutes, then fill and serve, or bake until hot.

Fillings for crepes can range from leftover beef stroganoff to whipped cream and fruits. These thin pancakes are one of the best ways to use leftovers, so use your imagination and have fun! *Yield: 8 servings*

Ingredients

¾ cup flour

2 teaspoons chili powder

⅛ teaspoon salt

10 eggs, divided

¾ cup milk

⅓ cup water

¼ cup sour cream

1 jalapeño pepper, minced

2 tablespoons butter

4 green onions, minced

1 cup shredded sharp cheddar cheese

2 tomatoes, chopped

Tex-Mex Egg Crepes

- Mix flour, chili powder, and salt. In small bowl, beat 2 eggs with milk and water; add to flour mixture; whisk.

- Wipe an 8-inch crepe pan with some oil and place on medium heat. Add a scant ¼ cup batter; swirl to cover bottom; cook until set. Repeat with remaining batter.

- In large bowl, beat 8 eggs with sour cream and jalapeños. Melt 2 tablespoons butter in large skillet; scramble eggs.

- Divide egg mixture among crepes; top with remaining ingredients, roll and serve.

Plain Crepes

For plain crepes, combine flour and salt in medium bowl. Beat eggs with milk and water and add to flour mixture; whisk until smooth. You can store the batter in the fridge up to 2 days. For sweet crepes, add 2 tablespoons of sugar to the flour mixture. Cook as directed. Freeze crepes, well wrapped, up to 6 months. Thaw at room temperature.

Fruit Filled Crepes

Make sweet crepes as directed and cool completely. For filling, combine 2 cups chopped strawberries, 1 cup raspberries, and 1 cup blueberries with 2 tablespoons sugar; let stand for 5 minutes. Fold in 2 cups frozen nondairy whipped topping, thawed, along with ½ cup strawberry preserves. Fill crepes, roll up; sprinkle with powdered sugar.

Make Crepe Batter

Cook Crepes

- You can use a blender or food processor to mix the crepe batter instead of a whisk.

- Just combine the eggs, milk, and water in the blender and blend until combined.

- Add the flour and seasonings and blend just until the batter is smooth; no longer. Let the batter stand for 5 minutes before making the crepes.

- Don't overmix crepe batter, no matter which method you use. Overmixing will make the crepes tough.

- It's all in the wrist! Tip the pan back and forth so the batter swirls and evenly covers the bottom of the pan.

- Don't stack crepes on top of each other when they come out of the pan or they will stick.

- Place the hot cooked crepes on clean kitchen towels until they have cooled.

- Stack with foil, plastic wrap, or waxed paper between each crepe. They can be stored in the refrigerator up to 4 days.

EGGS

BEEF STIR-FRY

Quick stir-fry with tender beef and savory vegetables is an excellent quick dinner

Stir-frying is a quick cooking method developed in Asian countries. The actual cooking time is about five to ten minutes.

Have all of the ingredients ready and waiting to go into the wok or skillet. You can prepare the ingredients ahead of time; in fact, some ingredients, like marinating meat, benefit from time in the refrigerator.

You don't need a wok to stir-fry, but you do need a sturdy saucepan and a heat-resistant spatula. Don't use nonstick equipment to stir-fry, since you need to scrape the bottom to remove pan drippings.

Almost any meat and vegetable combination is delicious, so enjoy experimenting. *Yield: 6 servings*

Ingredients

¼ cup low-sodium soy sauce

2 tablespoons white wine vinegar

1 tablespoon honey

½ cup beef broth

1 tablespoon minced gingerroot

1 tablespoon cornstarch

1 teaspoon sesame oil

⅛ teaspoon pepper

1 pound sirloin tip steak

2 tablespoons peanut oil

2 cups snow peas

½ cup chopped green onion

1 (15-ounce) can baby corn, drained

1 red bell pepper, chopped

Beef and Vegetable Stir-Fry

- In medium bowl, combine the first 8 ingredients.

- Slice steak into ½-inch x 4-inch pieces against the grain and add to marinade. Cover and refrigerate for 12–24 hours.

- Heat wok or large skillet over medium-high heat. Add pea- nut oil. Drain beef, reserving marinade. Stir-fry beef until browned and remove.

- Add vegetables to pan; stir- fry until crisp-tender. Return beef and reserved marinade to wok; stir-fry until beef is tender and sauce is thick- ened. Serve over hot cooked rice.

~ VARIATIONS ~

Beef Mushroom Stir-Fry

In resealable plastic bag, mix 2 tablespoons cornstarch, 3 tablespoons teriyaki sauce, 1 tablespoon minced ginger-root, 2 cloves minced garlic, and 1 cup beef stock. Add 1 pound round steak, cut into strips; marinate for 2 hours in fridge. Stir-fry 1 cup each chopped onion, celery, and mushrooms in 2 tablespoons peanut oil. Add drained beef, then marinade; stir-fry until beef is done.

Beef Pepper Stir-Fry

Combine 1 tablespoon grated gingerroot, 2 tablespoons cornstarch, 1 cup beef broth, and 2 cloves minced garlic with 1 pound round steak, cut into strips; marinate. Drain beef, reserving marinade. Heat 2 tablespoons oil; stir-fry beef until pink; remove. Stir-fry 1 chopped onion, and 1 each red and yellow bell pepper. Add beef and marinade; stir-fry until sauce is thickened.

Prepare Ingredients

- Until you're experienced at cutting foods, work slowly and with a ruler to measure the size of the chopped ingredients.

- If you are preparing the food ahead of time, refrigerate each separately in a closed plastic bag.

- Don't refrigerate meats longer than the recipe states, or they may become mushy.

- You can marinate the vegetables with the meats if you'd like, for even more flavor. Serve these stir-fry recipes over hot cooked rice.

Stir-Fry

- The stir-fry technique isn't difficult to achieve. Be sure that you turn all of the foods with your spatula.

- Reach into the edges of the pan so no food overcooks. Be sure to remove foods when the recipe specifies.

- Always stir the marinade or sauce mixture before adding to the wok or skillet, because the cornstarch can settle to the bottom.

- Always serve stir-fried food immediately; have your guests waiting for the food.

61

PAN-FRIED BEEF

Cook beef for a few minutes, add some ingredients for a sauce, and you have an elegant dinner

Pan-frying is an excellent quick and easy cooking technique. For beef to cook in a short amount of time, it usually has to be pounded thin or cut into strips.

Very thin pieces of meat that have been pounded are called paillards, also known as cutlets. Cook the cutlets as is or coat them with a seasoned flour mixture or breadcrumbs.

This type of cooking automatically creates a sauce, whether or not the meat has been marinated. The pan drippings left behind when the meat is cooked are full of flavor; add broth and stir vigorously to release them, add a bit of butter, swirl, and pour over the beef. *Yield: 4 servings*

Ingredients

1 pound sirloin steak

2 tablespoons olive oil

2 tablespoons red wine vinegar

½ teaspoon garlic salt

⅛ teaspoon pepper

1 tablespoon minced fresh rosemary

1 tablespoon fresh thyme leaves

2 tablespoons butter

½ cup beef broth

French Beef Paillards

- Cut steak into 4 serving pieces. Place on plastic wrap and sprinkle with a bit of water. Top with more plastic wrap. Pound until ⅛ inch thick. Remove plastic wrap.

- Mix oil, vinegar, salt, pepper in baking dish. Add beef, cover; marinate 20 minutes.

- Remove steaks from marinade; rub rosemary and thyme into meat. Heat butter in skillet over high heat.

- Add steaks; cook 1–2 minutes per side until browned. Remove meat and cover; add broth to pan. Cook 2 minutes. Pour over steaks; serve.

~ VARIATIONS ~

Mustard Strip Steaks

Rub 4 strip steaks with 2 tablespoons each olive oil and mustard; sprinkle with salt, pepper, 1 tablespoon dried thyme, 1 tablespoon mustard seed; let stand for 10 minutes. Heat 2 tablespoons oil in pan; cook steaks for 3–5 minutes on each side. Remove; add ½ cup broth and 2 tablespoons Dijon mustard; boil and pour over steaks.

Burgundy Tenderloin

Pound 4 tenderloin steaks until ½ inch thick; sprinkle with salt, pepper, and 1 teaspoon dried oregano; cover with ½ cup burgundy wine. Let stand for 10 minutes. Drain and cook in 2 tablespoons oil for 4–6 minutes on each side. Remove steak; add wine mixture; bring to a boil. Add 2 tablespoons butter, swirl, and pour over steaks.

Pound the Beef

- When pounding beef, be fairly gentle. You don't want to tear or rip the meat.

- If pounding a tenderloin or chuck steak, cut into individual pieces, then place cut side up on waxed paper.

- Start at the center and work out toward the edges of the beef.

- You can use the flat side of a meat mallet or a rolling pin. It may help to sprinkle the meat with a little water before you start.

Pan-Fry

- After the steak has marinated, many of the fibers have been weakened by the acid.

- This is the perfect time to add more flavor with dry rubs. Sprinkle on herbs, spices, peppers, and sugar.

- Be careful with dry rubs that contain a large amount of sugar, because they can burn easily on the high heat of the skillet.

- When the beef is done, let sit for 5 minutes; then, unless you're serving each piece, slice across the grain.

BROILED STEAK

Broiling is just like grilling; it adds great caramelized flavor to simple steaks

Broiling is just like grilling, but you do it indoors. The secret to broiling is to preheat the broiler, and cook with the oven door open. This high heat mimics the heat from a grill. Position the food 4–6 inches from the heat source and watch it carefully.

You may need to move the steaks around and turn the broiling pan so the meat is evenly cooked. Don't walk away from the oven, because the meat can go from caramelized to charred in seconds.

Marinades, dry rubs, mops, and pastes can add great flavor to broiled steaks. If these sauces contain sugar, they will caramelize on the meat, creating a delicious crust. *Yield: 4 servings*

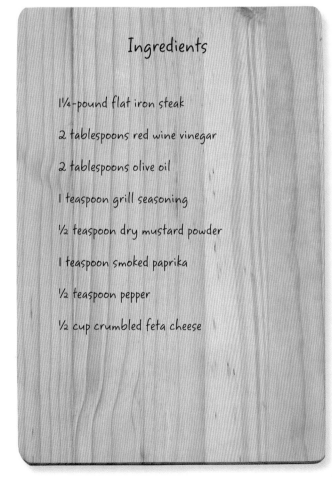

Ingredients

1¼-pound flat iron steak

2 tablespoons red wine vinegar

2 tablespoons olive oil

1 teaspoon grill seasoning

½ teaspoon dry mustard powder

1 teaspoon smoked paprika

½ teaspoon pepper

½ cup crumbled feta cheese

Broiled Spicy Feta Steak

- Place steak in glass baking dish. In small bowl, combine remaining ingredients except cheese and mix well. Rub into both sides of steak.

- Marinate at room temperature for 30 minutes or in the refrigerator for 8–24 hours.

- Arrange rack 4 inches from heat source and preheat broiler. Drain steak, pat dry, and place on broiler rack.

- Broil for 6–7 minutes per side, turning once, until steak is medium rare. Remove, top with cheese, cover with foil, and let stand for 5 minutes, then serve.

Steak houses have a secret for creating that rich, almost charred crust on their steaks. They add butter to the steak after it's cooked. The steaks are placed under a salamander, or industrial broiler, and broiled until the butter starts to char. You really can't replicate this at home, but melting butter onto a seared steak is delicious.

• • • • RECIPE VARIATION • • • •

Broiled Rib Eye Steak: Brush 4 boneless rib eye steaks with olive oil; rub with a mixture of 1 teaspoon salt, ¼ teaspoon pepper, ½ teaspoon dry mustard, 1 tablespoon brown sugar, and 1 teaspoon dried oregano. Let stand for 10 minutes. Broil 6 inches from heat source for 8–10 minutes, turning once, until desired doneness. Top each steak with a pat of butter and serve.

Marinate Steak

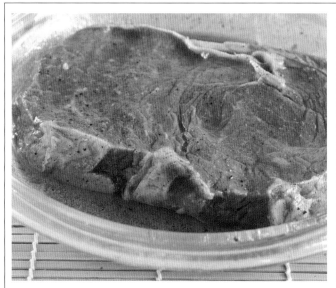

- Any marinade can be used for the steak. There are lots of bottled versions on the market.

- Salad dressings are also good choices for steak marinade. The tougher the steak, the longer it should marinate in the fridge.

- Round steak and flank steak should be marinated. Flat iron steaks, rib eye, sirloin, and T-bone steaks don't need a marinade.

- Be sure to pat the meat dry after it's removed from the marinade so the surface caramelizes.

Broil Steak

- The steak should be 4–6 inches from the heat source for best results. And make sure the broiler is preheated.

- Don't turn the steak until the top is browned and crusty. Use tongs or a spatula.

- To test doneness, cut a small slit into the steak to see the color. Medium rare should be a deep pink. Medium steaks are a lighter pink color.

- Or test using a meat thermometer. Rare is 140 degrees, medium 150 degrees, and well done 160 degrees F.

BEEF IN THE SKILLET

One-dish meal in the skillet uses ground beef for a hearty recipe

One-dish meals are one of the best ways to save time in the kitchen. All you need to add to these recipes is some bread, perhaps a cool salad, and dessert.

One-dish skillet meals are usually faster to make than oven meals. And you don't even need a kitchen! An electric skillet and a spoon work just fine.

Ground beef is the perfect ingredient upon which to base a skillet meal. It's inexpensive, delicious, and everyone loves it. It can be formed into meatballs or Salisbury steak, or browned with onions and garlic.

A skillet recipe is a great last minute choice for entertaining. Keep ingredients on hand to make your own favorite recipes. *Yield: 5 servings*

Ingredients

¼ cup crushed buttery round crackers

1 egg

1 (10.75-ounce) can condensed French onion soup, divided

¼ teaspoon pepper

1¼ pounds 80 percent lean ground beef

¼ cup flour

2 tablespoons olive oil

2 tablespoons butter

1 onion, chopped

3 cloves garlic, minced

1 (8-ounce) package sliced mushrooms

½ cup chili sauce

2 tablespoons Dijon mustard

2 teaspoons Worcestershire sauce

Classic Salisbury Steak

- Mix cracker crumbs, egg, 2 tablespoons soup, pepper; mix well, then add beef.

- Form into 5 oval patties. Dredge in flour, shaking off excess. Heat oil in large skillet; brown patties on both sides on medium heat.

- Remove patties to plate.

Drain fat from skillet; add butter; cook onion, garlic, and mushrooms 5 minutes.

- Add remaining soup, chili sauce, mustard, and Worcestershire sauce; mix well. Return patties to skillet, bring to a simmer, cover, and simmer for 15–20 minutes until beef is cooked.

~ VARIATIONS ~

Beef Meatball Skillet

Cook 1 chopped onion and 3 cloves minced garlic in 2 tablespoons oil. Add 1 (8-ounce) package sliced mushrooms, 1 (14-ounce) can diced tomatoes, 2 cups beef broth, salt, pepper, and dried thyme. Add 16 ounces frozen cooked meatballs; simmer 15 minutes. Add 2 cups egg noodles; simmer 8 minutes. Add ½ cup sour cream with 2 tablespoons flour; simmer until thickened.

Beef Steak and Potato Skillet

Toss 1 pound thinly sliced round steak with 3 tablespoons flour, 1 teaspoon each paprika, salt, dried oregano, and ⅛ teaspoon pepper; brown in 3 tablespoons butter. Add 2 potatoes, diced, 1 chopped onion, and 3 cloves garlic. Add 2 cups beef broth and diced tomato; simmer for 15 minutes. Add 1 cup Alfredo sauce; simmer.

Shape into Patties

- Like meatloaf and meatballs, these patties must be handled gently or they will be tough.

- Mix the ingredients for the patties first, then add the beef and mix just until combined; don't overmix.

- You can make the patties ahead of time; dredge them in flour and brown when you want to eat.

- When browning the patties, don't turn them until they easily release from the skillet for the best color and crust.

Add Sauce and Finish

- After the skillet is drained, don't wipe it out or wash it. Not only does this save time, it adds flavor.

- You want the drippings from the patties, which are on the bottom of the pan, to blend into the sauce.

- You can add more vegetables to this skillet meal for nutrition; green bell pepper, zucchini, or summer squash are good choices.

- Serve this skillet meal over hot cooked rice or mashed potatoes to soak up the sauce.

GRILLED STEAK

Steak on the grill is one of the classic recipes of summer, all year round

Your grill is an ideal quick cooking appliance. If you own a gas grill, you can heat it up, start cooking, and finish in under twenty minutes. A charcoal grill takes a bit longer to start.

Grilled foods have a slightly smoky taste and develop wonderful caramelization on the surface. Sugars and proteins on the food break down, then recombine to form hundreds of compounds that give grilled foods their complex taste.

When grilling, always build a two-level fire. On a gas grill, first heat all the burners, then turn one off so there's a cooler area to control cooking. On charcoal grills, leave a small space empty of coals.

Enjoy steak grilled to perfection. *Yield: 4 servings*

Mushroom Grilled Steak

Ingredients

2 tablespoons olive oil

3 tablespoons red wine vinegar

1 tablespoon honey

2 cloves garlic, minced

1 teaspoon grill seasoning

1/8 teaspoon pepper

1½ pounds flat iron steak

1 (8-ounce) package button mushrooms

1 (8-ounce) package cremini mushrooms

- In large plastic bag, combine oil, vinegar, honey, garlic, seasoning, and pepper and mix well.

- Cut steak into 4 portions. Add to marinade along with mushrooms, close bag, and turn bag over several times to distribute marinade. Let stand for 30–40 minutes.

- Preheat grill to medium. Drain steak and pat dry. Grill steak over direct heat for 8–10 minutes, turning once, until medium.

- At the same time, drain mushrooms and add to a grill basket; grill, turning basket, until mushrooms are tender, about 7 minutes.

~ VARIATIONS ~

Rib Eye Steak with Feta Butter
Brush 4 boneless rib eye steaks with olive oil and sprinkle with salt, pepper, and grill seasoning. Let stand for 10 minutes. Meanwhile, in small bowl combine ¼ cup butter, ⅓ cup crumbled feta cheese, ½ teaspoon dried oregano, ½ teaspoon grated lemon zest, and 3 tablespoons chopped parsley. Grill steak to desired doneness, then remove, top with butter mixture, and serve.

Delmonico Steak
In plastic bag, combine 3 tablespoons each olive oil, Worcestershire sauce, minced onion, and steak seasoning. Add ¼ teaspoon pepper and ½ teaspoon salt. Marinate round steaks in refrigerator for 18–24 hours. Prepare grill, drain steak, pat dry, and grill to desired doneness. Discard marinade.

Marinate Steak

- Marinade makes even tough steaks tender by breaking down the fibers in the meat. The acidic ingredient is key.

- Don't marinate the steaks longer than directed, or the fibers will break down too much and the steak will be mushy.

- Always marinate meat in the refrigerator unless marinating time is less than 30 minutes.

- Pat the steak dry before you place it on the grill for best caramelization. Don't turn the steaks until they release easily; then turn with tongs.

Grill Mushrooms

- A grill basket is a great way to grill smaller foods that might fall through the grill rack.

- Add the ingredients and lock the basket; place on the grill over direct heat.

- Then shake and turn the basket occasionally as the food cooks. Add the food in the basket after the steaks start cooking.

- If you'd like, you can boil the marinade for 2 minutes, add a bit of butter, and serve it as a sauce for the steaks.

STEAK WITH COMPOUND BUTTER

Flavored butter melting into steak is one of the easiest ways to dress up the meat

We all know that a great way to finish off a grilled steak is to top it with a pat of butter as it comes off the grill. But did you know you can dress up butter to make it even more special?

Compound butter is a mixture of butter and other ingredients like cooked garlic, herbs, spices, and cheeses. You can use it to top grilled chicken, pork, or seafood as well.

There's one caveat to making a compound butter; it doesn't store well. You can freeze these butters up to two weeks, but don't store them in the fridge longer than two days for food safety reasons. *Yield: 4 servings*

Ingredients

6 cloves garlic

2 tablespoons olive oil

½ teaspoon salt

⅛ teaspoon pepper

⅓ cup butter, softened

¼ cup crumbled blue cheese

1 teaspoon chopped fresh oregano

4 boneless rib eye steaks

1 teaspoon grill seasoning

¼ teaspoon pepper

Rib Eye with Roasted Garlic Butter

- Place unpeeled garlic cloves and oil in a small saucepan. Heat over medium heat until cloves turn golden brown.

- Remove cloves from oil and let cool. Squeeze flesh from cloves. Combine with salt, pepper, butter, blue cheese, and oregano in small bowl; refrigerate.

- Preheat grill to medium. Brush steaks with the oil from the garlic and sprinkle with grill seasoning and pepper.

- Grill steaks over medium direct heat, turning at least twice, about 12–14 minutes for medium rare. Top with butter; serve immediately.

70

~ VARIATIONS ~

Flat Iron Steaks with Pesto Butter

Marinate 4 flat iron steaks in a mixture of 2 tablespoons lemon juice, 1 tablespoon olive oil, ½ teaspoon salt, and ½ teaspoon dried basil for 2 hours in fridge. Meanwhile, combine ⅓ cup softened butter, ¼ cup minced fresh basil, 3 tablespoons grated Parmesan cheese, and 2 minced cloves of garlic. Mix well; chill. Drain steaks, pat dry; grill for 8–10 minutes; top with butter.

Steak with Lemon Herb Butter

For butter, combine ¼ cup softened butter with 1 tablespoon lemon juice, ½ teaspoon grated lemon zest, 2 teaspoons fresh thyme leaves, and ⅛ teaspoon pepper. Roll into a log, wrap in waxed paper, and chill for 2–3 hours. Grill steaks until desired doneness. Slice butter into rounds and place on steak; serve immediately.

Make Compound Butter

Grill Steak

- You can make compound butter with just a bowl and a spoon. Well-softened butter is the key to this method.

- Or you can combine the butter with the other ingredients in a food processor. Pulse until well mixed.

- You can form the butter into a log and chill, then cut rounds to top the steaks.

- Or just place the butter in a dish and spoon a dollop onto each steak for a more casual presentation.

- The key to grilled steaks is to leave them alone when they first go on the grill. Don't move the steaks until they release.

- Clean and oil the grill grate before you add the steaks. Oil the steaks, or, if they have been marinated, pat them dry.

- Turn the steaks at least twice. The first turn should be when they release from the grill.

- The final turn finishes the steaks. If you are brushing with marinade, this will "cook off" the marinade.

BROILED BURGERS

You can flavor burgers any way you'd like, from classic American to French

Ground beef is one of the most versatile meats in the supermarket. It can be crumbled into a pasta sauce, made into a meatloaf, formed into pinwheels, or shaped into burgers.

Burgers are easy to make and they can be flavored in many different ways. As long as you keep a basic proportion of ½–¾ cup additions per pound of beef, the meat will shape

easily and hold together well when broiling.

Handle the meat gently when making burgers. Combine all of the ingredients together except the meat and mix well. Then add the beef and mix gently with your hands just until combined. Less handling means juicier burgers.

Have fun with these recipes. *Yield: 4 servings*

Ingredients

¼ cup finely chopped onion

3 cloves garlic, minced

3 tablespoons butter, divided

2 tablespoons ketchup, plus more for serving

2 tablespoons mustard

1¼ pounds 80 percent lean ground chuck

4 onion buns, split

¼ cup mayonnaise

4 slices sharp cheddar cheese

1 tomato, sliced

Classic American Burgers

- Cook onion and garlic in 1 tablespoon butter until tender. Remove to large bowl; cool.

- Stir in 2 tablespoons ketchup and mustard, then add beef and mix. Form into 4 patties. Press into centers to make depression.

- Preheat broiler. Broil patties 6 inches from for 8–10 minutes, turning once, until 160 degrees F.

- Spread buns with softened remaining butter; broil until toasted. Spread with mayonnaise and ketchup, and top with burgers, cheese, tomato, and tops of buns.

~ VARIATIONS ~

Bacon Burger

Cook 4 slices bacon until crisp; crumble; place in large bowl. Add 2 cloves minced garlic, 2 tablespoons Worcestershire sauce, salt, pepper, and 1 egg. Add 1¼ pounds ground beef and mix gently. Form into 4 patties, press indentation in center, and broil until done. Serve on toasted onion buns with ketchup, mustard, and sliced tomato.

Greek Burgers

In small saucepan, cook ½ cup chopped onion and 2 cloves minced garlic in 1 tablespoon olive oil. Place in large bowl. Add 1 tablespoon each lemon juice and mustard, ½ teaspoon grated lemon zest, and ½ cup crumbled feta cheese. Add 1¼ pounds ground beef; shape into patties and press center. Broil until done; serve in toasted English muffins with feta and mayonnaise.

Mix Burger Ingredients

- All of the ingredients should be cooled before you add the ground beef so it doesn't start cooking.

- Don't handle the mixture too much after the beef has been added, and shape gently using your hands.

- You can shape the burgers ahead of time; cover and refrigerate up to 4 hours before cooking.

- Preheat the broiler before you add the hamburgers, and watch them carefully under the heat. Turn gently using a spatula.

Form Patties

- Many homemade hamburgers tend to puff up when they're cooked, making it difficult to add condiments.

- Press down in the center of each patty with a spoon or your fingers to prevent this.

- The meat will still swell during the cooking time, but because of the indentation, the final product will be flat.

- Never press down on the meat while it's cooking, or you'll press out all the juice and flavor.

MEATLOAF IN THE MICROWAVE

Microwave meatloaf stays moist and juicy when cooked in this special way

Yes, you can cook more in the microwave than popcorn and frozen dinners. Meatloaf cooks especially well because the mixture is dense. The energy moves easily through the meat, cooking it thoroughly but leaving it tender and juicy.

There are some special rules and regulations to follow when you're cooking in the microwave oven. Follow turning, stirring, and covering instructions to the letter.

With all microwave recipes, standing time is essential. This means the recipe must stand on a solid surface, not a rack, after cooking to let the heat distribute so the food is evenly cooked.

Think about different ways to flavor meatloaf, from Spanish olives and paprika to German spices. *Yield: 6 servings*

Ingredients

4 slices bacon

1 tablespoon olive oil

¼ cup finely chopped onion

3 cloves garlic, minced

⅓ cup chopped cremini mushrooms

⅓ cup crushed crisp rice cereal

½ teaspoon salt

⅛ teaspoon pepper

1 cup grated Swiss cheese

1 egg

1 pound extra lean ground beef

¼ cup chili sauce

2 tablespoons mustard

Bacon Swiss Meatloaf

- Cook bacon until crisp; drain, crumble and set aside. Drain pan and add olive oil, onion, garlic, and mushrooms; cook until liquid evaporates.

- Remove to large bowl, add bacon and cool slightly. Stir in cereal, salt, pepper, cheese, and egg. Add beef.

- Form into loaf in 1-quart microwave-safe dish. Cover; microwave on high 10–11 minutes to 155 degrees F.

- Mix chili sauce and mustard; pour over loaf. Microwave for 5–7 minutes longer or until 160 degrees F. Cover; let stand 10 minutes; slice.

Spanish Meatloaf

In large bowl, combine ¼ cup minced red onion, ¼ cup minced olives, 2 minced garlic cloves, ¼ cup chili sauce, ¼ cup ground almonds, ½ teaspoon paprika, ½ teaspoon salt and ⅛ teaspoon pepper. Add 1 pound ground beef; form into loaf. Place in dish; cover with 3 tablespoons chili sauce. Microwave as directed.

Sweet and Sour Meatloaf

Combine ¼ cup chili sauce, 1 egg, ½ cup crushed buttery crackers, 2 tablespoons sugar, 2 tablespoons apple cider vinegar, ½ teaspoon salt, ⅛ teaspoon pepper, and 2 tablespoons mustard; add 1 pound ground beef and mix. Shape into loaf, place in microwave-safe dish. Brush with ¼ cup ketchup and microwave as directed.

Cook Bacon and Onions

- Most ingredients should be cooked before being mixed into a meatloaf. The cooking time isn't long enough to make them tender.

- The bacon will soften when added to the ground beef, so make sure it's cooked very crisp and drained well.

- Cool the bacon and onion mixture before you add the cheese and meat, so everything mixes well.

- Mix gently but thoroughly by hand, just until all of the ingredients combine.

Finish the Meatloaf

- There are 3 tricks to the best microwave meatloaf. One is to not overmix the ingredients.

- The second is to follow cooking and standing times. Check the meatloaf with an instant-read thermometer to be sure of the temperature.

- And number 3: cover the meatloaf and let it stand on a solid surface for at least 10 minutes before you slice it.

- The temperature will rise about 5 degrees F when standing, to the safe temperature of 165 degrees F.

MICROWAVE CHILI

Rich and thick chili, made with beef and beans, is easy to make in the microwave

Chili is a classic quick and easy dish usually cooked on top of the stove. But the microwave is a faster way to cook it, and the flavors blend beautifully. With this recipe, you can have chili on the table in about twenty minutes.

Be sure to fully cook the ground beef with the onions before you add the other ingredients. Stir the beef occasionally to make sure that it breaks up and cooks evenly.

Once you've mastered the basic recipe, start having fun with it! Use ground chicken or turkey, try spicy pork sausage, or even use frozen vegetarian crumbles. Make it spicier with jalapeño or serrano peppers and use different types of beans. The sky's the limit! *Yield: 4 servings*

Ingredients

1 pound ground beef

1 onion, chopped

3 cloves garlic, minced

1 tablespoon chili powder

1 teaspoon ground cumin

1 (14.5-ounce) can diced tomatoes with onions and chiles, undrained

1 (8-ounce) can tomato sauce

1 (12-ounce) jar salsa

1 (15-ounce) can kidney beans, drained

¼ cup strong brewed coffee

2 tablespoons mustard

Salt and pepper to taste

1 tablespoon cornstarch

⅓ cup water

Spicy Tex-Mex Chili

- Crumble beef into 2 ½-quart microwave-safe dish. Add onion and garlic. Microwave mixture on high for 4 minutes, stirring once.

- Microwave on high for 2–3 minutes longer until beef is cooked. Drain off fat.

- Add remaining ingredients except cornstarch and water and stir well. Cover and microwave on high for 10–12 minutes until bubbly.

- Stir chili. Add mixture of cornstarch and water; stir well. Microwave on high for 2–3 minutes longer until thickened. Let stand for 5 minutes and serve.

~ VARIATIONS ~

Vegetable Beef Chili

Cook 1 pound ground beef, 1 chopped onion, 2 cups mushrooms, and 1 sliced yellow summer squash in microwave for 6 minutes; drain. Add 1 tablespoon chili powder, 1 cup salsa, 14-ounce can diced tomatoes, 1 cup beef broth, and 15-ounce can black beans; stir well. Cover; microwave on high for 10–12 minutes, stirring once. Serve with blue corn chips and shredded cheese.

Beef Chili with No Beans

Cook 1 pound ground beef, 1 chopped onion, 3 cloves garlic, and 1 chopped green bell pepper in microwave for 5 minutes; drain. Add 1 tablespoon chili powder, salt and pepper, 8-ounce can tomato sauce, 2 cups salsa, and ¼ cup tomato paste. Cover and microwave on high for 10–12 minutes, stirring once. Serve with Cotija cheese.

Brown Ground Beef

- The ground beef won't really "brown" in the microwave; it will lose its pink color. That's how you tell it's done.

- Onions, garlic, and other vegetables cook very well in the microwave oven.

- Be sure to stir the beef at least once during the cooking time so it cooks evenly.

- When you drain off fat, pour it into an empty can and store it in the freezer. When it's full, discard it.

Stir Chili

- When you stir the chili, use a hot pad to hold the dish because it will be hot.

- Stir gently, but be sure to get into the corners of the dish so food doesn't stick there and overcook.

- Always let the chili stand, covered, on a solid surface for at least 5 minutes after microwaving.

- Serve your finished chili with everything from sour cream to salsa, sliced avocados, chopped tomatoes, and shredded cheese.

DELUXE GRILLED BURGERS

Grown-up burgers use expensive but easily available ingredients for a special recipe

Grilling gives burgers a wonderfully smoky taste. There's something primal and satisfying about cooking meat over a fire.

Ground meat has to be cooked to an internal temperature of 165 degrees F for food safety reasons. Always check the temperature of the burgers before you serve them. An instant-read thermometer to test the temperature of meat is easy to use

and should be part of every quick and easy kitchen.

Build a 2-level fire when you cook your burgers so you can move them from higher to lower heat as needed. You don't want the outside to burn before the inside is fully cooked.

Add indulgent ingredients to your burgers. Cheeses, bacon and caramelized onions are all delicious. *Yield: 4 servings*

Ingredients

8 slices bacon

6 tablespoons butter, divided

½ cup finely chopped onion

2 cloves garlic, minced

3 tablespoons steak sauce

1¼ pounds 80 percent ground beef

1 teaspoon steak seasoning

4 kaiser buns

¼ cup Dijon mustard

¼ cup mayonnaise

4 thin slices sharp cheddar cheese

1 tomato, sliced

½ cup fresh basil leaves

Deluxe Beef Burger

- Cook bacon until crisp; drain on paper towels. Drain pan but don't wipe. Add 2 tablespoons butter.

- Cook onion, garlic, about 7 minutes. Place in large bowl. Add steak sauce, then ground beef; mix gently.

- Form into 4 patties 5 inches in diameter. Make indentation in center; top with seasoning and 2 teaspoons butter pats. Grill over direct medium heat 9–11 minutes.

- Butter buns and grill. Spread with mayonnaise and mustard. Top with burgers, cheese, tomato, bacon, basil, top half with bun; serve.

~ VARIATIONS ~

Onion Brie Burgers

Cook ½ cup minced onion and 2 cloves minced garlic in 2 tablespoons butter. Cool in large bowl. Add salt, pepper, and 1 teaspoon thyme leaves; work in 1 pound ground beef. Form into 8 thin patties. Top 4 with slices of Brie cheese; add remaining patties and seal edges. Grill over medium direct heat. Serve on English muffins with lettuce.

Butter Burger

Combine 3 tablespoons steak sauce, ½ teaspoon seasoned salt, and ⅛ teaspoon pepper in bowl. Add 1 pound ground beef and form into 4 patties, each around a pat of butter. Chill for 3–4 hours. Grill over medium direct heat until done; top with more butter. Serve on grilled buns with lettuce, tomato, and avocado.

Mix Ingredients

- Just as with meatloaf, burgers are better if the meat isn't handled much. Use a light touch.

- Combine all the other ingredients first before adding the meat. Work gently with your hands just until combined.

- The best beef for burgers has about 20 percent fat. Any less and the burgers will be dry. Any more and the meat may fall apart.

- You can chill the formed burgers until you're ready to cook; just add another minute or 2 to grilling time.

Grill Burgers

- Make sure that the coals are burned down to a gray ash covering, or that the gas grill has been preheated, before adding the meat.

- For medium heat, you should be able to hold your hand over the grill for 5 seconds before you have to pull it away.

- Never press down on the burgers when on the grill. That will just press the juice and flavor out.

- Have fun garnishing burgers; use guacamole, salsa, basil leaves, or ethnic mustards.

MEATBALLS WITH PASTA

Quick cooking meatballs with tender pasta in a flavorful sauce are just plain delicious

Frozen, fully cooked meatballs are one of the best convenience items in the grocery store. Always have a bag or two in the freezer and you'll be able to whip up pasta dishes, meatball sandwiches, and soups in seconds.

There are several sizes and flavors of frozen meatballs on the market. For main dishes, choose the larger meatballs. You can find them in Italian and plain flavors. Follow package instructions for thawing and heating. Make your own meatballs, cook them, and freeze to use in many recipes. Meatballs are easy to make and inexpensive. Once you've mastered the recipe, have fun with ethnic flavors and variations. German, Spanish, or Tex-Mex meatballs would be delicious. *Yield: 6 servings*

Ingredients

- 2 tablespoons olive oil
- 1 onion, chopped
- 4 cloves garlic, minced
- 1 (6-ounce) can tomato paste
- 1 cup beef broth
- 2 (14.5-ounce) cans diced tomatoes, undrained
- 1 (8-ounce) can tomato sauce
- 1 teaspoon salt
- ¼ teaspoon pepper
- 1 teaspoon dried basil leaves
- ½ teaspoon dried oregano leaves
- 1 (16-ounce) package frozen meatballs, thawed
- 1 (16-ounce) package spaghetti pasta

Classic Italian Spaghetti and Meatballs

- Cook onion and garlic in olive oil until tender, about 7 minutes.

- Add tomato paste; stir, then let stand until paste starts to brown in spots. Stir in remaining ingredients except pasta. Simmer 45–55 minutes; stir occasionally.

- Cook pasta until al dente according to package directions. Drain pasta, reserving ½ cup cooking water, and add pasta to sauce.

- Cook and stir, adding reserved pasta water if necessary, until blended.

80

~ VARIATIONS ~

Homemade Meatballs

In medium bowl, combine 1 beaten egg with 2 tablespoons water, ¼ cup Italian-seasoned dry breadcrumbs, ¼ cup grated Parmesan cheese, 1 teaspoon dried basil, ½ teaspoon salt, and ⅛ teaspoon pepper. Add 1 pound ground beef. Form into 1-inch meatballs. Bake at 350 degrees F for 20–30 minutes until thoroughly cooked. Cool and freeze.

Meatball Hoagies

Bring 16-ounce jar of pasta sauce to a simmer. Add 1 pound frozen fully cooked meatballs along with 1 chopped green bell pepper; simmer for 15–20 minutes until meatballs are hot. Toast 4 hoagie buns, brush with olive oil, and add meatball mixture. Top with grated provolone cheese and serve.

Start the Sauce

- Cooking onions and garlic is a simple step that adds lots of flavor to pasta sauces.

- Make sure that the onions and garlic cook until tender to get rid of harsh compounds and make them sweet and mellow.

- Browning a bit of concentrated tomato paste is a great quick way to add slow-cooked taste to sauces.

- Watch carefully; you don't want the paste to burn, just brown. Stir to incorporate the brown bits into the sauce.

Add Meatballs and Simmer

- Let the frozen meatballs thaw in the refrigerator, not on the counter, overnight to make the recipe faster.

- If the fully cooked meatballs are thawed, the sauce only has to simmer for 15–20 minutes until they're hot.

- Add more vegetables to the sauce for more nutrition. Sliced mushrooms, chopped bell peppers, and shredded carrots are good additions.

- Cook these vegetables along with the onions and garlic so they are tender and add flavor to the sauce.

81

QUICK SKILLET MEATBALLS

Some ground beef, a skillet, and a few other ingredients make a quick and easy meal

Meatballs are a quick and easy dinner choice, and they are so versatile, too. Your own homemade meatballs are a great shortcut ingredient.

To make ahead of time, make the meatballs and cook them completely. Let cool for thirty minutes, then refrigerate until cold. Freeze meatballs in a single layer on a cookie sheet, pack into hard-sided containers, label, and freeze up to three months. To thaw, let stand in the fridge overnight. You can also add them frozen to recipes and simmer until hot.

Flavor your meatballs according to your favorite ethnic cuisine. Caribbean meatballs could be made with a bit of crushed pineapple and minced jalapeño peppers. *Yield: 6 servings*

Ingredients

½ cup soft breadcrumbs

⅓ cup buttermilk

3 cloves garlic, minced

3 green onions, minced

1 teaspoon salt

⅛ teaspoon pepper

1 teaspoon dried marjoram leaves

1¼ pounds 90 percent lean ground beef

¼ pound Gouda, cut into ½-inch cubes

1 (18-ounce) jar pasta sauce

½ cup heavy cream

⅓ cup grated Parmesan cheese

Cheese Stuffed Meatballs

- In large bowl, combine breadcrumbs, buttermilk, garlic, onion, salt, pepper, and marjoram and mix.

- Add beef; mix just until combined. Form 2 tablespoons beef mixture into a ball; press a cheese cube into the center; mold meat around cheese. Repeat; chill for 2 hours.

- In large saucepan, bring pasta sauce to a simmer. Add meatballs and bring back to a simmer.

- Cover and simmer for 20 minutes without stirring. Gently stir in cream, sprinkle with Parmesan, and serve.

Garden Meatball Skillet

Use same meatball recipe; don't stuff with cheese. Brown meatballs in 2 tablespoons olive oil. Remove meatballs from skillet; add 1 chopped onion, 3 chopped carrots, 1 cup sliced mushrooms; cook until tender. Sprinkle with 2 tablespoons flour, salt, and pepper. Add 14 ounces beef broth, meatballs, and 14-ounce can diced tomatoes. Simmer until meatballs are cooked and sauce is thickened.

Spicy Meatballs and Rice

Use the same meatball recipe; add 1 minced jalapeño pepper; omit cheese. Brown meatballs in 2 tablespoons oil. Remove meatballs. Add 1 chopped onion; cook until tender. Add 1½ cups rice; sauté. Add 4 cups beef broth, 1 tablespoon chili powder, and meatballs. Cover; simmer 25 minutes; add 2 cups frozen peas; simmer until hot.

Fill Meatballs with Cheese

- Chop the ingredients included in the meatballs to a fine dice and make them about the same size.

- Handle the beef mixture gently; don't compress it too much around the cheese or the meatballs will be tough.

- Be sure that the cheese is fully covered and in the center of the meatballs or it can leak out during cooking.

- You can make and stuff the meatballs ahead of time; refrigerate for up to 8 hours.

Add Meatballs to Sauce

- Because the fat content of the ground meat is so low, you can cook the meatballs directly in the sauce.

- The meatballs will be very tender because they aren't browned first, and the sauce will have more meaty flavor.

- If you use a ground meat with more fat, you can brown the meatballs first, then drain off the fat and proceed with the recipe.

- You can serve this or any skillet meatball recipe with cooked pasta or rice.

LOW-FAT CHICKEN STIR-FRY

Chicken is perfect for stir-fry recipes, especially when cooked with these flavorful ingredients

Stir-fried chicken is a wonderful choice for a quick and easy meal. You don't need a lot of oil to stir-fry food. Just 1 or 2 tablespoons will work well, especially if the food has been marinated. Stir-fried meals are automatically low in fat.

The chicken is almost always marinated in a mixture of cornstarch, soy sauce, and other ingredients to make it tender.

All tender vegetables, like onions, bell peppers, zucchini, and mushrooms, stir-fry beautifully and don't need advance preparation.

Marinate the chicken up to 8 hours. Any longer, and the marinade will start to toughen the fibers in the meat. *Yield: 4 servings*

Ingredients

2 tablespoons cornstarch

3 tablespoons low-sodium soy sauce

1 tablespoon grated gingerroot

1 tablespoon brown sugar

⅛ teaspoon pepper

3 cloves garlic, minced

½ cup chicken broth

4 boneless, skinless chicken breasts

2 tablespoons peanut oil

1 onion, chopped

1 (8-ounce) package sliced mushrooms

1 red bell pepper, chopped

3 cups frozen edamame, thawed

Chicken Edamame Stir-Fry

- Combine cornstarch, soy sauce, ginger, brown sugar, pepper, garlic, and chicken broth.

- Cut chicken into 1-inch pieces and add to broth mixture; chill 20 minutes.

- Heat oil in wok or large skillet. Drain chicken and add; stir-fry until almost cooked, about 4 minutes. Remove chicken from pan.

- Add onion and mushrooms; stir-fry for 3–4 minutes. Add bell pepper, edamame, and chicken; stir-fry for 2 minutes. Stir broth mixture and add; stir-fry for 3–4 minutes. Serve over rice.

Spicy Chicken Stir-Fry

Combine 1 cup chicken broth, 3 tablespoons each soy sauce, cornstarch, and lime juice, 2 minced jalapeños, and 4 cubed chicken breasts. Refrigerate for 4 hours. Drain; stir-fry chicken in 2 tablespoons oil. Remove; add 1 sliced yellow summer squash, 1 sliced red bell pepper, and 2 cups sliced mushrooms. Stir-fry; add chicken and marinade; stir-fry.

Classic Chicken Stir-Fry

Combine 3 tablespoons each cornstarch and soy sauce, 1 tablespoon each grated gingerroot and brown sugar, 3 cloves garlic, and 1 cup chicken broth. Add 4 cubed chicken breasts; refrigerate for 4 hours. Drain; stir-fry chicken in 2 tablespoons oil. Remove; add 1 chopped onion, 1 cup sliced carrots, 2 cups sliced mushrooms; stir-fry. Stir marinade and add with chicken; stir-fry.

Prepare Ingredients

Marinate Chicken

- Place ingredients in separate bowls after preparation so you can add them all at once to the wok or skillet.

- To cut an onion, cut it in half and pull off the skin. Place cut side down on board. Cut horizontally, then vertically, then across.

- Prepare bell peppers by cutting in half. Pull out the seeds and membranes. Place skin side down and cut.

- Trim off the bottoms of mushrooms and place cap side down; slice through the stem.

- Always use low-sodium soy sauce, unless you're using a tablespoon or less. The regular variety is very high in sodium.

- You can add other flavorings to the chicken marinade. Think about using honey mustard, sweet and sour, or Tex-Mex flavors.

- For sweet and sour, combine equal amounts of cider or rice wine vinegar and sugar; add cornstarch and chicken broth.

- Tex-Mex flavors would use chili powder, cumin, lime juice, and salt and pepper along with the cornstarch and broth.

PAN-FRIED PAILLARDS

Paillards of chicken will become one of your go-to recipes with these easy recipes

Paillards are very thin pieces of meat, either cut thin or pounded very thin. They cook in just a few minutes, so have to be very well flavored.

Pan-frying is the best way to cook paillards because they won't dry out. You can add a sauce to the paillards to add flavor and moisture. The sauce is made after the paillards are cooked, using the pan drippings, and then poured over the paillards.

If you're going to cut the meat into thin pieces, it will be easier if the meat is partially frozen first. Place in the freezer for thirty to forty minutes, remove and quickly slice.

This is one of the most versatile recipes; use your favorite vegetables and flavors. *Yield: 6 servings*

Ingredients

6 boneless, skinless chicken breasts

1 teaspoon salt

¼ teaspoon pepper

1 tablespoon chili powder

½ teaspoon cumin

⅓ cup flour

3 tablespoons olive oil

1 onion, chopped

4 cloves garlic, minced

2 jalapeño peppers, minced

1 cup chicken broth

2 tablespoons lime juice

2 cups cherry tomatoes

2 tablespoons butter

⅓ cup chopped cilantro

Tex-Mex Chicken Paillards

- Place chicken in a plastic bag; gently pound until about ¼ inch thick. Sprinkle with salt, pepper, chili powder, and cumin, then dredge in flour.

- Heat olive oil over medium heat in large skillet; sauté chicken, turning once, until golden brown, about 4–5 minutes, and remove.

- Add onion, garlic, and jalapeños to pan; sauté for 5 minutes. Add broth, juice, and tomatoes and simmer.

- Return chicken to pan and cook for 1–2 minutes until hot. Swirl in butter and sprinkle with cilantro.

Honey Mustard Paillards

Butterfly 4 small chicken breasts: Hold knife parallel to work surface. Cut almost through; open up chicken. Pound to ¼ inch thick; dredge in ¼ cup flour, salt, pepper, and ½ teaspoon dry mustard. Cook chicken 1–2 minutes on each side in 2 tablespoons butter; remove. Add ½ cup chicken broth, ¼ cup honey mustard, and 2 tablespoons honey; swirl and pour over meat.

Lemon Pesto Paillards

Pound 4 chicken breasts, and dredge in ¼ cup flour, 1 teaspoon lemon zest, salt, and pepper. Cook in 2 tablespoons butter 1–2 minutes on each side. Remove chicken to plate. Add ½ cup pesto, 2 tablespoons lemon juice, and ½ cup chicken broth to pan; boil and pour over chicken.

Pound Chicken

- To pound the meat, place in a heavy duty plastic bag, since plastic wrap, parchment paper, or waxed paper can tear.

- Start pounding from the center of the meat, working to the outside edges. Check the thickness frequently.

- Pound firmly but gently so you don't tear or rip the meat. If there are holes, the chicken will easily overcook and not be as pretty.

- Coat the chicken with flour to help protect it from the heat and thicken the pan sauce.

Finish Sauce

- If you use about the same amount of sauce mixture, the recipe will turn out every time.

- For liquid, you can use chicken broth, sweet and sour sauce, or any other Asian marinade.

- Swirl in butter at the very end of cooking time to finish the dish. This adds a silky texture and rich taste to the simple pan sauce.

- Add fresh chopped herbs at the very end so they keep their bright color and flavor.

CHICKEN ENTREES

SAUTÉED CHICKEN COATINGS

Boneless, skinless chicken breasts can be coated with everything from cornflakes to nuts

Chicken is the perfect last minute recipe for dinner, especially when it's coated with a crisp and flavorful mixture.

You can use almost anything you'd like for the coating mixture. Crushed cereal, ground nuts, fresh or dried bread-crumbs, panko, and cheeses are good bases for coatings. Flavor them with everything from dried herbs and spices to fresh herbs and citrus zests. The meat will cook more evenly and the coating will be perfectly browned if you flatten the chicken before coating and cooking. A rolling pin or meat mallet can be used to flatten the chicken.

Make a quick pan sauce from the drippings, pour over the chicken, and serve in minutes. *Yield: 6 servings*

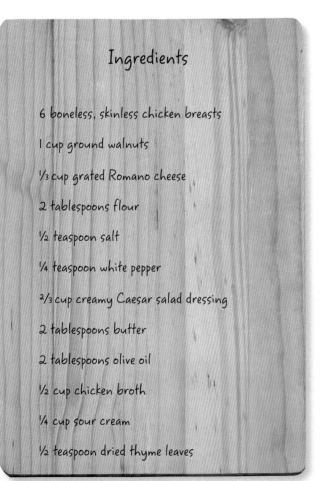

Ingredients

6 boneless, skinless chicken breasts

1 cup ground walnuts

⅓ cup grated Romano cheese

2 tablespoons flour

½ teaspoon salt

¼ teaspoon white pepper

⅔ cup creamy Caesar salad dressing

2 tablespoons butter

2 tablespoons olive oil

½ cup chicken broth

¼ cup sour cream

½ teaspoon dried thyme leaves

Crisp Walnut Caesar Chicken

- Place chicken in plastic bag; pound until ¼ inch thick.

- In shallow bowl, combine walnuts, cheese, flour, salt, and pepper. Coat chicken in salad dressing, then press into walnut mixture to coat; let stand for 5 minutes.

- In large saucepan, melt butter and olive oil over medium heat. Add chicken, 3 pieces at a time, and sauté for 2–4 minutes on each side until thoroughly cooked.

- Remove chicken and cover. Add broth, sour cream, and thyme to skillet and bring to a boil. Pour over chicken to serve.

Brown Sugar Pecan Chicken

Pound 6 chicken breasts to ¼ inch thick. On plate, combine ¾ cup ground pecans, ¼ cup dry breadcrumbs, 3 tablespoons brown sugar, salt, and pepper. Dip chicken in ½ cup honey mustard, then press into pecan mixture to coat. Cook in 3 tablespoons butter for 4–6 minutes. Remove, add 1 cup chicken broth to pan, boil, and pour over chicken.

Chicken Parmesan

Pound 6 chicken breasts. Combine ½ cup dried Italian breadcrumbs, ⅓ cup grated Parmesan cheese, ½ teaspoon oregano, and ½ teaspoon salt. Dip chicken into 2 beaten eggs, then into breadcrumb mixture. Cook in 3 tablespoons butter until golden brown. Meanwhile, heat 3 cups pasta sauce in pan. Pour sauce over chicken; top with 1 cup shredded Mozzarella cheese.

Mix Coating Ingredients

- The coating mixture should be well mixed so each piece of chicken gets an equal amount of seasoning.

- You don't have to pound the chicken before coating. If you don't, cook for 4–6 minutes on each side over medium-low heat until done.

- The amount of coating needed will depend on the size of the breasts. Add more if necessary.

- You could substitute ground pecans, cashews, or pine nuts for the walnuts in this recipe if you'd like.

Coat Chicken

- Dip the chicken into the dressing until completely coated, then gently shake off the excess. Use more dressing if you run short.

- Drop the chicken into the coating mixture, scoop more of the coating mixture on top of the chicken, and press.

- The chicken should be evenly and completely coated, with no empty spots.

- Let the chicken dry on a wire rack for 5–7 minutes before sautéing so the coating stays on the chicken.

CHICKEN ENTREES

BAKED CHICKEN

Chicken cooks to juicy perfection in the oven, flavored so many ways

Baked chicken will always come out tender and juicy because this cooking method is gentler than broiling or sautéing.

You can bake plain chicken breasts or thighs, coat them with flour or envelop them in a sauce, stuff boneless chicken breasts, or bake a cut up whole chicken. The baking times will be different, but the method is the same.

At 350 degrees F, boneless, skinless chicken breasts bake for 20 minutes. Boneless, skinless chicken thighs bake for 40–50 minutes. A whole, cut up chicken bakes for 1¼ hours. Bone-in, skin-on chicken breasts bake for 35–45 minutes.

Cook chicken breasts to a final temperature of 170 degrees F, thighs and whole chickens to 180 degrees F. *Yield: 4 servings*

Ingredients

4 boneless, skinless chicken breasts

½ teaspoon salt

⅛ teaspoon white pepper

4 thin slices prosciutto

¼ cup chopped black olives

2 cloves garlic, minced

¼ cup slivered almonds, toasted

4 (½-inch x 3-inch) sticks manchego cheese

⅔ cup grated Cotija cheese

2 red bell peppers, sliced

1 cup dry white wine

2 tablespoons olive oil

Spanish Chicken Roll Ups

- Preheat oven to 325 degrees F. Pound chicken until ¼ inch thick and place on work surface. Sprinkle with salt and pepper.

- Top each breast with 1 slice prosciutto, olives, garlic, almonds, and 1 piece manchego cheese. Roll up; fold in ends to enclose filling.

- Press chicken rolls in Cotija cheese to coat. Place in glass baking dish and add peppers. Pour wine and olive oil into dish.

- Cover and bake for 30–40 minutes, until chicken is thoroughly cooked. Serve with the sliced peppers.

Crispy Herb Chicken
Combine 1 cup crushed cornflakes, 1 tablespoon dried parsley, ½ cup grated Romano cheese, 1 teaspoon salt, and 1 teaspoon each dried basil and thyme. Dip 12 boneless, skinless chicken thighs in 2 beaten eggs, then dip into cornflake mixture. Place in baking dish, drizzle with 2 tablespoons melted butter, and bake at 350 degrees F for 30–40 minutes until done.

Sticky Baked Chicken
In medium saucepan, cook 1 chopped onion in 2 tablespoons olive oil. Add ¼ cup soy sauce, ½ cup seafood cocktail sauce, ½ cup honey, 4 cloves minced garlic, salt, and pepper; simmer for 5 minutes. Place 1 cut up whole chicken in baking dish; pour sauce over. Bake at 375 degrees F for 1 hour until done.

Prepare Filling

- You could chop the prosciutto and cheese and combine all the ingredients before filling the chicken.

- Or just layer the ingredients on the chicken before rolling it up. Tuck in the sides to enclose the filling.

- Don't overfill the chicken breasts. If there's too much filling, it will just leak out of the chicken and burn on the pan.

- The filling should be well seasoned and complete in itself, since the chicken won't flavor it while it's cooking.

Roll To Enclose Filling

- Be sure that there is enough chicken around the filling to enclose it completely.

- Secure the chicken bundles with toothpicks or metal picks. Or use a strand of spaghetti; it will cook along with the chicken.

- You could add other quick-baking vegetables to the pan with the chicken. Be sure they will cook in the time specified.

- Mushrooms, chopped onions, or zucchini would be good choices for chicken breasts. For whole chicken, choose cubed potatoes or carrots.

GRILLED CHICKEN BREASTS

Chicken on the grill is perfect and gorgeous, especially when marinated in a savory dressing

Grilling chicken adds another layer of flavor to this tender and mild meat. The grill automatically caramelizes the chicken skin or coating because of the very high heat. You can add smoke flavor with additions like wood chips or fruit vines.

Put these additions directly on a charcoal fire, or in a small pan placed under the grate on a gas grill. Wood chips should be soaked for 1 hour before adding to the grill; herbs and vines do not need to be soaked.

Build a two-level fire when grilling chicken. Boneless, skinless thighs and breasts can be grilled completely over direct heat. Brown whole chickens and cut-up chickens over direct heat, then finish over indirect heat. *Yield: 4 servings*

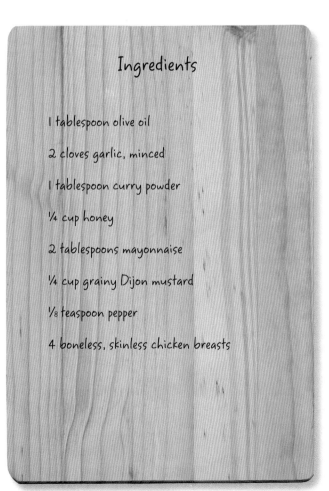

Ingredients

1 tablespoon olive oil

2 cloves garlic, minced

1 tablespoon curry powder

¼ cup honey

2 tablespoons mayonnaise

¼ cup grainy Dijon mustard

⅛ teaspoon pepper

4 boneless, skinless chicken breasts

Curried Honey Chicken Breasts

- In small microwave-safe dish, combine oil, garlic, and curry powder. Microwave on high for 1–2 minutes until garlic is fragrant.

- Remove and stir in remaining ingredients except chicken. Place chicken in glass baking dish; marinate in refrigerator 30 minutes or up to 24 hours.

- Prepare grill for direct medium heat. Remove chicken from marinade; reserve marinade.

- Grill for 5–7 minutes on each side, turning once and basting with reserved marinade, until thoroughly cooked.

Grilled Citrus Chicken

Combine 3 tablespoons each lime juice, lemon juice, and brown sugar, ¼ cup Dijon mustard, 1 teaspoon salt, ⅛ teaspoon pepper, 1 teaspoon grated lemon zest, and 3 cloves minced garlic. Add 6 boneless, skinless chicken breasts and marinate for 30 minutes or refrigerate for 12–24 hours. Grill over direct medium heat for 5–6 minutes per side until done. Discard marinade.

Grilled Teriyaki Chicken

In plastic bag, combine ⅓ cup teriyaki sauce, ¼ cup lemon juice, 4 cloves minced garlic, 2 tablespoons low-sodium soy sauce, 2 tablespoons honey, and ¼ teaspoon cayenne pepper. Add 5 boneless, skinless chicken breasts; marinate for 30 minutes or refrigerate for 12–24 hours. Drain, discard marinade. Grill for 6–8 minutes per side until chicken is thoroughly cooked.

Microwave Garlic and Curry Powder

Grill Chicken

- Curry powder is heated along with the garlic because the heat deepens and develops the flavors.

- Watch the mixture in the microwave carefully so it doesn't burn. If the garlic does burn, discard it and start over.

- The honey in the marinade flavors the chicken and adds moisture. It will also caramelize beautifully on the grill.

- Discard any remaining marinade after you've brushed the chicken with it once. There isn't enough to serve as a sauce for the chicken.

- Grill the chicken until an instant-read meat thermometer registers 165 degrees F.

- The chicken should stand for 5–6 minutes after grilling. The temperature will go up to 170 degrees F before serving.

- You can grill this chicken on an indoor dual contact grill. Grill for half the time, since the chicken cooks on both sides.

- If you use a stovetop grill, have the vent fan going full power, since the marinade will smoke as the chicken grills.

ROTISSERIE CHICKEN SKILLET MEALS

Start with a rotisserie chicken and you'll have a skillet dinner on the table in minutes

Every grocery store offers rotisserie chicken. These fully cooked chickens are tender and juicy and offer a wealth of possibilities for quick and easy meals.

The chicken should be very hot when you purchase it. Be sure to take it home immediately. Use it or refrigerate it as soon as you get home.

You can cut up the chicken as you would a roasting chicken and serve it in large pieces, or you can remove each section of light and dark meat and shred or cut it into small pieces.

Use the chicken within two days. Leftovers, including the bones and skin, can be frozen to make broth. *Yield: 6 servings*

Ingredients

½ rotisserie chicken

2 tablespoons olive oil

I red bell pepper, chopped

2 cloves garlic, minced

I (16-ounce) package fettuccine pasta

I (15-ounce) jar four-cheese Alfredo sauce

⅔ cup basil pesto

2 cups frozen peas, thawed

⅓ cup grated Parmesan cheese

Pesto Chicken and Fettuccine

- Remove chicken from bones and skin and shred; set aside. Bring a large pot of salted water to a boil.

- In large skillet, heat oil over medium heat. Add bell pepper and garlic; cook and stir for 3 minutes.

- Cook fettuccine until almost al dente. Meanwhile, add Alfredo sauce, pesto, and chicken to skillet; bring to a simmer.

- When fettuccine is cooked, drain and add to skillet with peas. Cook and stir over medium heat until mixture is blended and hot. Top with cheese and serve.

Skillet Chicken Cordon Bleu
Chop enough cooked chicken to equal 3 cups; set aside. Cook 1 chopped onion and 3 cloves garlic in 2 tablespoons olive oil. Add 1 cup chopped ham and chicken; cook until hot. Add 16-ounce jar low-fat Alfredo sauce and simmer. Add 1 cup shredded Swiss cheese and 1 cup frozen peas; cook until hot. Serve over cooked pasta.

Skillet Chicken Cacciatore
Chop enough cooked chicken to equal 3 cups; set aside. Cook 1 chopped onion and 2 cloves garlic in 3 tablespoons olive oil. Add 1 chopped green bell pepper, 8 ounces sliced mushrooms, 1 teaspoon Italian seasoning. Add 14-ounce can diced tomatoes, ¼ cup tomato paste, and ½ cup chicken broth. Simmer 10 minutes, add chicken; simmer until hot. Sprinkle with minced parsley.

Remove Meat from Chicken

- It's not difficult to remove the meat from the chicken. Just use a sharp knife and work slowly until you're good at it.

- Place the chicken on the counter and cut along the backbone on each side.

- Then cut along the bottom of each breast to remove it. Shred, slice, or chop the meat.

- Then turn the chicken over and cut the meat from the drumsticks, wings, and thighs. Freeze the bones to make into stock or broth.

Cook Pasta and Sauce

- You can find jars of low-fat Alfredo sauce. Low-fat pesto is hard to find. To reduce the fat content, add more minced basil to the sauce.

- Undercook the pasta slightly, as it will finish cooking in the sauce.

- If it's undercooked at this point, it will absorb some flavor from the sauce.

- You don't need to cook the mixture much once the pesto and pasta have been added. Keep the mixture moving by gently manipulating it with tongs.

CHICKEN ENTREES

CHICKEN BURGERS

Add a few ingredients to ground chicken for a delicious, fresh burger

Chicken burgers are a nice change from the traditional beef burger. They're lower in fat, and since the meat is milder than beef, can be flavored in an infinite number of ways.

Ground chicken can be difficult to find at the grocery store. You can ask the butcher to grind some for you, or you can do it at home.

Just cut up some raw, chilled, boneless, skinless chicken breasts and/or thighs and place in a food processor. Pulse the meat until it's coarsely ground. Don't go overboard; if you grind too much the burgers will be mushy.

Ground chicken should be used or frozen within one day for food safety reasons. Enjoy these easy recipes. *Yield: 4 servings*

Ingredients

1 tablespoon olive oil

½ cup minced onion

⅓ cup shredded carrots

⅓ cup soft breadcrumbs

1 egg

½ teaspoon grill seasoning

1¼ pounds ground chicken

4 onion buns, split

4 slices Muenster cheese

2 avocados, sliced

Avocado Chicken Burgers

- In small skillet, heat olive oil over medium heat. Add onion and carrots; cook and stir until tender, about 5 minutes.

- Remove to large bowl; let cool. Add breadcrumbs, egg, and seasoning; mix. Add chicken; mix gently. Form into 4 patties; and chill for 2–3 hours.

- Grill burgers on direct medium heat for 5–6 minutes per side until thoroughly cooked.

- Grill buns, add cheese to chicken, and cook for 1–2 minutes. Top burgers with avocado; serve on buns.

Buffalo Chicken Burgers

Cook ¼ cup minced celery in oil. Add breadcrumbs, ½ teaspoon Tabasco, ¼ cup blue cheese, and 2 tablespoons chicken broth. Omit onion, carrot, Muenster, and avocado. Top with blue cheese dressing and serve on toasted, buttered sourdough buns with sour cream, tomato and lettuce.

Thai Chicken Burgers

In bowl, combine ½ cup panko breadcrumbs, 2 tablespoons low-sodium soy sauce, 2 cloves minced garlic, 1 tablespoon curry paste, 3 tablespoons minced red onion, 1 tablespoon lime juice, 2 tablespoons peanut butter, and 2 drops mint extract. Add 1 pound ground chicken. Form into 4 patties and grill until done. Serve in pita breads with a mixture of mayonnaise, lime juice, and hot pepper sauce.

Mix Burger Ingredients

Grill Burgers

- Ingredients like onion, garlic, and carrots must be cooked before the ground chicken is added.

- The cooking time on the grill isn't long enough to cook these vegetables. They will be tough if not cooked first.

- Work with ground chicken just as you do ground beef; mix all other ingredients first, then add chicken and mix gently.

- Don't overwork the chicken mixture, and don't press the burgers together too hard or they will be tough.

- Chicken burgers are more delicate and tender than beef burgers, so handle with care.

- The chilling time is important, so don't skip it. It gives the chicken mixture time to set up and the breadcrumbs time to absorb liquid.

- You may want to grill the chicken burgers on a grill mat instead of directly on the grate.

- Don't press down on the burgers when they are cooking, or you'll press out liquid and lots of flavor.

GROUND POULTRY

97

DELUXE TURKEY BURGERS

Brie cheese is a fabulous addition to tender and juicy turkey burgers

Like chicken burgers, turkey burgers are a great change of pace. Ground turkey meat is easier to find in the marketplace. You can make your own in a food processor.

In the store, you'll find both white meat and a mix of white meat/dark meat ground turkey. Either one works well for turkey burgers. Choose the white meat version for less fat, or the mixed version for more flavor.

The all-white-meat burgers do need more additions be-

cause the meat is so low in fat. Sauté some onion in a bit of olive oil, or add some sour cream or shredded cheese for moisture.

Flavor your turkey burgers with any combination of herbs, spices, cheeses, and vegetables and enjoy. *Yield: 4 servings*

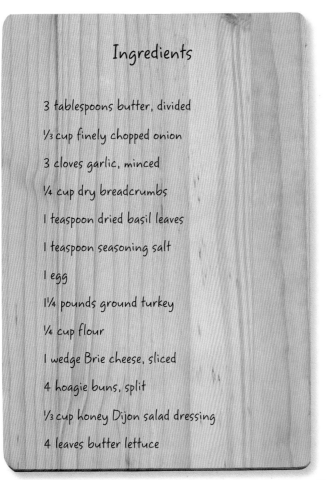

Ingredients

3 tablespoons butter, divided

⅓ cup finely chopped onion

3 cloves garlic, minced

¼ cup dry breadcrumbs

1 teaspoon dried basil leaves

1 teaspoon seasoning salt

1 egg

1¼ pounds ground turkey

¼ cup flour

1 wedge Brie cheese, sliced

4 hoagie buns, split

⅓ cup honey Dijon salad dressing

4 leaves butter lettuce

French Brie Turkey Burgers

- In large saucepan, melt 1 tablespoon butter; cook onion and garlic until tender. Remove to large bowl; cool.

- Add breadcrumbs, basil, salt, and egg; mix. Add turkey; mix gently with hands. Form into 4 patties; make indentation in center; chill for 2–3 hours.

- In same saucepan, melt 2 tablespoons butter. Coat patties with flour; cook in butter, turning once, for 9–11 minutes.

- Remove burgers from heat, add Brie; cover. Grill buns in saucepan. Spread buns with dressing, top with lettuce, burgers, and bun tops.

Tex-Mex Turkey Burgers

Cook ½ cup each minced onion and red bell pepper, and 2 each minced garlic cloves and jalapeño peppers until tender. Remove from heat; add ½ cup crumbled tortilla chips; let stand for 5 minutes. Add 1¼ pounds ground turkey. Form into patties and cook as directed. Serve on toasted hamburger buns with Pepper Jack cheese, mayo, salsa, tomatoes, and sliced avocado.

Greek Turkey Burgers

Combine ⅓ cup dried breadcrumbs; 1 egg; ½ cup crumbled feta cheese; ½ teaspoon each dried oregano, basil, and dill; and ¼ cup minced olives. Add 1¼ pounds ground turkey and mix; form into patties. Cook as directed. Serve on toasted hoagie buns with lettuce, tomato, mayo, and mustard.

Shape Patties

- The turkey mixture will be more delicate than a ground beef mixture, so handle gently. Over handling will make the burgers tough.

- It's always a good idea to chill poultry burgers before cooking, especially before grilling.

- You can use a grill mat if you want to grill. These nonstick perforated sheets will stop the burgers from falling apart.

- If it's hard to shape the burgers, refrigerate the mixture before you shape it into patties.

Melt Cheese on Top

- Brie is a delicate and rich cheese. For easier slicing, try putting it in the freezer for about 10 minutes before you slice.

- The rind on Brie cheese is edible, but the texture is very different from the cheese itself.

- You can remove the rind if you'd like for a more consistent topping on the burgers.

- For even more indulgent flavor, add some sliced avocados to the burgers along with the lettuce and dressing.

GROUND POULTRY

SALSA MEATBALLS

Mexican ingredients like salsa and cumin add a spark of flavor to chicken meatballs

Making meatballs is the same as making meatloaf or burgers. Combine all of the extra ingredients first, then add the ground chicken or turkey and mix just until combined.

The chicken mixture, again, will be quite delicate. So baking or broiling the meatballs is a better choice than trying to cook them in a saucepan.

An easy way to make meatballs, as well as meatloaf, is to cook a sauce, then use part of that sauce as an addition to the ground meat. The meatballs are then flavored very well from the inside out.

You can serve the meatballs and sauce over hot cooked rice, cooked pasta, or mashed sweet potatoes. *Yield: 6 servings*

Ingredients

2 tablespoons olive oil

1 onion, chopped

3 cloves garlic, minced

1 (16-ounce) jar chunky salsa

2 teaspoons chili powder

½ teaspoon cumin

½ teaspoon salt

⅛ teaspoon pepper

½ cup soft breadcrumbs

1 egg

1 pound ground chicken

1 (8-ounce) can tomato sauce

Mexican Spicy Chicken Meatballs

- In large saucepan, heat olive oil over medium heat. Add onion and garlic; cook and stir until tender.

- Add salsa, chili powder, cumin, salt, and pepper; remove from heat. Combine ⅓ cup of this mixture with breadcrumbs and egg in large bowl.

- Add chicken; mix well. Form into 18 meatballs. Place on greased broiler rack; broil meatballs until light brown, turning once.

- Add meatballs to salsa mixture along with tomato sauce; simmer for 9–12 minutes until chicken is thoroughly cooked.

Parmesan Chicken Meatballs

Combine 1 egg, ⅓ cup grated Parmesan cheese, ⅓ cup dried breadcrumbs, ¼ cup minced red onion, 2 cloves minced garlic, salt, and pepper. Add 1 pound ground chicken. Form into 1-inch balls. Bring 26-ounce jar pasta sauce to a boil; add meatballs. Simmer for 15–25 minutes until meatballs are cooked. Serve over pasta.

Buffalo Chicken Meatballs

Cook ⅓ cup minced onion and 2 minced cloves garlic in 2 tablespoons butter. Place in bowl; add 2 tablespoons hot sauce, ¼ cup bottled Alfredo sauce, and ¼ cup breadcrumbs. Add 1 pound ground chicken; form into meatballs. Brown in 2 tablespoons olive oil; drain. Add 1¾ cups Alfredo sauce, 1 cup chopped celery; simmer for 20–25 minutes. Add 1 cup blue cheese; serve over pasta.

Prepare Ingredients

- Let the sautéed mixture cool for a bit before you add the chicken. It doesn't have to be completely cool.

- If you like it spicy, add a lot more chili powder. You could also add some minced jalapeño or serrano peppers.

- The heat level of the salsa you choose will also affect the flavor. Remember that the chicken is very mild.

- If your family isn't used to hot foods, choose a mild salsa with green chiles instead of jalapeño peppers.

Broil Meatballs

- Watch the meatballs carefully under the broiler. You may need to turn them several times, moving the meatballs slightly each time.

- Turn the meatballs with a pair of tongs, and handle gently. Spray the broiler pan with nonstick cooking spray before broiling.

- Because the meatballs don't cook completely under the broiler, you can't stop at this point and refrigerate them.

- After the meatballs broil, add them directly to the pasta sauce and finish cooking.

GROUND POULTRY

MICROWAVE CHICKEN QUICHE

Yes, you can make quiche in the microwave; just a few tricks make it perfect

Quiches used to be considered exotic and difficult to make. Nothing could be further from the truth! A quiche is simply a main dish pie based on beaten eggs and cheese. That's it!

Quiches are usually baked in the oven. That heat is needed to brown the crust and set the egg custard. But twenty years ago, people started making quiches in the microwave oven.

There are a few tricks to microwave quiche cooking. Because the crust won't brown, you'll need to color it somehow. Use spices like chili powder or cinnamon, or dark liquids like soy sauce or Worcestershire sauce. And follow cooking, rotating, and standing times to the letter.

Now invent your own microwave quiche! *Yield: 6 servings*

Ingredients

1 (9-inch) pastry shell

2 teaspoons soy sauce

1 tablespoon butter

1 pound ground chicken

1 onion, chopped

3 cloves garlic, minced

1 red bell pepper, chopped

3 eggs

2/3 cup light cream

1 teaspoon dried thyme leaves

1/2 teaspoon salt

1/8 teaspoon cayenne pepper

1 cup grated Muenster cheese

1/2 teaspoon paprika

Chicken Onion Quiche

- Rub edge of shell with soy sauce; prick with fork. Microwave on high 5–7 minutes, until surface looks flaky.

- In saucepan, melt butter; add chicken, onion, and garlic; cook until meat browns. Add bell pepper, cook 2 minutes longer.

- Drain; place in crust. In bowl, beat eggs, cream, thyme, salt, and cayenne pepper. Add cheese; pour into crust. Sprinkle with paprika.

- Microwave on 75 percent power for 19–25 minutes until knife inserted comes out clean. Let stand 10 minutes; serve.

Havarti Dill Chicken Quiche

Prepare crust as directed. Cook 1 pound ground chicken, 1 chopped onion, and 3 cloves garlic in 2 tablespoons butter in microwave. Add ²/₃ cup milk, 3 eggs, 1 teaspoon dried dill, and ½ teaspoon salt. Place 1½ cups Havarti cheese in pie shell; pour chicken mixture over. Sprinkle with ¼ cup grated Parmesan cheese. Cook as directed.

Chicken Divan Quiche

Prepare crust as directed. Cook 1 pound ground chicken and 1 chopped onion in 2 tablespoons butter in micro-wave. Add 2 cups frozen broccoli florets, thawed and drained, 3 eggs, 1 cup light cream, ¼ cup Parmesan cheese, and 2 tablespoons flour. Place 1 cup cheddar cheese in crust, top with chicken mixture; sprinkle with 1 teaspoon paprika. Cook as directed.

Cook Filling Ingredients

- You can cook the filling ingredients in a saucepan or in the microwave oven.

- To cook in the microwave, place in microwave-safe dish. Microwave for 4 min-utes on high power; remove and stir.

- Continue microwaving for 1-minute intervals until chicken and veggies are tender. Place in crust and proceed with recipe.

- The filling ingredients can be hot when you put them in the crust, and when pouring the egg mixture over them.

Precook Pie Crust

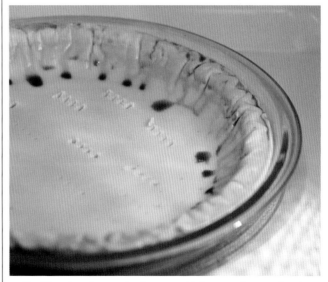

- Cooking the piecrust in the microwave is easy, but you need to know a few rules.

- The crust won't brown in the microwave. You can use a browning agent like Kitchen Bouquet, or a spice like curry powder.

- Make sure that you let the crust, then the filled cooked pie, stand on a solid surface after cooking.

- The solid surface keeps the heat in the pie, where it will redistribute, finishing the pie to perfection.

GROUND POULTRY

TURKEY PASTA SAUCE

Ground turkey is the perfect addition to a classic pasta sauce; serve over a fun pasta shape

Pasta and a rich tomato sauce is a classic quick cooking recipe. All you really need is a jar of pasta sauce, some seasonings, cheese, and pasta.

But that basic recipe can be varied in so many ways. Adding ground turkey is an excellent way to add protein, flavor, and texture to any pasta sauce.

These sauces don't need to cook for a long time. Just a few minutes of simmering will blend flavors.

Make a Tex-Mex turkey pasta sauce by adding jalapeño peppers and salsa to the recipe, or add dried herbes de Provence and roasted red bell peppers for a French turkey pasta sauce. Enjoy experimenting! *Yield: 6 servings*

Ingredients

1 tablespoon olive oil

1 pound ground turkey

1 onion, chopped

4 cloves garlic, minced

1 (6-ounce) can tomato paste

2 (14-ounce) cans diced tomatoes, undrained

1 cup tomato juice

2 teaspoons sugar

½ teaspoon salt

1½ teaspoons dried basil leaves

½ teaspoon dried oregano leaves

¼ teaspoon pepper

1 (16-ounce) package spaghetti

½ cup grated Romano cheese

Spaghetti with Tomato Turkey Sauce

- In large saucepan, heat olive oil; add turkey, onion, and garlic. Cook and stir until turkey is tender; drain.

- Add tomato paste; let brown in spots, then add tomatoes, juice, and remaining ingredients except spaghetti and cheese.

- Let the sauce simmer, stirring occasionally. Bring a large pot of salted water to a boil. Cook pasta until al dente.

- Drain pasta, reserving ¼ cup cooking water. Add pasta to sauce, adding water if necessary; cook 2 minutes. Sprinkle with cheese; serve.

Ground turkey is marked several ways in the supermarket. Ground turkey breast is more expensive than a light and dark meat combination. The light and dark meat combo is marked "lean ground turkey," while the breast is labeled "ground turkey breast." Or they may be marked "extra lean" for white meat and "lean" for the combination. Ask the butcher if you are unsure.

Turkey Sausage Marinara: Cook 1 pound ground turkey sausage, 1 chopped onion, 3 cloves garlic, and 1 green bell pepper in skillet. Add 18-ounce jar marinara sauce, 8-ounce can tomato sauce, ½ teaspoon each dried oregano and basil, and ½ cup white wine. Simmer 15–20 minutes; serve over 12 ounces cooked spaghetti with grated Romano cheese.

Cook Sauce

- Because ground turkey is so mild, you can use any type of flavoring or seasoning in your pasta sauce recipe.

- You could substitute a large jar of pasta or marinara sauce for the tomato paste, tomatoes, juice, sugar, salt, and seasonings.

- Ground chicken can be substituted for the ground turkey in a 1:1 ratio. The remaining ingredients stay the same.

- Stir the sauce frequently, scraping along the bottom so it doesn't burn and all the ingredients meld together.

Cook Spaghetti

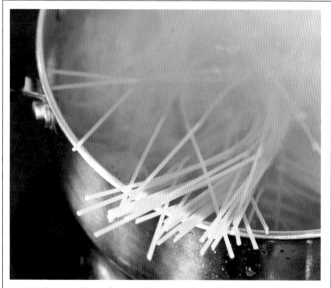

- Stir the spaghetti frequently while it's cooking so it doesn't stick together.

- The water has to be at a full boil all the time to get the pasta to absorb the water and soften.

- When the pasta is cooked al dente, there will still be a slight bit of firmness and a small white line in the center.

- Take a bite and see what you think. If the pasta tastes good to you, it's done.

ONE-DISH SKILLET MEALS

Shredded broccoli and vegetables add great flavor and texture to ground chicken

Ground chicken is perfect for a skillet meal. It cooks quickly and stays tender, and it's an excellent foil for other strongly flavored ingredients.

You can use skillet chicken as the base for other recipes; this is also a great way to use leftovers. Top some shredded lettuce or spinach with the hot chicken mixture for a delicious salad. Use the skillet mixture to fill enchiladas or tacos, or serve it over hot cooked pasta.

Because these meals cook quickly, have all of the ingredients prepared before you start cooking. A skillet meal isn't very different from a stir-fried meal; the cooking time is just a bit longer.

Use your favorite flavors and vegetables. *Yield: 6 servings*

Ingredients

4 slices bacon

1 pound ground chicken

1 onion, chopped

3 cloves garlic, minced

5 cups shredded red cabbage

1 cup shredded carrot

1¼ cups water, divided

½ cup apple cider vinegar

⅓ cup sugar

½ cup low-fat sour cream

2 tablespoons mustard

1 teaspoon salt

½ teaspoon caraway seed

¼ teaspoon pepper

German Chicken with Slaw Skillet

- In large skillet, cook bacon until crisp; crumble and set aside. Drain all but 2 tablespoons bacon drippings.

- Add chicken, onion, and garlic; cook and stir until chicken is almost done. Remove food from skillet.

- Add cabbage and carrots to skillet along with ¼ cup water; cover and simmer until cabbage is almost tender.

- In small bowl, combine remaining ingredients. Add to skillet along with chicken mixture; cook and stir for 3–4 minutes until sauce thickens and vegetables are tender. Top with bacon.

Chicken Taco Salad

Cook 1 pound ground chicken with 1 chopped onion, 2 cloves garlic, and 2 jalapeño peppers until done. Add 15-ounce can drained black beans, 8 ounces tomato sauce, and 1 cup salsa; simmer. Serve over shredded lettuce with 2 cups tortilla chips, 2 cups Pepper Jack cheese, 4 chopped tomatoes, and ½ cup sour cream.

Thai Chicken Skillet

Cook 1 pound ground chicken with 2 chopped red bell peppers, 1 chopped onion, 2 garlic cloves, and 1 tablespoon minced fresh ginger. Add ¼ cup peanut butter, 1 cup chicken broth, ½ cup coconut milk, 2 tablespoons soy sauce, 1 tablespoon lime juice, and 2 teaspoons curry powder; simmer until thickened. Serve over hot cooked rice.

Chop or Shred Cabbage

Add Sauce to Skillet

- To chop cabbage, first remove the outer wilted leaves. Cut the cabbage in half and cut out the core.

- Place the cabbage, cut side down, on work surface. Cut several times parallel to the work surface.

- Then cut cabbage from the rounded side to the flat side, forming strips. Finally, cut against those cuts to form cubes.

- Or you could shred the cabbage using a food processor. Follow directions for the appliance.

- Depending on what you're cooking with the chicken, you may want to remove it from the skillet after it's done.

- If you're using longer-cooking foods like cabbage or potatoes, remove the chicken while those foods cook.

- The best way to cook cabbage so it doesn't waft aromas through the house is to cook it quickly.

- You could use a packaged cole slaw mix in place of the cabbage and carrot. Or use grated zucchini or chopped mushrooms.

GROUND POULTRY

PORK STIR-FRY

Stir-fry pork with some fresh fruits for a nice twist on a classic recipe

Pork isn't a common stir-fry ingredient in Asian cuisines. But it's a great addition to this super quick meal. You can use cut up pork chops, cubed pork tenderloin, or strips of boneless pork loin. Or use cubes of fully cooked ham. If you do use ham, don't marinate it, and add it at the end of stir-frying, when you add the sauce.

Using fruit in stir-fries is a bit different from using vegetables. The fruit doesn't cook as long, but you still want it to heat through and release some juice. A light hand with the spatula is necessary, as it is very quick cooking.

Other good fruits for this recipe include plums, nectarines, and mangos. *Yield: 6 servings*

Ingredients

2 tablespoons cornstarch

2 tablespoons sugar

¼ cup apple cider vinegar

½ cup pineapple juice

½ cup chicken broth

½ teaspoon salt

⅛ teaspoon cayenne pepper

1 pound pork tenderloin, cubed

2 tablespoons peanut oil

1 red onion, chopped

3 cloves garlic, minced

2 peaches, peeled and sliced

1 cup pitted cherries

Fruited Sweet and Sour Pork

- In medium bowl, combine cornstarch, sugar, vinegar, pineapple juice, broth, salt, and pepper. Add pork; let stand for 10 minutes.

- Drain pork, reserving marinade. Heat peanut oil in large skillet or wok. Add pork; stir-fry until pork is browned; remove from skillet with slotted spoon.

- Add onion and garlic; stir-fry until tender, 5 minutes. Return pork to skillet with marinade and fruit.

- Bring to a simmer; stir-fry gently until pork is cooked and sauce is thickened. Serve over hot cooked rice.

Peeling soft fruits like peaches can fry your nerves. A stiff blade can remove a lot more than the skin. Look for soft-bladed peelers, like the Trio Tri-Blade Peeler. It has 3 blades in the handle: one for hard vegetables like carrots, another to make julienne strips, and a third serrated blade perfect for peaches, plums, and tomatoes.

Apple Pear Pork Stir-Fry: Make the marinade in the recipe, except substitute apple juice for pineapple juice; marinate same pork for 10 minutes. Drain and stir-fry in 2 tablespoons peanut oil; remove. Add 1 chopped onion, 2 sliced apples, and 1 sliced pear. Stir-fry until crisp-tender. Return pork to skillet along with marinade; stir-fry until thickened.

Prepare Sauce

- A wire whisk is the best tool to combine sauces with cornstarch. The wires mix the cornstarch in with the liquids so there are no lumps.

- Be sure to whisk the marinade again when you add it to the wok to finish the dish so the cornstarch is redistributed.

- You can use any fruit juice in the marinade. Try pear or mango nectar or cherry or orange juice.

- You could substitute honey or brown sugar for the granulated sugar in the marinade.

Stir-Fry

- Make sure that all of the ingredients are prepared and waiting before you start cooking.

- The onion and garlic, stir-fried after the pork, add moisture to the pan to help lift pan drippings.

- Pit the cherries over a sink or a bowl so you hear every pit come out of the cherry. You don't want to bite down on a pit.

- Stir the mixture gently, but be sure to scrape the surface of the wok so the sauce doesn't burn.

PORK ENTREES

FIVE-INGREDIENT PORK PACKETS
Pesto and tender veggies make these grilled packets a breeze

Packets are a combination of food placed in heavy duty foil, then grilled to perfection. These delicious and super easy one-dish meals are the ultimate quick dinner: no cleanup, and excellent flavor.

Because the food cooks all together in a sealed packet, it steams. This means that the flavors of the foods mingle as they cook. As a bonus, steaming is one of the healthiest ways to cook. You need little or no added fat, and vitamins aren't lost as the food cooks. With just five ingredients, all of the food has to be the best quality possible. Don't skimp, or try to use food that is not at peak quality. Every food and every flavor is important. *Yield: 6 servings*

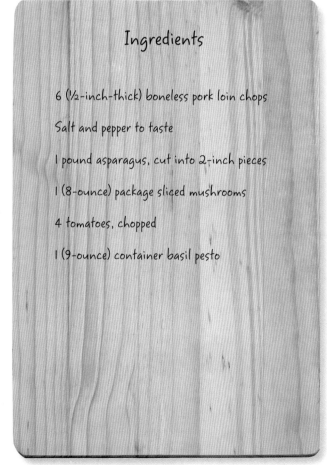

Ingredients

6 (½-inch-thick) boneless pork loin chops

Salt and pepper to taste

1 pound asparagus, cut into 2-inch pieces

1 (8-ounce) package sliced mushrooms

4 tomatoes, chopped

1 (9-ounce) container basil pesto

Pork Pesto Packets

- Prepare and heat grill. Tear off 6 sheets of heavy duty aluminum foil 18 inches x 12 inches.

- Place chops on foil; sprinkle with salt and pepper. Divide asparagus, mushrooms, and tomatoes over chops.

- Spoon pesto over food. Fold foil over and secure with double folds, allowing some room for heat expansion.

- Grill packets over direct medium heat, turning and moving around frequently, for 20–25 minutes, until pork is 155 degrees F on a meat thermometer and vegetables are tender.

~ VARIATIONS ~

Pork Rice Packets

Combine 1½ cups instant brown rice with 1½ cups water and 2 teaspoons chili powder; let stand for 10 minutes. Place on foil, topped by 4 boneless pork chops, 2 cups thawed frozen corn, 1 cup salsa, and 1 cup shredded cheddar cheese. Fold packets using a double fold and grill as directed.

Italian Pork Packets

Place 4 ½-inch-thick boneless pork loin chops on heavy duty foil. Add 2 cups frozen stir-fry vegetables, thawed, and 1 chopped red onion. Drizzle with ½ cup zesty Italian salad dressing and top with 1½ cups chopped tomatoes. Fold using double fold, then grill as directed.

Place Food on Foil

- You can make these packets ahead of time if you'd like. They will keep in the fridge until it's time to cook.

- Packets are also an excellent way to entertain. Put out a selection of foods and let your guests build their own.

- Keep the food in a fairly small area on the packet. You should be able to fit 6 on an average-sized grill.

- You can mark individual packets, which will look the same on the grill, with grill charms or markers on the foil.

Make a Double Fold

- To make a double fold, first be sure that your foil piece is large enough.

- It should be at least 18 inches long. Place the food in the center, then bring the long sides together.

- Fold once, then twice. Then make a double fold on the short ends of the packet, fastening securely.

- Be sure to leave some air space in the packet to allow for heat expansion as the food cooks. And tell your guests to be careful of steam!

PAN-FRIED PORK CHOPS
Apple and pork are natural partners in this simple and quick recipe

Pan-frying is an excellent way to cook tender pork chops. The trick is first to sear the chops to develop a good brown color and caramelization, then finish cooking them in a sauce so they stay tender and juicy.

The thickest pork chops you can use for this method are about 1 inch. Thinner chops work well too; they just cook for a shorter period of time. If you have thicker chops, try pounding them so they cook through in the time specified.

You can cook everything in one pan if you'd like. Just cook the chops first and cover to keep warm; then make the sauce, add the chops, and heat until done and the sauce is slightly thickened. *Yield: 6 servings*

Ingredients

½ cup apple cider

2 tablespoons low-sodium soy sauce

6 (1-inch-thick) pork loin chops

5 tablespoons butter, divided

1 cup pecan pieces

1 onion, chopped

¼ cup brown sugar

2 tablespoons honey

⅛ teaspoon nutmeg

⅛ teaspoon cardamom

2 Granny Smith apples, peeled and sliced

Apple Pecan Pork Chops

- In plastic bag, combine cider and soy sauce; add chops. Let stand for 15 minutes.

- Drain pork chops, reserving marinade. In saucepan, toast pecans in 3 tablespoons butter; remove.

- Add onion; cook 5 minutes, then add remaining ingredients, including marinade, except pork and pecans; simmer.

- Meanwhile, in another skillet heat 2 tablespoons butter and sauté pork chops until done, about 5–8 minutes on each side. Add to first pan and simmer for 3–4 minutes. Sprinkle with pecans.

Creamy Mushroom Pork Chops

Sprinkle 6 boneless pork chops with 1 teaspoon seasoned salt and ⅛ teaspoon pepper. Heat 2 tablespoons olive oil in large skillet; add chops. Brown on medium-high heat. Add 1 chopped onion and 2 cups sliced cremini mushrooms; cook for 2 minutes. Add 16-ounce jar Alfredo sauce and 4-ounce jar sliced mushrooms, undrained. Simmer for 20 minutes.

Blue Cheese Chops

Salt and pepper 6 1-inch chops; dredge in ⅓ cup flour. Brown chops in 3 tablespoons butter in large skillet. Add 2 chopped onions and 4 cloves minced garlic. Cook until chops are done, about 15–20 minutes longer. Remove pork. Add ½ cup each chicken broth and cream; boil for 2 minutes. Return chops to skillet; sprinkle with ½ cup blue cheese; cook 2-3 minutes.

Brown Pork Chops

- When browning the chops, be sure to leave them alone until they easily release from the pan. Turn with tongs instead of a spatula to be sure.

- When they release, the chops are seared and have developed lots of flavor through caramelization.

- The pork is done when an instant-read meat thermometer registers 155 degrees F, or medium. The meat will be slightly pink.

- Pork no longer needs to be cooked to well done for food safety reasons.

Add Sauce

- The sauce will become thicker as it simmers while the pork chops cook in the other pan.

- Stir the sauce occasionally as it cooks, making sure to scrape the bottom of the pan with the spoon or spatula so it doesn't burn.

- The pork simmers in the sauce just long enough to finish cooking and to absorb some liquid.

- You could substitute sliced pears for the apples in this recipe. Use pears that are just barely ripe.

113

SAUSAGE KABOBS

Kabobs can be flavored in so many ways; this Asian recipe is delicious

Threading meat onto skewers and cooking on the grill, in a pan, or under the broiler is a great quick and easy cooking method.

Use precooked sausage for this type of recipe. The time on the grill isn't long enough to thoroughly cook raw sausages.

Metal skewers are better than bamboo when you're cooking this much food. The sausages are heavy, and you don't want the skewers to burn and fall apart when the food is cooking.

Tender vegetables like bell peppers and mushrooms can be grilled without precooking. If you want to use harder vegetables like potatoes or carrots, precook them in boiling water until almost tender, then thread onto the skewers and grill to perfection. *Yield: 6 servings*

Ingredients

⅓ cup teriyaki sauce

2 tablespoons low-sodium soy sauce

3 tablespoons honey

2 teaspoons sesame oil

3 cloves garlic, minced

2 tablespoons minced gingerroot

2 tablespoons rice wine vinegar

⅛ teaspoon cayenne pepper

2 red bell and 1 yellow bell peppers, sliced

1 (8-ounce) package cremini mushrooms

4 green onions, cut into 2-inch pieces

1½ pounds cooked Polish sausage

Asian Sausage Kabobs

- In bowl, combine teriyaki sauce, soy sauce, honey, sesame oil, garlic, gingerroot, vinegar, and cayenne pepper. Add vegetables; marinate for 15 minutes.

- Drain vegetables, reserving marinade. Slice sausage into 1½-inch chunks. Prepare and preheat grill.

- Thread ingredients onto 6 metal skewers, alternating sausage with the vegetables.

- Grill kabobs over direct medium heat, turning frequently and brushing with marinade, until sausage is hot and vegetables are tender.

There are several types of precooked sausages, including cooked, smoked, and dried. Sausages that are cooked and smoked include kielbasa, also known as Polish sausage, and chorizo. Fresh sausages that are dried, and usually eaten cold, include salami and summer sausage. Sausages that are cooked but not smoked include cooked knackwurst and Braunschweiger; just reheat these, and don't overcook them.

• • • • RECIPE VARIATION • • • •

Italian Potato and Sausage Kabobs: Precook 8 small red potatoes, halved, and 4 carrots, cut into chunks, in boiling water for 6–8 minutes. Combine ½ cup zesty Italian salad dressing and ¼ cup sour cream for marinade. Thread skewers with 1½ pounds kielbasa, 8 ounces mushrooms, potatoes, and carrots. Grill as directed, brushing with reserved marinade.

Mix the Glaze

- Teriyaki sauce is made from soy sauce, ginger, garlic, and a sweetener like brown sugar or honey.

- You can find low-sodium versions of the sauce. Hoisin sauce makes a good substitute, for a slightly more complex flavor.

- Sesame oil has a very strong flavor, which is why it's used in such small quantities.

- Use gingerroot by first peeling with a vegetable peeler, then finely chopping or grating the flesh.

Thread Food on Skewer

- When you thread the food on the skewer, be sure to pierce the thickest part.

- You can put the food on the skewer ahead of time; just cover the assembled skewers and refrigerate until it's time to grill.

- Grill over direct medium

heat, turning the skewers occasionally as the food browns. Use hot pads to protect your fingers.

- You can purchase skewer racks or holders, which hold the skewers in position and make them easier to turn.

PORK MEDALLIONS

Tender, coated pork chops are topped with a creamy sauce

Medallions are pieces of meat cut thin and pounded thinner to cook very quickly. A sauce is added to work the flavorful pan drippings into the recipe and help keep the meat moist.

You can use pork tenderloin or pork chops to make medallions. Pork tenderloin is easier to work with and is naturally more tender than chops, so it's a better choice.

Pound the meat gently but firmly. Do not use the spiked side of a meat tenderizer. The bottom of a heavy saucepan,

a rolling pin, or the smooth side of a tenderizer is the best choice for flattening the meat.

Flavor these medallions any way you'd like. The mild meat is complemented by any herb, spice, vegetable, or fruit. *Yield: 8 servings*

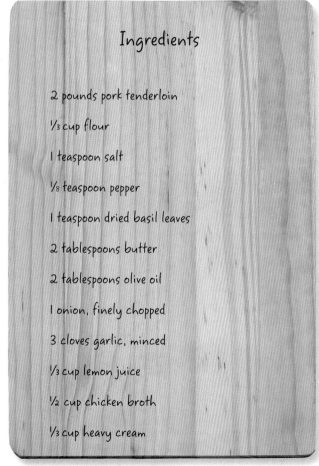

Ingredients

2 pounds pork tenderloin

⅓ cup flour

1 teaspoon salt

⅛ teaspoon pepper

1 teaspoon dried basil leaves

2 tablespoons butter

2 tablespoons olive oil

1 onion, finely chopped

3 cloves garlic, minced

⅓ cup lemon juice

½ cup chicken broth

⅓ cup heavy cream

Pork Medallions with Lemon

- Slice pork into 1-inch pieces, but slice the thin ends into 2-inch pieces. Combine flour, salt, pepper, and basil on plate.

- Dredge pork in flour mixture; place on waxed paper. Pound until ⅓ inch thick.

- Melt butter and oil in skillet

on medium heat. Brown pork on both sides, 2–3 minutes; remove from heat.

- Add onion and garlic to pan; cook to loosen pan drippings. Add lemon juice, broth, and cream; boil until sauce is reduced. Return pork to pan and heat 2 minutes; serve.

Pork Medallions with Mushrooms

Pound pork as directed, using dried thyme in place of basil. Sauté pork as directed. Remove pork from pan and add 1 chopped onion, 2 cups sliced mushrooms, 2 cloves minced garlic to pan; sauté to loosen pan drippings. Add 1 cup chicken broth and 2 tablespoons lemon juice to pan; boil until reduced. Add medallions; simmer 2 minutes.

Mustard Pork Medallions

Pound pork as directed, using 1 teaspoon dried tarragon instead of basil. Sauté pork as directed. Remove pork from pan and add 1 chopped onion and 2 cloves minced garlic; sauté. Add ⅓ cup white wine, ⅓ cup chicken broth and ¼ cup cream to skillet; boil. Add 2 tablespoons Dijon mustard and medallions; simmer and serve.

Pound Medallions

- You can use waxed paper or heavy duty plastic bags to hold the pork while you pound it.

- The flour is pounded into the meat so it forms a nice crust when the medallions are sautéed.

- The pounding action also pushes the seasonings into the meat.

- Be sure that you don't pound so hard that the meat rips or tears. Evenly pounded meat cooks more uniformly and makes a pretty presentation.

Finish Sauce

- Lemon and basil are natural partners, and they add a delicious brightness to tender pork medallions.

- When you add the liquid to the hot pan, a lot of steam will rise; be careful and stand back so you don't get burned.

- You can substitute low-fat evaporated milk for the cream to make the dish lower in fat.

- Garnish the finished dish with some thinly sliced lemons and a sprig or 2 of fresh basil.

PORK ENTREES

SLOW-COOKER PORK AND RICE

Wild rice and pork make a delicious casserole reminiscent of the Midwest

The slow cooker is one of the best quick and easy cooking techniques. The long, slow cooking turns even tougher cuts of meat into butter-like tenderness. And the actual hands-on work time for you is usually under twenty minutes.

It's important to layer food in the slow cooker in a specific way. Vegetables cook more slowly than meats so they are placed in the bottom of the appliance so they are closer to the heat source. Grains have to be covered by liquid, so they're placed in the bottom too.

Brown rice, wild rice, barley, quinoa, and farro are all good choices for cooking in the slow cooker. White rice tends to overcook. *Yield: 6 servings*

Ingredients

4 slices bacon

6 thin boneless pork chops

¼ cup flour

1 teaspoon salt

⅛ teaspoon pepper

1 teaspoon dried marjoram leaves

1 onion, chopped

2 cloves garlic, minced

4 cups chicken broth

2 cups uncooked wild rice

1 (16-ounce) jar four-cheese Alfredo sauce

Wild Rice Pork Casserole

- In large saucepan, cook bacon until crisp; drain, crumble, and set aside.

- Dredge pork in mixture of flour, salt, pepper, and marjoram. Brown in pan drippings on both sides; remove from pan.

- Cook onion and garlic in pan until tender, about 5 minutes. Add broth and bring to a simmer.

- Place wild rice in 4-5-quart slow cooker. Top with broth mixture; layer pork chops, bacon, and Alfredo sauce on top. Cover and cook for 7–8 hours until rice is tender and pork is cooked.

Pork Chops with Brown Rice

Brown chops as directed in 2 tablespoons butter. In slow cooker, layer 2 cups long-grain brown rice, 16-ounce package baby carrots, and 2 chopped onions, then chops. To skillet, add 4 cups chicken broth, 2 tablespoons sugar, 3 tablespoons apple cider vinegar, 2 tablespoons soy sauce, ½ cup chili sauce. Boil; pour over chops. Cook on low for 8–9 hours.

Pork with Wild and Brown Rice

Cube 6 boneless pork chops; toss with seasonings as directed. Place 1 cup brown rice and 1 cup wild rice in slow cooker. Top with 4 cups vegetable or chicken broth. Add 2 chopped onions, 3 cloves minced garlic, and 2 cups sliced mushrooms. Top with pork. Cover and cook on low for 8–9 hours, stirring once during cooking time.

Brown Pork in Skillet

- Make sure that the bacon is very crisply cooked so it doesn't get soggy or limp in the slow cooker.

- The bacon will soften a bit, but will retain a nice, slightly chewy texture after long hours of cooking.

- Only cook the chops until they brown. This shouldn't take longer than 4–5 minutes.

- The onion and garlic are cooked in the pan to remove the pan drippings from the sautéed chops.

Layer Food in Slow Cooker

- The pan drippings hold much of the flavor in this dish. The brown bits are caramelized, with lots of complex compounds.

- Be sure that the rice is covered with the broth before you add the chops, bacon, and Alfredo sauce.

- Keep the cover on the slow cooker while it's cooking. The lid creates a seal that holds in the heat and moisture.

- Every time you lift the lid you need to add 20 minutes to the total cooking time.

PORK ENTREES

HAM STIR-FRY
Ham is the perfect stir-fry meat for one of the quickest meals ever

A stir-fry meal can be on the table in literally minutes, especially if you choose a precooked meat like ham. Ham shouldn't be marinated, as is it flavorful and tender enough, so skipping that step shaves at least ten minutes off the preparation time.

You can actually find cubed or diced ham in the supermarket in the prepared meats section, so you don't even have to do that work. And look in the produce section of the super-

market, too, for stir-fry vegetables and fruits. Everything from grated carrots to chopped pineapple to trimmed sugar snap peas is available, ready and waiting.

Have fun creating your own quick and easy stir-fry recipes using ham. *Yield: 4 servings*

Ingredients

1 (15-ounce) can pineapple tidbits

½ cup chicken broth

1 tablespoon curry powder

⅛ teaspoon pepper

½ teaspoon ground ginger

2 tablespoons cornstarch

2 tablespoons oil

1 onion, chopped

3 cloves garlic, minced

2 cups cubed ham

2 cups red grapes

2 cups hot cooked brown rice

Curried Ham and Fruit Stir-Fry

- Drain pineapple, reserving juice. In small bowl, combine reserved juice, chicken broth, curry powder, pepper, ginger, and cornstarch.

- In large skillet, heat oil over medium-high heat. Add onion and garlic; stir-fry until tender, about 5 minutes.

- Add ham; stir-fry until ham starts to brown around edges, about 5–6 minutes longer. Add pineapple and grapes.

- Stir pineapple juice mixture and add to skillet. Stir-fry until food is hot and sauce thickens, about 3–4 minutes. Serve over rice.

Think about the kinds of flavors that typically go with ham when you're inventing your own marinade and glaze recipes. Sweet and tart fruits like pineapple, pear, and peaches are naturals. Combine them with sharper flavors like barbecue sauce, onion, garlic, and mustard. Sugar or honey mellows the mixture, while herbs like basil or mint add fresh flavor.

• • • • RECIPE VARIATION • • • •

Ham and Pea Stir-Fry: For sauce, combine 1 cup chicken broth with 2 tablespoons each cornstarch, soy sauce, and mustard. Stir-fry 1 onion in 2 tablespoons oil; add 2 cups sugar snap peas, 1 cup sliced mushrooms, 1 red bell pepper, and 2 cups cooked ham. Stir and add sauce along with 2 cups frozen baby peas. Stir-fry until sauce bubbles and thickens. Serve over rice.

Prepare Ingredients

Stir-Fry

- Use a sharp utility knife to cut the fruit and onions into about the same size cubes.

- If the grapes are large, cut them in half. Work slowly, because they have a tendency to roll around.

- Have all the ingredients ready to go and waiting before you heat the wok. There's no time to prepare ingredients after the cooking has started.

- Divide the ingredients into bowls according to when they are added to the wok.

- You'll develop your own method and rhythm of stir-frying after a few tries.

- Use a metal or heatproof spatula so you can cover the most surface area with each turn of the wok.

- Always stir the sauce or marinade before you add it to the wok, because the cornstarch settles to the bottom.

- Cook your rice in a rice cooker; then it will be ready and waiting for you when the food is done.

HAM AND FRUIT PACKETS

Whether grilled or baked, these special packets are perfect for last minute entertaining

These packets can be cooked on the grill or baked in the oven. On the grill, you must use heavy duty foil to keep the food from burning, and so the packet doesn't burn up.

Don't overfill the packets, whether you're grilling or baking them. There has to be room in the packet to allow for steam and for expansion as the food heats.

In the oven, place the packets on a cookie sheet, even if you're using heavy duty foil, since the packets can leak. On the grill, it doesn't matter if the packets leak, but pay attention. When you're removing the packets from the grill, you don't want to spill hot liquid on yourself. *Yield: 4 servings*

Ingredients

1 pound ham steak

1 (15-ounce) can sweet potatoes

3 peaches or nectarines

1 red onion, chopped

2 cloves garlic, minced

½ cup peach nectar

2 tablespoons honey

1 teaspoon ground ginger

⅛ teaspoon pepper

Ham and Peach Packets

- Cut ham into 1-inch x 3-inch strips. Tear off 4 18-inch x 12-inch sheets of heavy duty foil.

- Drain sweet potatoes, discarding juice. Cut sweet potatoes into 1-inch pieces. Peel peaches and slice; just slice nectarines, if using.

- Divide ham, sweet potatoes, peaches or nectarines, onion, and garlic among foil strips.

- In small bowl combine remaining ingredients; drizzle over food. Fold up and seal packets; grill over direct medium heat for 17–23 minutes until food is hot.

~ VARIATIONS ~

Baked Ham Packets
Cut 4 12-inch x 18-inch pieces of parchment paper. Fold in half crosswise and unfold. Combine 2 cups instant brown rice with 1½ cups chicken broth; let stand 5 minutes. Place on parchment. Top with green pepper rings, 3 cups chopped ham, 1 chopped onion. Divide 14-ounce can diced tomatoes among packets. Fold up. Bake at 400 degrees F for 35–45 minutes.

Pesto Ham Packets
Cut 1 ham steak into 4 pieces. Place on heavy duty foil. Top each with 2 sliced plum tomatoes, 1 chopped green bell pepper, 2 cups frozen corn. Combine ¾ cup basil pesto with ⅓ cup sour cream; spoon over food. Fold up and grill over direct medium heat for 12–18 minutes until food is hot.

Place Food on Foil

- You can use canned or frozen peaches if the fresh aren't readily available or in season.

- Drain canned peaches well. Thaw frozen peaches and drain them, too. Too much water will dilute the flavors.

- A finished packet should be about a 6-inch x 8-inch rectangle, whether foil or parchment.

- To fold parchment, start at one end and crimp the paper closed; keep crimping all the way around to the end.

Fold Foil Packets

- Be careful pulling the packets off the grill or out of the oven. They will be very hot.

- The parchment paper will start to brown and may burn a little; that's okay.

- You can cut a large X in the center of the packets to

open them up, or unfold the foil or paper.

- And be sure to warn your guests about the steam that will billow out when they open the packets.

123

GRILLED HAM STEAK

Ham steak is one of the best cuts in the supermarket for super quick and easy meals

A ham steak is fully cooked, so all you're doing on the grill is re-heating it and adding some caramelization and smoky flavor.

Since the time on the grill will be quick, you'll have to stagger how you cook other foods. Tender vegetables like bell peppers, mushrooms, and tomatoes can be cooked at the same time as the ham, but others, including potatoes and carrots, should either be precooked or put on the grill long before the ham.

There are so many ways to flavor this tender cut of ham. Try a sauce made with curry powder and chutney and grill pineapple and peaches. Or use zesty Italian dressing and grill bell peppers and onions. *Yield: 4 servings*

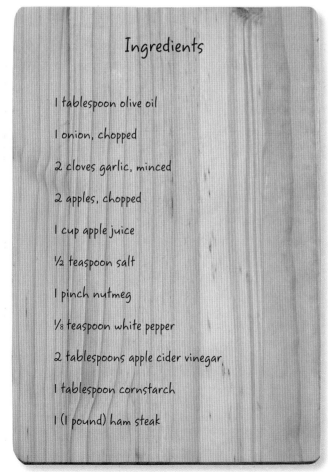

Ingredients

1 tablespoon olive oil

1 onion, chopped

2 cloves garlic, minced

2 apples, chopped

1 cup apple juice

½ teaspoon salt

1 pinch nutmeg

⅛ teaspoon white pepper

2 tablespoons apple cider vinegar

1 tablespoon cornstarch

1 (1 pound) ham steak

Ham Steak with Apples

- In medium saucepan, heat olive oil over medium heat. Add onion and garlic; cook and stir, about 5 minutes.

- Add apples and sauté for 3 minutes. Add apple juice, salt, nutmeg, and pepper; bring to a simmer.

- Simmer sauce for 8–10 minutes until apples are tender. Stir in vinegar and cornstarch; simmer until thickened, about 2 minutes.

- Grill ham on direct medium heat, turning once and brushing with apple mixture, until hot and glazed, 9–10 minutes. Serve ham with remaining sauce.

~ VARIATIONS ~

Cranberry Ham Steak
In saucepan, cook 1 chopped onion and 2 cloves minced garlic in 2 tablespoons olive oil. Add ⅓ cup seafood cocktail sauce, 2 tablespoons Dijon mustard, 1 cup whole berry cranberry sauce, and ⅓ cup dried cranberries; simmer for 10 minutes. Grill a 1-pound ham steak, brushing occasionally with sauce, until hot, about 10–15 minutes. Serve with sauce.

Peachy Ham Steak
In saucepan, cook 2 minced shallots in 1 tablespoon olive oil. Add 1 cup minced peaches, ½ cup peach nectar, ⅓ cup peach jam, 2 tablespoons lemon juice, and ⅛ teaspoon pepper; simmer for 10 minutes. Grill a 1-pound ham steak as described, brushing occasionally with sauce, until hot, about 10 minutes. Serve with sauce.

Technique Focus 1

Technique Focus 2

- You can prepare the glaze or sauce ahead of time if you'd like. If the sauce uses perishable ingredients, refrigerate.

- Just cool it to room temperature, cover, and then reheat before you start grilling.

- Substitute other fruits and fruit juices in place of the apples and apple juice. Chopped pears and nectar, or pineapple tidbits would work.

- Because the ham is fully cooked, you don't have to worry about boiling the sauce after it's been in contact with the meat.

- Use a silicone brush to baste the ham on the grill for easiest cleanup. You can use an ordinary pastry brush.

- Or think about making a grill brush with bunches of herbs. For this recipe, tie sprigs of thyme together.

- Turn the ham with tongs. If you turn it with a spatula, you'll scrape off the sauce.

- Let the ham sit on the grill until it releases easily. Make sure the grill is clean and oiled before you begin.

HAM SKILLET

Add a few ingredients and a sauce to ham for a delicious skillet meal ready in minutes

A skillet meal is cooked entirely in one skillet. There's just one pan to wash, which facilitates cleanup. And when you start with fully cooked ham, the cooking process is even faster.

The difference between a stir-fry and a skillet meal is that there is usually a longer cooking time in the skillet meal. The food doesn't have to be constantly manipulated with a spat-ula or spoon. And there are times when the covered skillet is left to simmer for a few minutes.

These meals can be flavored with any favorite ethnic cuisines. A Tex-Mex skillet would use jalapeño peppers, salsa, tomatoes, corn, and chopped ham. An Italian ham skillet could use basil, onions, red bell pepper, and fusilli pasta. *Yield: 4 servings*

Ingredients

2 tablespoons olive oil

1 onion, chopped

3 cloves garlic, minced

1 green and 1 red bell pepper, chopped

1 (15-ounce) can great northern beans, drained

1 cup frozen edamame, thawed

2 cups chopped ham

⅔ cup chicken broth

1 tomato, chopped

1 teaspoon dried thyme leaves

⅛ teaspoon white pepper

Ham and Bean Skillet

- In large skillet, heat olive oil over medium heat. Add onion and garlic; cook and stir until tender, about 5 minutes.

- Add bell peppers; cook and stir for 3 minutes longer. Add beans, edamame, ham, and chicken broth; bring to a simmer.

- Add tomato, thyme, and pepper and stir. Bring mixture back to a simmer; cover and simmer for 7–9 minutes until vegetables are tender.

- Serve this mixture over hot cooked couscous or rice; sprinkle with chopped parsley.

~ VARIATIONS ~

Italian Pasta Ham Skillet
Cook 2 cups gemelli pasta in boiling water until al dente. Meanwhile, cook 1 chopped onion and 2 cloves garlic with 2 tablespoons olive oil. Add 1 chopped red bell pepper, 3 cups cubed ham, and 1 teaspoon dried Italian seasoning. Stir in pasta and 1½ cups chicken broth; simmer for 4 minutes. Sprinkle with ½ cup Romano cheese.

Tex-Mex Ham Rice Skillet
Cook 1 chopped onion and 2 minced jalapeños in 2 tablespoons oil. Add 1 cup long-grain rice, 3 cups cubed ham, and 1 cup salsa. Cover and simmer for 20–25 minutes until rice is tender. Stir in 1 cup Pepper Jack cheese and ½ cup sour cream, and remove from heat. Let stand 5 minutes, then serve.

Add Bell Peppers to Skillet

- The onions and garlic are cooked first because they take a longer time to become sweet and tender.

- If you like bell peppers very crisp, add them when you add the tomato at the end of cooking time.

- Edamame are soybeans. You can find them, frozen, in the health food section of your supermarket.

- To make this dish even easier, use 2 cups frozen onion and bell pepper stir-fry mix, thawed and drained.

Finish Sauce

- The tomato will add more liquid to the skillet. If you squeeze out the seeds and jelly, it will add less.

- If the sauce isn't thick enough, add 1 tablespoon cornstarch in 2 tablespoons water; simmer 4–5 minutes.

- It's not a good idea to try to make skillet meals ahead of time, for the best texture. They don't hold very well.

- You can rewarm leftovers and eat them, either as is or as a sandwich wrap or salad topping.

HAM IN PHYLLO

For those special breakfasts, or a late night dinner, a phyllo roll is beautiful and distinctive

Phyllo, also called filo or fillo dough, is paper-thin sheets of nonfat dough used in Greek cooking. You can find it in the frozen dessert section of any supermarket.

The dough is layered with butter or other ingredients, including honey, cooking spray, or flavored oils, then baked until crisp. It's easy to work with, but you do have to follow rules.

Thaw according to package directions, usually overnight in the refrigerator. There are quick thawing options, too.

Cover the thawed dough as you work with individual sheets, because it dries out and becomes brittle very quickly.

Once you've learned how to work with this dough, fill it with any lightly sauced food. *Yield: 6 servings*

Ingredients

½ cup basmati rice

½ cup chicken broth

½ cup apple juice

2 tablespoons butter

1 Granny Smith apple, peeled and chopped

2 cups chopped ham

1 teaspoon dried marjoram leaves

½ cup ricotta cheese

1 cup shredded cheddar cheese

16 (9-inch x 15-inch) sheets frozen phyllo, thawed

¼ cup butter, melted

Butter-flavored cooking spray

Ham and Apple in Phyllo

- Preheat oven to 375 degrees F. In saucepan, combine rice, chicken broth, and apple juice; simmer for 20 minutes.

- In medium skillet, melt butter; cook apple 2 minutes. Add ham and marjoram; remove from heat. Add rice; let cool for 15 minutes; stir in cheeses.

- Brush one phyllo sheet with butter. Layer 8 sheets, alternate brushing with butter and spraying with cooking spray; top with half of ham mixture. Roll, brush with butter. Repeat.

- Place on cookie sheet. Bake 25–35 minutes until browned. Cut into thirds.

······· GREEN ● LIGHT ·············

Your refrigerator manual is your friend! It's important that you actually read the manual. Some refrigerators have drip pans that must be periodically emptied, and you must clean the refrigerator coils periodically. Keep the manual in a cupboard near the refrigerator so you can refer to it as necessary.

···· RECIPE VARIATION ····

Potato Ham in Phyllo: In skillet, cook 1 chopped onion and 2 cloves garlic in 2 tablespoons butter. Add 1 chopped green bell pepper, 2 cups chopped ham, 2 cups frozen thawed hash brown potatoes, and 10-ounce package refrigerated Alfredo sauce. Add 1 cup Swiss cheese. Roll up in phyllo and bake as directed in recipe.

Prepare Filling

Layer Phyllo Dough

- The filling should have a sauce, but that sauce shouldn't overwhelm the food.

- The sauce also has to be thick so the phyllo dough, which is quite delicate, can contain it. A runny sauce will make the phyllo soggy.

- You can make the filling ahead of time and refrigerate it. Layer the phyllo and fill it when you want to eat.

- Other good fillings include ham mixed with a thawed frozen spinach soufflé, or scrambled eggs with ham.

- The phyllo does rip easily, so handle it gently. If it does rip, just layer it on a solid sheet and brush with more butter.

- The butter will help repair rips, and the layering process automatically fixes them.

- Brush the butter mixture sparingly over the dough. Don't soak the dough; the butter should lightly coat most of it.

- Serve this recipe immediately so the dough is as crisp as possible. Reheat leftovers in a toaster oven on a rimmed cookie sheet.

SLOW-COOKER HAM CASSEROLE

Potato and ham in a creamy rich sauce are perfect partners in the slow cooker

Ham is a great food to cook in the slow cooker. As with other methods, you don't have to worry about doneness. And ham just won't overcook in the low, slow heat of this appliance.

Since all you're doing is reheating the ham, place it on top in the slow cooker. Other foods, like root vegetables, rice, and grains, should be on the bottom. Just pour a sauce or broth over everything, cover it, and let it start cooking. Dinner will be ready and waiting for you.

Cubed or sliced ham cooks best in the slow cooker, especially when combined with other ingredients in a casserole. It will release some salty juices to flavor the entire dish to perfection. *Yield: 6 servings*

Ingredients

2 tablespoons olive oil

1 onion, chopped

4 cloves garlic, minced

1 (16-ounce) jar four-cheese Alfredo sauce

2 cups shredded Havarti cheese

1 cup sour cream

1 (32-ounce) package frozen hash brown potatoes, thawed

2 cups cubed ham

2 green bell peppers, chopped

Creamy Potato and Ham Casserole

- In medium skillet, heat olive oil over medium heat. Add onion and garlic; cook and stir for 5 minutes.

- Stir in Alfredo sauce, cheese, and sour cream; cook and stir until melted. Spray a 4–5 quart slow cooker with nonstick cooking spray.

- Layer potatoes, ham, green bell pepper, and cheese sauce in slow cooker, ending with cheese sauce.

- Cover and cook on low for 7–8 hours or until mixture browns around the edges and potatoes are tender.

~ VARIATIONS ~

Slow-Cooker Ham and Beans
Combine 1 chopped onion, 3 cloves minced garlic, 3 (28-ounce) cans pork and beans, drained, 15-ounce can drained black beans, ½ cup ketchup, ½ cup chili sauce, ¼ cup mustard, ¼ cup brown sugar, and 4 cups chopped ham in a 5-quart slow cooker. Cover and cook on low for 8–9 hours.

Slow-Cooker Ham and Potatoes
In 5-quart slow cooker, combine 2 chopped onions, 4 cloves minced garlic, 32-ounce bag frozen hash brown potatoes, thawed and drained, and 3 cups chopped ham. Combine 16-ounce can Alfredo sauce, ½ cup sour cream, and 2 cups grated Swiss cheese; stir into slow cooker. Cover and cook on low for 7–9 hours.

Prepare Ingredients

- Experts advise not to cook frozen food in the slow cooker for safety reasons.

- It can cool down the other foods and keep them in the danger zone of 40 degrees F to 140 degrees F too long.

- Make sure the potatoes are thawed and well drained. Liquid doesn't evaporate from the slow cooker.

- You could use refrigerated shredded potatoes in place of the frozen hash browns. Drain them well before use.

Fill Slow Cooker

- Look for low-fat Alfredo sauces. You can find them in the regular grocery store, in the pasta aisle, and the refrigerated foods aisle.

- You could use low-fat sour cream and cheese as well, to dramatically reduce the fat content in this recipe.

- When cooking and baking, don't use all nonfat products, as the texture and flavor will be compromised.

- Use a mixture of low-fat and nonfat products for best results.

STIR-FRIED SALMON

Stir-frying isn't a common way to prepare salmon, but it's quick and delicious

There aren't many recipes for stir-fried fish, with the exception of shrimp and scallops. Most fish is too delicate to withstand the rough and tumble environment of the wok. But salmon is different.

Salmon and tuna are good choices for a stir-fry recipe because they are sturdy. You still need to use a gentle hand, but the fish will keep its shape in the wok or skillet.

Once cut into cubes, the salmon can be marinated for a few minutes. Never marinate longer than twenty minutes, or the fish's texture can be compromised.

Salmon will cook in the wok in just a few minutes, so it's added at the very end of the cooking time. *Yield: 4 servings*

Ingredients

1¼ cups orange juice

2 tablespoons cornstarch

¼ cup orange marmalade

1 tablespoon soy sauce

3 tablespoons honey

½ teaspoon salt

⅛ teaspoon pepper

1 pound salmon fillet, skin removed

1 onion, chopped

2 green bell peppers, sliced

2 nectarines, sliced

2 tablespoons peanut oil

Orange Stir-Fried Salmon

- In medium bowl, combine the first ingredients. Cut salmon into 1-inch cubes and add to marinade.

- Meanwhile, prepare onion, peppers, and nectarines. Heat oil in large skillet or wok over medium-high heat.

- Add onion; stir-fry for 3 minutes. Drain salmon, reserving marinade. Add salmon with bell peppers to skillet; stir-fry for 3 minutes.

- Stir marinade and add to skillet along with nectarines; stir-fry for 3–5 minutes until salmon is cooked and sauce has thickened. Serve over hot cooked rice.

Salmon Nectarine Stir-Fry
Combine ½ cup each apple juice and chicken broth; 2 tablespoons each soy sauce, cornstarch, and mustard; and ⅛ teaspoon pepper. Marinate 1 pound cubed salmon and for 15 minutes. Stir-fry 1 chopped red onion and 2 green bell peppers in 2 tablespoons oil. Add 2 sliced nectarines and drained salmon; stir-fry. Add sauce and stir-fry until bubbly.

Salmon Black Bean Stir-Fry
Combine 1 cup chicken broth, 2 tablespoons rinsed, minced, and fermented black beans, 2 tablespoons each cornstarch, soy sauce, and cider vinegar. Marinate 1 pound cubed salmon for 10 minutes. Stir-fry 1 red onion, 2 cloves garlic, and 2 cups green beans in 2 tablespoons oil. Add salmon; stir-fry, then add sauce with 1 can drained black beans.

Marinate Salmon

Stir-Fry

- When buying salmon, look for firm and shiny flesh that's a bright pink color, with a fresh sea smell.

- Remove skin from the salmon before marinating for best results. This will make the salmon more delicate.

- There may be some pin bones in the salmon. Feel them with your fingers and pull out with tweezers.

- Toss the salmon with the marinade until it's coated, then let it stand while you prepare the other ingredients.

- After the sauce has been added to the wok or skillet, let it stand for 1 minute to start heating.

- Then carefully stir, using the spatula to scrape the bottom of the wok or skillet to move the food around.

- The stir-fry is ready when the sauce becomes clear, bubbles, and thickens.

- Have the rice perfectly cooked, hot, and ready and waiting for you in a rice cooker. Serve the stir-fry immediately.

LOW-FAT STEAMED FISH
Steaming is a quick and healthy way to cook, and the presentation is spectacular

Steaming is a wonderful and healthy way to cook fish. It's also a very quick method of cooking. The food is usually put into one or more steamer baskets—metal or bamboo contraptions that have holes in the bottom to let steam through.

The steamer baskets should be tightly covered to keep the steam moving around the food. And the food has to be carefully arranged in the baskets. Make sure that the food is placed in a single layer in the baskets, unless the recipe specifies otherwise.

The baskets should be rearranged every two to three minutes when cooking, so all of the food cooks evenly. Move the bottom basket to the top. *Yield: 4 servings*

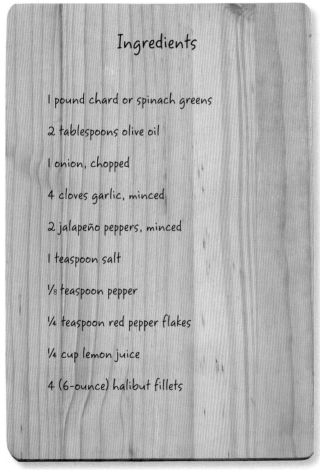

Ingredients

1 pound chard or spinach greens

2 tablespoons olive oil

1 onion, chopped

4 cloves garlic, minced

2 jalapeño peppers, minced

1 teaspoon salt

⅛ teaspoon pepper

¼ teaspoon red pepper flakes

¼ cup lemon juice

4 (6-ounce) halibut fillets

Steamed Fish with Spicy Greens

- Immerse chard leaves in cold water, then shake off water. Dry and coarsely chop.

- In large skillet, heat oil over medium heat. Add onion, garlic, and jalapeño; cook and stir for 3 minutes.

- Add greens, salt, pepper, red pepper flakes, and lemon juice; cover and steam for 2 minutes until greens start to wilt.

- Line 4 steamer baskets with greens, top with fish, and drizzle with mixture from skillet. Steam food over simmering water, rearranging baskets, until fish is cooked, about 10–12 minutes.

·· · · RECIPE VARIATION· · · ·

Divide 3 cups sliced mushrooms among steamer baskets; sprinkle with 1 chopped red onion, 2 tablespoons grated gingerroot, and 3 cloves minced garlic. Sprinkle 6 orange roughy fillets with salt and pepper and place on mushrooms. Drizzle with a mixture of 3 tablespoons each chicken broth, soy sauce, and cider vinegar. Steam over simmering water for 15–20 minutes until done.

Place Food in Baskets

- You can use other liquids to add a bit of flavor to steamed foods.

- Broths, fruit juices, and wine are good choices for additions to the steaming water. You could also add aromatic ingredients like chopped onion, gingerroot, and herbs.

- You can add more food to the baskets if you'd like, but they must be quick cooking, like mushrooms or sliced peppers.

- Be sure to leave a bit of room around each piece of food so the steam can circulate and the food cooks evenly.

Rearrange Baskets

- Make sure that the bottom of the steamer basket does not touch the simmering liquid.

- If it does touch, carefully remove some of the liquid. You don't want the bottom layer of food to overcook.

- Use hot pads to protect your hands while you're rearranging the baskets, especially if they are made of metal.

- The same steam that gently cooks food can burn you in seconds. Be careful when rearranging the baskets.

FISH VEGETABLE PACKETS

Rice, fish, and lemon pair up in these easy one-dish meal packets cooked on the grill

Fish gets great flavor from other foods when they are cooked all together in foil packets on the grill. These packets can also be baked in the oven. Heavy duty foil works well for both methods.

If you're going to be cooking foods like rice, potatoes, or other long-cooking foods along with the fish, they need to be precooked first. Cook rice, grains, or pasta until they are almost done. They will finish cooking in the steam that builds up in the packets.

Because the heat is so intense underneath these packets when they are grilled, it's best if there is a layer of food like rice or pasta between the fish and the foil. *Yield: 4 servings*

Ingredients

1 tablespoon olive oil

1 onion, minced

1 cup long-grain white rice

2 cups chicken broth

3 tablespoons lemon juice

1 teaspoon grated lemon zest

1 (10-ounce) package Alfredo sauce

4 (6-ounce) orange roughy fillets

Salt and pepper to taste

1 fennel bulb, thinly sliced

1 lemon, thinly sliced

Lemon Rice Fish Packets

- In skillet, heat olive oil over medium heat. Add onion; cook and stir for 5 minutes. Add rice; cook and stir for 2 minutes.

- Add broth; cover and simmer for 15–20 minutes until rice is almost cooked. Stir in juice, zest, and Alfredo sauce.

- Tear off 4 sheets of heavy duty foil, 18 inches x 12 inches. Divide rice mixture on foil; top with fish fillets; sprinkle with salt and pepper.

- Place fennel and lemon on fish; wrap packets. Grill over direct medium heat for 18–23 minutes until fish flakes when tested.

Fish and Spinach Packets

Divide 4 cups of baby spinach among 4 sheets of heavy duty foil. Top with 1 chopped red onion, 2 cups chopped tomatoes, and 3 cloves minced garlic. Add 4 6-ounce fillets of cod. Drizzle with mixture of ⅓ cup chili sauce, 2 tablespoons lemon juice, salt, pepper, and 1 tablespoon brown sugar. Seal and grill as directed.

Thai Fish Packets

Divide 2 cups grated carrots among 4 sheets of foil. Top with ½ cup chopped green onion, 2 cloves garlic, and 2 tablespoons minced gingerroot. Top with 4 fish fillets, then sprinkle with mixture of ¼ cup chicken broth, 2 tablespoons honey, 2 tablespoons fish sauce, and ¼ teaspoon cayenne pepper. Bake at 400 degrees F for 18–23 minutes.

Partially Cook Rice

- The rice should be soft on the outside, with a firm inside when it is partially cooked.

- You can precook the rice ahead of time and chill it in the fridge. Reheat in the microwave before proceeding with the recipe.

- In the packets, the rice will continue cooking and will absorb flavors from the Alfredo sauce, the lemon juice, and the zest.

- You could substitute sliced bell peppers and mushrooms for the fennel if you'd like.

Arrange Food on Foil

- Alfredo sauce in 10-ounce containers is sold in the dairy section of the supermarket. You could use part of a 16-ounce jar.

- Move the packets around on the grill as they cook, to keep the food moving a bit and distribute the heat evenly.

- Use a spatula to move the packets. You can find large spatulas at most kitchenware stores.

- Warn your guests that there will be hot steam billowing from the packets when they're opened.

LOW-FAT BROILED FISH FILLETS

Three kinds of mustard make a crisp and flavorful coating on simple broiled fillets

Broiling is a dry heat, quick method of cooking that is similar to grilling. The food is placed 4–6 inches away from the heat source, which is turned to the highest temperature of the oven.

Because the food cooks so quickly, many fish fillets don't need to be turned. Fish is usually cooked for 10 minutes per inch of thickness. A ½-inch-thick piece of fish cooks for 5 minutes.

The heat from the broiler is quite intense, so a sauce is sometimes added to the fish. As on the grill, the sauce caramelizes in the heat, adding another layer of flavor.

Any fairly thick sauce, flavored any way you'd like, can be used with the fish. *Yield: 6 servings*

Ingredients

⅓ cup honey mustard salad dressing

2 tablespoons Dijon mustard

½ teaspoon mustard seeds

¼ cup sour cream

2 tablespoons orange juice

6 (5–6-ounce) orange roughy fillets

½ teaspoon salt

⅛ teaspoon white pepper

1 orange, cut into wedges

2 tablespoons minced fresh dill

Three-Mustard Broiled Fish

- Preheat broiler. In small bowl, combine dressing, mustard, mustard seeds, sour cream, and orange juice.

- Place fish fillets on broiler pan and sprinkle with salt and pepper. Broil fish 6 inches from heat for 3 minutes.

- Spoon mustard mixture on fish and broil for 4–6 minutes longer until fish flakes when tested with fork and mustard mixture browns.

- Remove fish from heat and serve immediately, garnished with orange wedges and fresh dill.

Curried Mahi Mahi Fillets
Combine ¼ cup pineapple juice, 2 tablespoons olive oil, 1 tablespoon curry powder, 1 tablespoon grated ginger-root, ½ teaspoon salt, and ⅛ teaspoon pepper in small bowl. Place 4 fillets in glass baking dish and pour marinade over; marinate for 20 minutes. Broil 6 inches from heat for 5 minutes per ½ inch of thickness.

Bacon Halibut
Broil 8 slices of bacon until partially cooked. Bacon will still be pliable. Sprinkle 4 orange roughy fillets with salt and pepper and wrap each with 2 pieces of bacon. Brush with mixture of 2 tablespoons honey, 2 tablespoons mustard, and 2 tablespoons cider vinegar. Broil, turning once, until bacon is crisp and fish is cooked.

Mix the Glaze

Broil the Fish

- You can make the glaze ahead of time and refrigerate it until you're ready to cook. The thin layer will warm up quickly under the broiler.

- The glaze can be varied easily by using more sour cream and omitting the mustard ingredients.

- Add ingredients like honey, orange zest, minced herbs like basil and tarragon, or cheeses.

- The same mustard mixture will taste very different if you add some grated cheese and different herbs.

- Be sure not to leave the oven while the fish is broiling. The glaze can go from perfectly browned to burned in seconds.

- If the fish is thicker than ½ inch, turn it over after the first 5 minutes, then apply the glaze mixture.

- The doneness test for fish is if it flakes. That means that the fish comes apart at the natural muscle lines.

- The fish will also turn opaque when it's perfectly cooked. These 2 doneness tests are reliable.

MICROWAVE SALMON

A quick fruit chutney, also made in the microwave, tops tender salmon in this fabulous recipe

The microwave is an excellent method for cooking fish. This appliance works by making molecules in the food move quickly, which generates heat. The heat moves throughout the food, cooking it. Follow directions for the amount of heat, cooking time, stirring, and rearranging food carefully. And be sure that you understand doneness tests.

Microwave cooking also demands standing time. After cooking, the food must stand on a solid surface, not a wire rack, to let the heat redistribute and finish cooking the food.

You can also use the microwave to cook sauces and condiments to accompany the main dish. *Yield: 6 servings*

Ingredients

2 cups blueberries

½ cup minced onion

½ teaspoon ground ginger

⅓ cup apple cider vinegar

½ cup brown sugar

2 tablespoons cornstarch

6 (4–5-ounce) skinless salmon fillets

1 teaspoon salt

⅛ teaspoon white pepper

1 teaspoon dried thyme leaves

¼ cup orange juice

Microwave Salmon with Blueberry Chutney

- In medium microwave-safe bowl, combine blueberries, onion, ginger, vinegar, and brown sugar.

- Cover and microwave on high for 2 minutes, remove, and stir. Add cornstarch, mix well, and microwave for another 2 minutes. Remove and cool.

- Place salmon in microwave-safe dish. Sprinkle with salt, pepper, and thyme. Add orange juice.

- Cover and microwave on high for 8–12 minutes, rearranging salmon once, until salmon flakes. Let stand for 5 minutes, then serve with chutney.

~ VARIATIONS ~

Honey Mustard Salmon
Place 6 fillets of salmon in a microwave-safe dish. Sprinkle with salt, pepper, and ½ teaspoon dried dill weed. Combine ¼ cup honey mustard salad dressing with 2 tablespoons coarse brown mustard and 2 tablespoons honey. Spread over salmon. Pour 2 tablespoons orange juice into dish. Microwave on high for 8–12 minutes. Let stand 5 minutes.

Microwave Parmesan Salmon
Place 6 salmon fillets in microwave-safe dish. Sprinkle with salt, pepper, and 1 teaspoon dried thyme. In bowl, mix 10-ounce container Alfredo sauce with ½ cup Parmesan cheese and ½ cup chopped green onion. Pour over fish and microwave as directed. Let stand 5 minutes.

Make Blueberry Chutney

- This chutney can be made with other fruits. Substitute chopped peaches or nectarines, or chopped strawberries or pears.

- You can make the chutney ahead of time. Refrigerate it up to 2 days. It can be served cold with the fish, or reheat it in the microwave.

- To reheat the chutney, microwave on 50 percent power for 2–3 minutes, stirring once, then let stand.

- You can cook the salmon as directed and serve with another sauce, including mango chutney.

Cook Salmon

- You can ask your fishmonger or butcher to remove the salmon skin from the fillets. Or do it yourself with a very sharp knife.

- Feel carefully in the salmon with your fingers for any pin bones, which are very tiny.

- Remove the bones, if there are any, with tweezers and discard. You can do this ahead of time.

- Salmon can be served slightly undercooked in the center, but only if you're sure that your source is impeccable.

141

QUICK FISH SOUP

Greek seasonings are the perfect complement to tender and mild fish in this simple soup

Fish and soup are natural partners. Because fish cooks quickly, it's added at the end of cooking time.

Quick soups rely on ingredients like boxed stocks and broths. These products have a long-cooked taste with no work on your part. Look for low-sodium broths. Not only are they better for you, but they usually taste better because the manufacturer can't rely on salt. Flavor these soups any way you'd like. As long as you cook the ingredients for the appropriate time, you can make fish soups out of everything from potatoes and carrots to apples and pears.

Have fun inventing your own fish soups, using flavors from Tex-Mex heat to subtle French to spicy Creole. *Yield: 6 servings*

Ingredients

3 tablespoons olive oil

1 onion, chopped

3 cloves garlic, minced

2 cups baby carrots, sliced lengthwise

2 (14.5-ounce) cans diced tomatoes, undrained

3 cups chicken broth

½ cup long-grain white rice

1½ pounds fish fillets, cubed

¼ cup lemon juice

⅓ cup chopped parsley

Salt and pepper to taste

Greek Fish Soup

- In large pot, heat olive oil over medium heat. Add onion, garlic, and carrots; cook and stir for 5 minutes.

- Add tomatoes and chicken broth; bring to a simmer. Reduce heat to low and simmer for 15 minutes.

- Add rice; cover and simmer for 18 minutes until rice is partially cooked. Stir in fish and bring to a simmer.

- Cover and simmer for 7–8 minutes until fish flakes when tested with fork. Stir in lemon juice and parsley, season to taste, and serve.

~ VARIATIONS ~

Creole Fish Soup
Cook 1 onion and 2 cloves garlic in 2 tablespoons butter. Add 14-ounce can diced undrained tomatoes, 4 cups chicken broth, 2 bay leaves, 2 teaspoons chili powder, and ⅛ teaspoon cayenne pepper; simmer. Add 2 cups frozen corn, 1 cup chopped celery, and 1 pound cubed cod. Simmer for 8–10 minutes until fish flakes easily. Remove bay leaves.

Creamy Fish and Corn Soup
Cook 1 chopped onion and 3 cloves garlic in 2 tablespoons butter. Add 3 cups frozen hash brown potatoes; cook until thawed. Add 3 cups water, 15-ounce can creamed corn, and 15-ounce jar four-cheese Alfredo sauce; simmer. Add 1 pound cubed fish, 2 cups milk, 2 cups corn, 1 teaspoon thyme, salt, and pepper; simmer.

Prepare Ingredients

- You can prepare ingredients like onions, garlic, and carrots ahead of time. Cover and refrigerate until you're ready.

- The ingredients are first simmered in oil to provide a good base for the soup.

- The size of pot you choose depends on the recipe. A 3-quart saucepan will hold 12 cups, while a 5-quart stock pot holds 20 cups.

- For this quick cooking soup, cut the ingredients fairly small so they cook evenly in the short time frame.

Add Broth to Pot

- You could use brown or wild rice if you'd like. Just simmer for 30 minutes instead of 18, then add fish.

- A homemade stock is easy to make. Combine 2 pounds chicken pieces with 3 quarts water, onions, garlic, and carrots.

- Add salt, pepper, and herbs like thyme and tarragon. Simmer the stock for 2–3 hours. Then cool, strain, and freeze in ¼-cup portions.

- This homemade stock can be substituted, in a 1:1 ratio, for purchased stocks and broths.

SHRIMP STIR-FRY

Shrimp is spicy and tender in this simple stir-fry recipe

Shrimp is one of the best foods to stir-fry because it cooks so quickly. It can be flavored so many ways, and pairs beautifully with almost any fruit or vegetable.

Shrimp doesn't have to be marinated before it's stir-fried, because the fish doesn't readily absorb flavors. It's also perfectly tender if not overcooked, so doesn't need the marinade's tenderizing properties.

You can use shrimp as a substitute for the meat in any clas-

sic stir-fry recipe. There's just one caveat; don't overcook it. Shrimp is done when it curls and turns pink. If overcooked, it will be tough and rubbery.

Flavor shrimp with bold ingredients like fermented black beans, or with sweet and gentle flavors like thyme and fruit. Enjoy these recipes. *Yield: 4 servings*

Ingredients

½ cup chili sauce

3 tablespoons low-sodium soy sauce

2 tablespoons honey

2 tablespoons cornstarch

½ teaspoon crushed red pepper flakes

1 cup chicken broth

3 tablespoons peanut oil

1 pound raw shrimp, peeled and deveined

1 onion, chopped

1 (16-ounce) bag frozen stir-fry vegetables, thawed

Spicy Red Shrimp Stir-Fry

- In small bowl, combine chili sauce, soy sauce, honey, cornstarch, red pepper flakes, and chicken broth.

- In large skillet or wok, heat peanut oil over medium-high heat. Add shrimp; stir-fry for 2–3 minutes until shrimp curl and turn pink. Remove shrimp from wok.

- Add onion; stir-fry for 3 minutes. Add drained vegetables; stir-fry for 3–4 minutes until vegetables are hot.

- Stir chicken broth mixture and add to skillet along with shrimp. Stir-fry for 2–3 minutes until sauce bubbles and thickens. Serve over hot cooked rice.

Szechuan Shrimp

Combine ½ cup chicken broth, ¼ cup seafood cocktail sauce, 2 tablespoons soy sauce, 1 tablespoon cornstarch, 1 tablespoon brown sugar, ⅛ teaspoon cayenne pepper, and ½ teaspoon ginger. Stir-fry 1 pound raw shrimp in 2 tablespoons oil; remove. Stir-fry 1 onion, 1 jalapeño pepper, and 2 cloves garlic. Add shrimp and sauce; stir-fry.

Sesame Shrimp

Combine ¼ cup teriyaki sauce, ½ cup chicken broth, 1 tablespoon cornstarch, 2 teaspoons sesame oil, ½ teaspoon ginger, ⅛ teaspoon cayenne pepper, and 2 cloves garlic. Stir-fry 1 pound shrimp in 2 tablespoons oil; remove. Add 1 chopped onion and 1 sliced red bell pepper. Add shrimp and sauce; stir-fry. Sprinkle with 2 tablespoons toasted sesame seeds.

Make Red Sauce

Stir-Fry

- You could substitute ketchup or seafood cocktail sauce for the chili sauce for a milder recipe.

- If you like bolder flavors, add some minced onion or garlic to the sauce, or add a minced serrano pepper.

- Or add spices and herbs. Add a bit of curry powder for spice, or fresh herbs like thyme or rosemary.

- The sauce can be made ahead of time; just cover it and keep it in the fridge until you're ready to cook.

- The shrimp is stir-fried first to make sure it has good contact with the hot oil and cooks very quickly.

- Remove the shrimp to a clean plate and continue with the recipe. It will be reheated when the sauce is added.

- Make sure that you drain the thawed frozen vegetables very well; you want them to fry, not steam.

- If they are too wet, the oil will spatter when the vegetables are added, which is a safety hazard.

SEAFOOD PACKETS

Tender orange roughy can be flavored so many ways, but this lemon sauce is superb and easy

Fish is one of the best foods to cook in packets with other ingredients. Because it's so mild it can be paired with many other foods. And the food cooks in a packet by steaming— the ideal way to cook delicate fish.

These packets are one-dish meals that cook on the grill or in the oven. The presentation is really beautiful; perfect for a celebration or party. And you can make the packets ahead of time, so they just cook for a few minutes and you're ready to eat.

Flavor these packets any way you'd like. You can use flavored yogurt, your favorite salad dressing, or just slices of lemon with herbs, salt, and pepper. *Yield: 4 servings*

Ingredients

4 (5–6-ounce) orange roughy fillets

Salt and pepper to taste

½ cup lemon yogurt

1 teaspoon grated lemon zest

2 tablespoons lemon juice

2 tablespoons honey

1 tablespoon chopped fresh dill

2 tomatoes, sliced

1 yellow summer squash, sliced

Lemon Dill Fish Packets

- Tear off 4 12-inch x 18-inch sheets of heavy duty aluminum foil. Spray centers with nonstick cooking spray.

- Place fish in center of foil; sprinkle with salt and pepper. In bowl, combine remaining ingredients except tomatoes and squash.

- Arrange tomatoes and squash on top of fish. Spoon on lemon sauce; add more salt and pepper.

- Fold up packets using a double fold, leaving room for expansion. Grill on direct medium heat for 9–12 minutes until fish flakes when tested with fork.

~ VARIATIONS ~

Hawaiian Shrimp Packets
Slice 1 red onion thinly and divide among 4 sheets of parchment paper. Divide 1¼ pounds raw shrimp on the onion and top with 15-ounce can drained pineapple tidbits. Add 1 chopped red bell pepper. Combine ¼ cup pineapple juice with ¼ cup teriyaki sauce and drizzle over food. Bake at 400 degrees F for 20–25 minutes.

Fish and Pepper Packets
Slice 1 red, 1 yellow, and 1 green bell pepper; divide among 6 pieces of heavy duty foil. Top each piece with 1 tilapia fillet. Top with 1 thinly sliced lemon. Combine ⅓ cup seafood cocktail sauce with ¼ cup chicken broth; drizzle over food. Fold up packets; grill over direct medium heat for 15–20 minutes.

Make Lemon Sauce

Layer Seafood with Veggies

- Lemon yogurt is a good shortcut ingredient that's healthy too. You can find it in full-fat and low-fat versions.

- You could substitute low-fat sour cream for a richer flavor. Just add another half teaspoon of grated lemon zest.

- Make the sauce ahead of time and keep it in the fridge up to 4 days.

- Then when you want to grill, just assemble the packets, add the sauce, and get ready to eat.

- If the fish fillets are quite thin and delicate, put some of the vegetables underneath them as well as on top.

- The vegetables will steam and act as a shield for the fish against the intense heat. They also flavor the fish.

- You could substitute other quick cooking vegetables for the squash and tomatoes.

- Sliced mushrooms, bell peppers, zucchini, jarred baby corn, or corn cut off the cob would be delicious.

BROILED SHRIMP KABOBS

Broiling tender shrimp for just a few minutes makes them smoky and sweet

Shrimp, along with other seafood, broils to perfection in just a few minutes. The broiler is a good choice for cooking seafood, especially if you'd like to grill but the weather isn't cooperating.

Shrimp, threaded on skewers, is a fun and easy way to prepare dinner and to entertain. Preparation is dictated by the types of foods you thread on the skewers with the shrimp.

Tender vegetables and fruits can be broiled along with the shrimp because they cook in about the same amount of time. Longer cooking veggies like potatoes, cauliflower, and carrots should be parboiled or precooked in the microwave before adding to the shrimp. Use your imagination and enjoy creating your own shrimp skewers. *Yield: 4 servings*

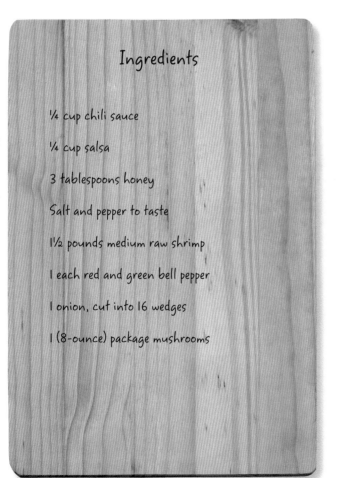

Ingredients

¼ cup chili sauce

¼ cup salsa

3 tablespoons honey

Salt and pepper to taste

1½ pounds medium raw shrimp

1 each red and green bell pepper

1 onion, cut into 16 wedges

1 (8-ounce) package mushrooms

Tex-Mex Shrimp Kabobs

- In large bowl, combine chili sauce, salsa, honey, and salt and pepper. Add shrimp, bell pepper, onion, and mushrooms and toss to coat.

- Cover and refrigerate for 15–20 minutes. Drain shrimp and vegetables, reserving marinade. Preheat broiler.

- Thread shrimp and vegetables on metal skewers. Spray broiler pan with cooking spray; place kabobs on pan.

- Broil 6 inches from heat for 5–7 minutes, turning once and brushing with reserved marinade, until shrimp curl and turn pink and vegetables are crisp-tender.

Broiled Spicy Shrimp

Combine 2 cloves minced garlic, ½ cup minced onion, ¼ cup olive oil, ¼ cup seafood cocktail sauce, 1 tablespoon apple cider vinegar, ½ teaspoon salt, and 1 teaspoon dried basil. Add 1½ pounds raw peeled shrimp; marinate for 30 minutes. Thread on skewers and broil shrimp 6 inches from heat for 2–4 minutes per side until curled and pink.

Shrimp Nectarine Skewers

Combine 3 tablespoons lemon juice, 2 tablespoons honey, 2 minced cloves garlic, 1 tablespoon tequila, 2 minced jalapeño peppers, and ⅛ teaspoon cayenne pepper. Skewer 1½ pounds raw large shrimp, 4 green onions, and 4 sliced nectarines on skewers. Grill on medium direct heat, brushing often with the sauce, until shrimp turn pink.

Prepare Vegetables

- Don't marinate the vegetables and shrimp longer than the recipe specifies. The vegetables will be soggy and the shrimp tough.

- You can make the marinade ahead of time and keep it in the fridge until you're ready to eat.

- The onions will probably fall into pieces when cut into such a small wedge. Thread them on toothpicks before skewering them.

- Remove the toothpicks before you put the skewers under the broiler, because they're so small.

Thread Food on Skewers

- When you're using tender, quick cooking vegetables, you can use bamboo skewers, soaked in water for 30 minutes.

- Metal skewers can be used over and over again and don't burn up under the broiler.

- Be careful handling the skewers; because they are metal, they transmit heat. Use hot pads or heatproof gloves.

- Place the food on the skewers with a little bit of space between each piece so the food cooks evenly.

MICROWAVE SHRIMP

Shrimp scampi is flavored with garlic, butter, and lemon; the microwave makes it super quick

Shrimp cook very well in the microwave oven. You do have to be careful about stirring and standing times so the tender meat doesn't overcook.

Since shrimp are fairly dense, standing times are important so the heat can move evenly through the flesh. Make sure that the dish stands on a solid surface, not on a wire rack, so

heat doesn't escape from the bottom of the dish.

You can substitute shrimp for the meat in any recipe. Just make sure that all the other ingredients are almost cooked before you add the shrimp. The shrimp cook in 3–5 minutes.

Be adventurous pairing shrimp with flavorings and ingredients. *Yield: 4 servings*

Ingredients

¼ cup butter

3 tablespoons olive oil

1 onion, chopped

6 cloves garlic, minced

⅓ cup white wine

¼ cup lemon juice

1 teaspoon grated lemon peel

1½ pounds large raw shrimp

1 cup sugar snap peas

1 cup frozen baby peas

Microwave Shrimp Scampi

- In 2-quart shallow microwave-safe baking dish, combine butter, olive oil, onion, and garlic.

- Microwave on high for 2–3 minutes, stirring once during cooking time, until onion and garlic are crisp-tender.

- Add wine, lemon juice, and lemon peel; microwave for 1 minute until hot. Add shrimp and sugar snap peas; stir to coat.

- Cover and microwave on high for 2 minutes. Add frozen baby peas; microwave on high for 1–3 minutes until shrimp curl. Let stand on solid surface for 5 minutes.

Old Bay Shrimp and Veggies

Cook 2 minced shallots in 2 tablespoons olive oil and 2 tablespoons butter for 4–5 minutes at 100 percent power. Add 2 cups trimmed green beans and 2 chopped tomatoes; microwave for 4 minutes. Add 1 pound raw large shrimp sprinkled with 2 teaspoons Old Bay Seasoning. Microwave for 2 minutes, stir, microwave for 2–4 minutes longer until done.

Zesty Shrimp and Asparagus

Combine 1 pound asparagus, cut into 2-inch pieces, 1 chopped red onion, 2 cloves minced garlic, and ⅓ cup zesty Italian salad dressing. Microwave on high for 3 minutes and stir. Add 1 pound raw large shrimp along with 2 tablespoons lemon juice, ½ teaspoon salt, ⅛ teaspoon cayenne pepper. Microwave for 2 minutes, stir, then microwave 2–4 minutes longer until done.

Prepare Shrimp

Microwave Shrimp

- To prepare raw unpeeled shrimp, first pull off the legs. Then cut off the head if it's still attached.

- Run a small, sharp knife along the back of the shrimp and gently pull off the shell. Make sure you remove it completely.

- There may be a dark line running along the curved back of the shrimp. Cut along it and rinse to remove.

- You can prepare the shrimp well in advance of cooking time. Store, tightly covered, in the refrigerator.

- All microwave ovens cook unevenly. They create hot spots and cool spots. This is why the food has to be moved around.

- Be sure that you stir the food and the sauce very well. Overcooking food may make it unpalatable, but undercooking can be dangerous.

- If some of the shrimp seem to be cooking more slowly, arrange them around the outside edge of the dish.

- Similarly, if they are cooking too fast, put them in the center of the dish.

GRILLED SHELLFISH

Grilled clams and mussels make an easy and spectacular main dish perfect for company

Shellfish, which includes clams, mussels, and oysters, cook beautifully on the grill. The grill adds wonderful smoky flavor to these tender and flavorful meats.

The shellfish can be cooked directly on the grill grate, or can be placed in an aluminum pan or roaster.

Clams, mussels, and oysters will cook at different times, so you have to pay attention when they're on the grill. Remove the shellfish as soon as the shells open; place in a warmed bowl and cover with foil or a lid to keep them warm.

Savory and spicy flavors work best with these slightly salty and rich foods. Soy sauce, wine, cocktail sauces, and hot peppers are delicious, so include them in your creations. *Yield: 4 servings*

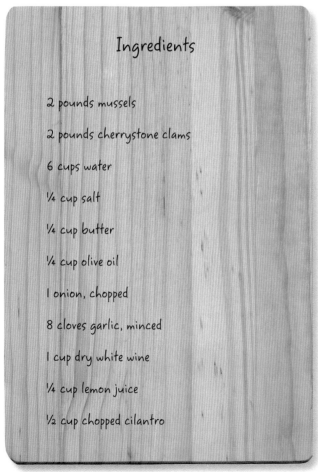

Ingredients

2 pounds mussels

2 pounds cherrystone clams

6 cups water

¼ cup salt

¼ cup butter

¼ cup olive oil

1 onion, chopped

8 cloves garlic, minced

1 cup dry white wine

¼ cup lemon juice

½ cup chopped cilantro

Grilled Clams and Mussels

- Scrub mussels and clams; remove beards from mussels. Discard open shellfish. Soak in mixture of water and salt for 10 minutes.

- Place roasting pan on grill over medium-high heat. Add butter and olive oil; heat for 2 minutes.

- Add onion and garlic; cook and stir for 4–5 minutes. Add wine and lemon juice and bring to a simmer.

- Add mussels and clams; to grill. Cover and grill for 8–12 minutes until shellfish open. Add to roasting pan and stir; serve with dipping sauce.

Curried Mussels

Scrub 4 pounds mussels and pull beards off using needlenose pliers. Discard open or cracked mussels. In saucepan, combine ½ cup butter with 1 chopped onion and 4 cloves minced garlic. Add 1 tablespoon curry powder, ½ teaspoon salt, and ⅛ teaspoon cayenne pepper; cook for 3 minutes. Grill mussels until opened; discard unopened shells. Serve with butter.

Dipping Sauce

In small bowl, combine ½ cup finely crumbled goat cheese, ¼ cup chopped cilantro, 1 teaspoon grated lemon peel, ⅛ teaspoon pepper; mix well. Chill until ready to serve. Serve with grilled clams and mussels.

Soak Shellfish

- Pull the beards, which are the wiry threads, off the mussels using small needle-nose pliers.

- You can try to soak shellfish before cooking; soak in a mixture of water and salt or corn meal. Neither is really proven to remove sand.

- There shouldn't be much sand in cleaned shellfish. Just scrub the shells gently but thoroughly and rinse.

- Oysters are grilled just like clams and mussels; they may take a few more minutes on the heat.

Discard Bad Shellfish

- There's a strict rule about shellfish and food safety. When raw, clams and mussels should be tightly closed.

- Tap on an open shell; if it doesn't close, discard it along with any shellfish with cracks or chips.

- After cooking, the clams and mussels must be open. Discard any that are closed.

- If you're serving this as a main dish, you'll need about 1 pound of shellfish per person. As an appetizer, ⅓ pound per person.

SEAFOOD

SCALLOP SKILLET DISH

Tender and mild scallops are the perfect partner with pasta and pesto

Scallops are small nuggets of shellfish that are creamy, white, and delicate. There are two kinds of scallops: bay and sea. It's easy to remember which is which: Bay scallops are smaller than sea scallops because a bay is smaller than the sea.

Beware of calico scallops, which are often marked as bay scallops. They aren't as sweet and can be tougher.

Bay scallops are sweeter and more tender than sea scallops. Buy what you need. Bay scallops are good for sautéed dishes, while sea scallops are better for grilled skewers.

Use your nose when buying scallops. They should smell sweet and like seawater; not at all fishy or strong. Use them within one to two days. *Yield: 4 servings*

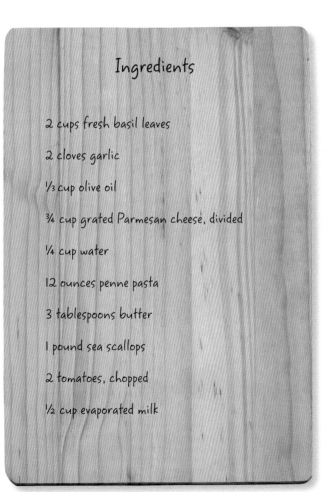

Ingredients

2 cups fresh basil leaves

2 cloves garlic

⅓ cup olive oil

¾ cup grated Parmesan cheese, divided

¼ cup water

12 ounces penne pasta

3 tablespoons butter

1 pound sea scallops

2 tomatoes, chopped

½ cup evaporated milk

Pesto Scallops with Pasta

- Bring a large pot of water to a boil. In blender or food processor, combine basil, garlic, olive oil, and ½ cup Parmesan cheese.

- Cover and blend or process until mixed. Gradually add enough water to form a thick sauce. Set aside.

- Add pasta to boiling water. In large skillet, melt butter over medium heat. Add scallops; cook, turning once, until browned.

- Drain pasta and add to skillet along with pesto, tomatoes, and milk. Cook and stir until sauce blends and tomatoes are hot, about 3–5 minutes.

Scallops and Asparagus

Cook 1½ cups brown rice in 3 cups chicken broth. Meanwhile, in large skillet melt 3 tablespoons butter with 1 tablespoon olive oil. Add 1 pound asparagus, trimmed and cut into 2-inch pieces, 3 cloves minced garlic, and 1 chopped onion; cook 5 minutes. Add 1 pound bay scallops, 2 tablespoons lemon juice, salt, pepper. and basil; cook for 5–8 minutes. Serve over rice.

Bacon Scallops

Cook 4 slices bacon; drain and crumble. Pour off drippings; add 2 tablespoons butter. Sear 1 pound sea scallops, turning once, until surface is golden brown; remove. Add ½ pound sugar snap peas and 2 cloves garlic; cook 3 minutes. Return scallops and bacon to skillet with ¼ cup honey mustard and ⅓ cup sour cream; cook 2-3 minutes. Serve over cooked pasta.

Prepare Pesto

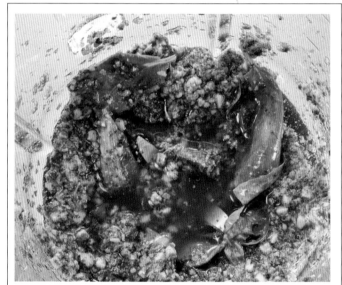

- The pesto can be prepared in a blender or food processor, or mixed by hand with a mortar and pestle.

- You can substitute baby spinach leaves for some of the basil to reduce cost and add nutrition. Or try cilantro leaves or parsley.

- The pesto can be made ahead of time; cover and refrigerate until ready to use.

- You can substitute a 9-ounce package of prepared pesto for the homemade version; just add with the tomatoes.

Combine Ingredients

- Sometimes scallops come with a small, tough muscle attached to one side that should be removed.

- This muscle will be exposed if you run your fingers over the scallop. Just pull it off and discard.

- The pasta finishes cooking in the sauce along with the pesto, so be sure to undercook it slightly.

- The pasta will absorb flavors from the sauce, including the garlic and cheese in the pesto and the tomatoes.

SEAFOOD

PASTA WITH TOMATO SAUCE

White wine is the surprising ingredient in a creamy tomato sauce tossed with tender pasta

Pasta tossed with a simple tomato sauce is the classic Italian dish. Italians don't use a lot of sauce in their pasta recipes, because they believe it smothers the taste of the pasta.

Pasta has to be cooked in a lot of boiling salted water. Italians say that the water should taste like the sea. Stir the pasta several times as it is cooking so it doesn't stick together.

When you're going to finish the pasta in a sauce, undercook it slightly in the boiling water. As it finishes cooking in the sauce, it will absorb some of those flavors.

Have fun using different sauces and flavorings to make these simple recipes. *Yield: 6 servings*

Ingredients

5 slices bacon

2 tablespoons olive oil

3 cloves garlic, minced

3 tablespoons tomato paste

¼ cup dry white wine

1 (16-ounce) jar pasta sauce

1 (16-ounce) package uncooked mostaccioli

½ cup heavy whipping cream

½ cup grated pecorino cheese

Mostaccioli with Wine Tomato Sauce

- Bring a large pot of salted water to a boil. Meanwhile, in large saucepan, cook bacon until crisp. Drain on paper towels, crumble, and set aside.

- Pour off bacon fat; do not wipe saucepan. Add olive oil and garlic; cook for 3 minutes.

- Add tomato paste; cook until paste begins to brown, about 4 minutes. Add wine; cook and stir to loosen pan drippings.

- Add pasta sauce; simmer for 10 minutes. Cook mostaccioli. Add to sauce with bacon and cream. Top with cheese and serve.

Hearty Pasta Sauce

Cook 1 pound pork sausage with 1 chopped onion and 2 cloves minced garlic until done; drain. Add 14-ounce can diced tomatoes, 6-ounce can tomato paste, 8-ounce can tomato sauce, 1 teaspoon sugar, 1 teaspoon dried basil, ½ teaspoon fennel seed, ¼ teaspoon pepper; simmer for 20 minutes. Serve over 16-ounce package linguine.

Pasta Alfredo

Cook 1 chopped onion and 3 cloves minced garlic in 2 tablespoons olive oil. Add 16-ounce jar Alfredo sauce, 3-ounce package cream cheese, 1 cup milk, and ⅓ cup grated Romano cheese; simmer 5 minutes. Add 12 ounces cooked and drained penne pasta; cook for 3–4 minutes longer. Sprinkle with ⅓ cup chopped parsley and more Parmesan cheese and serve.

Simmer Sauce

- The bacon fat adds flavor you really can't get any other way. Just a little bit makes a big difference.

- The white wine lifts off the pan drippings and incorporates them into the sauce. The alcohol will not completely burn off.

- Brown the tomato paste to add flavor to the sauce. The browned bits are caramelized. Don't let it burn.

- Because they're high in sugar, tomato sauces can burn fairly easily; stir frequently from the bottom.

Add Pasta

- Whenever you're cooking pasta with sauce, reserve some of the pasta cooking water.

- The water contains starch from the pasta, so it gives the sauce body even as it's diluting the texture.

- Any tomato sauce can be made smoother and richer with the addition of a dairy product. The proteins in the dairy product add a richer mouthfeel.

- Cream, evaporated milk, yogurt, crème fraîche, and cheese all take the sharp edge off tomato sauce.

PASTA

ORZO PASTA SALAD

Orzo pasta, which looks just like rice, is delicious tossed with a cheesy dressing in a main dish salad

Orzo is a delicious, tiny pasta that is shaped exactly like grains of rice. It is a great addition to cold or hot salads.

Many recipes will tell you to rinse the hot cooked pasta in cold water before adding it to the salad dressing and other ingredients. This does rinse off surface starch, but then the pasta doesn't absorb the flavors of the dressing.

You can make a pasta salad out of just about anything. Vegetables, meats, cheeses, and fruits all work well.

The amount of dressing looks like a lot, but the pasta will absorb it as it cools. You can add more of the dressing ingredients as needed if you think the salad needs it. *Yield: 8 servings*

Ingredients

½ cup plain yogurt

⅔ cup creamy Italian cheese salad dressing

⅓ cup grated Parmesan cheese

2 cups frozen sugar snap peas

2 cups baby frozen peas

2 cups frozen snow peas

1 (16-ounce) package orzo pasta

⅓ cup chopped green onion

Three-Pea Parmesan Orzo Salad

- Bring a large pot of salted water to a boil over high heat. Meanwhile, combine yogurt, salad dressing, and cheese in large bowl.

- Prepare snap peas, baby peas, and snow peas as directed on package. Drain and add to dressing.

- Cook pasta according to package directions until al dente. Drain and add to dressing along with green onions.

- Toss gently to coat ingredients with dressing. Cover and chill for 3–4 hours to blend flavors.

Orzo Fruit Salad

Combine ¾ cup orange yogurt, ¾ cup mayonnaise, 3 tablespoons each mustard and milk, and ½ teaspoon dried thyme. Add 16 ounces cooked and drained orzo, 1 cup diced ham, 2 cups chopped nectarines, 15-ounce can drained mandarin oranges, 2 cups red grapes, and ½ cup toasted sliced almonds. Stir well and chill.

Orzo Shrimp Salad

Combine ½ cup honey mustard salad dressing, ¼ cup olive oil, ½ cup plain yogurt and ½ teaspoon dried dill weed. Add 1 pound cooked medium shrimp, 16-ounce package cooked and drained orzo, 1 each chopped green, red, and yellow bell peppers, 1 cup chopped celery, and ½ cup crumbled blue cheese. Mix and chill.

Make Dressing

Cook Pasta

- The dressing should be smooth and well mixed before you add the salad ingredients.

- You can use any creamy salad dressing in this recipe: honey mustard, Caesar, Thousand Island, or blue cheese.

- You can cook the peas as directed on the package label, or you can simply thaw and drain them for a crunchier texture.

- Substitute foods like chopped bell peppers, mushrooms, cherry or grape tomatoes, or cooked green beans for the peas.

- Be sure to stir the orzo pasta often as it cooks, as it has a tendency to stick to the bottom of the pot.

- Salt the water generously. A handful of salt is an appropriate amount to flavor the pasta well.

- Drain the pasta well by pouring it into a colander. Shake to remove excess water and immediately stir it into the dressing.

- The salad should be chilled for 3–4 hours before serving. Stir the salad after it has chilled.

PASTA

NOODLE BOWLS

Slurpy noodle bowls, made with shrimp and veggies, are flavorful and very easy to make

Noodle bowls were made popular by the Vietnamese. They are literally bowls filled with cooked noodles, vegetables, meat, and lots of well-seasoned broth.

These bowls are actually sold as street food in Asian countries. The solids are eaten with chopsticks, and it's considered perfectly acceptable to slurp the food and liquid as you eat.

The broth must be of the highest quality because it's such an important part of the recipe. Your own homemade stock is easy to make, but the newer boxed stocks and broths on the market are very high quality.

Each bowl should be about ¼ noodles, ¼ meat and vegetables, then filled with the broth. *Yield: 4 servings*

Ingredients

2 tablespoons peanut oil

1 onion, chopped

3 cloves garlic, minced

6 cups chicken stock

3 tablespoons teriyaki sauce

¼ teaspoon red pepper flakes

½ teaspoon ground ginger

12 ounces buckwheat soba noodles

2 cups chopped green cabbage

1 pound cooked shrimp

1½ cups frozen baby peas, thawed

Shrimp and Cabbage Noodle Bowl

- Bring a large pot of water to a boil. Meanwhile, in large saucepan, heat peanut oil over medium-high heat.

- Add onion and garlic; stir-fry for 4–5 minutes until tender. Add stock, teriyaki sauce, red pepper flakes, and ginger; bring to a simmer.

- Cook soba noodles as directed on package until al dente. Meanwhile, add cabbage to saucepan; simmer for 3 minutes.

- Add shrimp and peas; simmer for 2 minutes. Stir in drained noodles; simmer 2–3 minutes. Serve in deep bowls with chopsticks.

• • • • RECIPE VARIATION • • • •

Beef Noodle Bowls: Cook 1 chopped onion, 1 tablespoon grated ginger, and 2 cloves garlic in 1 tablespoon oil. Add ½ cup beef sirloin, cut into thin strips; cook until brown; remove beef. Add 2 cups chopped red cabbage, 1 cup grated carrot, and 1 cup chopped mushrooms. Add 6 cups beef broth and beef; simmer 5 minutes. Add 2 cups noodles; simmer 5-6 minutes.

Simmer Broth

Add Noodles

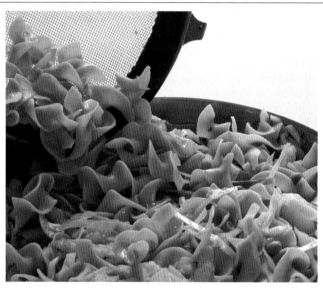

- To make your own broth, combine 2 pounds beef bones and 2 each chopped carrots and onions with 2 quarts water.

- Simmer for 3–4 hours until the broth tastes beefy. Strain, cool, and freeze in 1-cup portions until ready to use.

- You can make chicken broth by using chicken bones. Season the broth as you'd like, with salt, pepper, and herbs.

- Substitute hoisin sauce, soy sauce, or oyster sauce for the teriyaki sauce for a different taste.

- Because the noodles absorb a lot of water when they cook, they aren't cooked in the broth with the other ingredients.

- Soba noodles are thin and are made from buckwheat flour, and are the classic bowl noodle.

- You could also use *udon,* a thick pasta made from plain wheat flour. Or substitute ordinary linguine.

- This dish has to be served immediately; it won't wait. The noodles will continue to cook in the hot broth.

PASTA

PASTA SOUPS

Tortellini is the fast food of pasta when cooked in broth and vegetables

Soup is the ideal medium for pasta. You can cook the pasta right in the soup, which is not only quicker and easier, but flavors the pasta. There's a huge difference in taste and texture between pasta cooked in salted water and pasta cooked in broth.

A soup is only as good as its base. Usually, aromatics like onions, garlic, and spices are cooked in oil or with meat to start the soup. Then water or stock or other liquid is added, and ingredients like pastas are added at the end of cooking time.

You can make these soups with any combination of ingredients you'd like, and any ethnic flavoring and foods. *Yield: 6 servings*

Ingredients

1 pound spicy pork sausage

1 onion, chopped

3 cloves garlic, minced

3 cups frozen mixed vegetables

5 cups chicken broth

1 (14.5-ounce) can diced tomatoes, undrained

Salt and pepper to taste

1 teaspoon dried Italian seasoning

1 (20-ounce) package frozen cheese tortellini

⅓ cup grated Parmesan cheese

Tortellini Minestrone

- In large pot, cook sausage with onion and garlic until sausage is browned; drain well.

- Add frozen mixed vegetables; cook and stir for 3–4 minutes until vegetables start to thaw. Then add broth; bring to a simmer. Simmer for 8–9 minutes.

- Add tomatoes, salt, pepper, and Italian seasoning. Then add tortellini; simmer for 5–6 minutes until tortellini is hot and tender and vegetables are cooked.

- Stir soup gently, then sprinkle with Parmesan cheese and serve immediately.

Tomato Pasta Soup

Cook 1 onion and 3 cloves garlic in 2 tablespoons olive oil. Add 4 chopped plum tomatoes, 14-ounce can diced tomatoes, 1 teaspoon dried Italian seasoning, 2 cups tomato juice, 3 cups chicken broth, and 1 cup chopped celery; simmer for 10 minutes. Add 1 cup orzo pasta; simmer for 10–12 minutes until tender. Serve with Parmesan cheese.

Buffalo Chicken Pasta Soup

Cook 1 chopped onion, 2 stalks chopped celery, and 2 minced cloves garlic in 2 tablespoons butter. Add 2 tablespoons flour, ½ teaspoon salt, and ¼ teaspoon cayenne pepper; cook until bubbly. Add 5 cups chicken broth, 1 cup light cream, 2 cups cooked chicken, and 1 cup orzo; simmer 10 minutes; add 1 cup each shredded Swiss and crumbled blue cheeses.

Cook Soup Base

- Cooking onions and garlic with sausage in the first step helps flavor the whole pot of soup.

- You could add other vegetables to the soup if you'd like. There are many types and varieties of frozen mixed vegetables.

- Or you could chop and add fresh vegetables. Match the combination in your favorite frozen vegetable package or choose your own.

- Chopped bell peppers, green beans, sliced mushrooms, frozen corn, or sliced carrots are all good choices.

Add Remaining Ingredients

- If you'd like to substitute fresh tomatoes for the canned, just chop 6–7 plum or Roma tomatoes.

- Add them, juice and all, to the soup along with a pinch of salt. You may need to add a few tablespoons of tomato juice.

- Frozen tortellini are usually fully cooked, then frozen, so they aren't cooked in the soup.

- The tortellini are just reheated. When they are done, they'll float to the surface of the soup.

PASTA

MICROWAVE LASAGNA

Lasagna made in the microwave is a quick and delicious main dish for company

The microwave, believe it or not, is a great way to quickly cook almost any lasagna recipe. You can use the no-boil type of lasagna noodles to make sure they will be tender, but regular noodles work well as long as there's enough liquid in the recipe.

It's very important to follow microwaving power, rotating, and standing instructions when you're cooking a large cas-serole like lasagna. Be sure that your microwave has at least 800 watts of power to cook the lasagna in this time frame. If your microwave has less power, increase cooking time by 30–40 percent.

With just noodles, sauce, and cheese, you can make any flavor lasagna quickly and easily. *Yield: 10 servings*

Ingredients

1 tablespoon olive oil

1 pound ground chicken

1 onion, chopped

Salt and pepper to taste

1½ teaspoons dried Italian seasoning

1 (26-ounce) jar zesty spaghetti sauce

½ cup water

1½ cups ricotta cheese

2 eggs, beaten

¼ cup chopped chives

½ cup grated Parmesan cheese, divided

9 uncooked lasagna noodles

1 cup shredded mozzarella cheese

1 cup shredded provolone cheese

Chicken Microwave Lasagna

- In microwave-safe dish, combine olive oil, chicken, and onion. Microwave on high for 3 minutes, and stir.

- Microwave for 2 minutes longer, then drain. Stir in salt, pepper, seasoning, spaghetti sauce, and water.

- Combine ricotta, eggs, chives, and ¼ cup Parmesan. In 9-inch x 13-inch glass baking dish, layer chicken sauce, 3 noodles, half of the ricotta mixture, and mozzarella cheese.

- Repeat layers. Sprinkle ¼ cup Parmesan. Cover; microwave on high 15–20 minutes. Let stand 10 minutes.

Chicken Alfredo Lasagna

Combine 16-ounce jar Alfredo sauce with 1 cup milk. Layer 9 no-boil lasagna noodles, 3 cups cooked chicken, 10-ounce package thawed and drained frozen spinach, 2 cups mozzarella cheese, 1 cup ricotta cheese, and sauce mixture in microwave-safe dish. Top with ¼ cup Parmesan cheese. Microwave on high for 12–20 minutes, turning once. Let stand for 10 minutes.

Classic Beef Lasagna

Cook 1 pound ground beef, 1 chopped onion, and 3 cloves garlic until done. Mix with 26-ounce jar pasta sauce and ½ cup water. Mix 1 cup cottage cheese, ½ cup ricotta cheese, and 1 egg, Layer 9 uncooked lasagna noodles with beef mixture, cheese mixture, and 2 cups shredded mozzarella cheese. Microwave as directed.

Microwave Chicken

Prepare Ingredients

- Ground chicken has to be cooked in some kind of fat because it's so low in fat. Otherwise it will be dry.

- You can cook the chicken and onion in a saucepan on the stove if you're more comfortable with that method.

- Ground chicken, as with all ground meats, has to be thoroughly cooked. The final temperature should be 165 degrees F.

- You could substitute ground turkey or spicy or sweet Italian pork sausage for the chicken for more flavor.

- You could add more vegetables to this or any lasagna recipe for more color, flavor, and nutrition. The vegetables should be cooked.

- Frozen chopped spinach, thawed and thoroughly drained, is a classic addition, as are canned mushrooms.

- Since the lasagna can't be stirred, standing time to let the heat travel through the entire dish is important.

- Add a layer of four-cheese Alfredo sauce to the lasagna for more moisture and additional flavor.

PASTA

COUSCOUS SKILLET

Couscous is tiny pasta that cooks in a flash; stirred with chicken and vegetables, it's a hearty meal

Many people think that couscous is a grain, but it's a form of pasta. It's made from semolina wheat, available in two forms.

The large grains of couscous traditionally used in Moroccan cooking take a long time to prepare and cook. That's not the type of couscous called for in these recipes.

The second form is a very small grain, also made of semolina wheat, which is precooked. To prepare it, all you have to do is mix it with boiling liquid.

Because couscous is very mild, like pasta, to add flavor it's rehydrated in broths and flavored liquids, then combined with almost any food in almost any cuisine. *Yield: 6 servings*

Greek Couscous Skillet

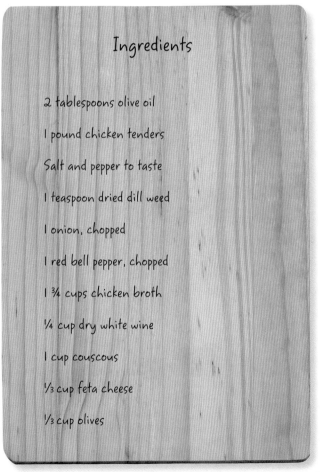

Ingredients

2 tablespoons olive oil

1 pound chicken tenders

Salt and pepper to taste

1 teaspoon dried dill weed

1 onion, chopped

1 red bell pepper, chopped

1 ¾ cups chicken broth

¼ cup dry white wine

1 cup couscous

⅓ cup feta cheese

⅓ cup olives

- In heavy skillet, heat oil over medium heat. Sprinkle chicken with salt, pepper and dill; sauté until browned, about 3–4 minutes. Remove from skillet.

- Add onion and bell pepper; cook and stir for 3 minutes. Return chicken to skillet; add broth and wine.

- Bring to a simmer; simmer for 2–3 minutes until chicken is thoroughly cooked. Stir in couscous.

- Cover and remove from heat. Let stand for 7–8 minutes. Uncover, add feta and olives; fluff with fork, and serve.

Tex-Mex Couscous Skillet

Cook 1 pound ground beef, 1 chopped onion, 3 cloves garlic, and 2 jalapeño peppers; drain. Add 1 green bell pepper, 2 cups corn, ½ cup salsa, and 1½ cups beef broth; bring to a simmer. Stir in 1 cup couscous; cover and remove from heat. Let stand 5 minutes, and stir in ½ cup Cotija cheese.

French Chicken Couscous Skillet

Cook 3 cubed chicken breasts, 1 chopped onion, and 3 cloves garlic in 2 tablespoons olive oil. Add 2 cups frozen green beans and 1 chopped red bell pepper. Add 2 cups chicken broth, 1 cup couscous, and 1 cup diced Brie cheese; stir, cover, and remove from heat. Let stand, fluff with fork, serve.

Simmer Ingredients

Add Couscous

PASTA

- To prepare chicken tenders, all you need to do is cut across them to form 1-inch cubes.

- For the most tender chicken, first brown it to add flavor to the dish, then remove it while the vegetables start cooking.

- Other ingredients you could use in this dish include trimmed and chopped green beans, thinly sliced carrots, and frozen peas.

- For even more authentic Greek flavor, use kalamata olives and stir in some lemon peel along with the couscous.

- Be sure that the couscous you use in this dish is precooked. Read the label and cooking instructions to make sure.

- The couscous will be perfectly rehydrated during the brief standing time. Fluff it with a fork when you're ready to eat.

- Make sure that the liquid is simmering before you add the couscous for best results.

- The liquid has to be very hot in order for the couscous to absorb it properly and rehydrate.

PASTA SALAD

Pasta is a natural for main dish salads, enveloped in creamy dressings with vegetables

Use your imagination when creating pasta salads. This delicious category of food is perfect for hot summer days and for when your house is full of company. You make it, put it in the fridge, and let everyone help themselves.

Be sure there's enough dressing for the salad, and that the dressing is the proper consistency. It should look like thick pancake batter. If it's thicker, it won't blend well with the other ingredients and the salad will be dry. Thinner, and the food won't be able to hold onto it, and you'll end up with a puddle of dressing in the bottom of the bowl.

Enjoy creating your own fresh pasta salads. *Yield: 8 servings*

Ingredients

¾ cup ranch salad dressing

¼ cup zesty Italian salad dressing

½ cup light mayonnaise

1 teaspoon dried basil leaves

⅓ cup grated Parmesan cheese

1 each red, yellow, and green bell peppers

1 pound crabmeat (real or imitation)

16 ounces frozen cheese tortellini

2 cups frozen baby peas, thawed

Italian Crab Pasta Salad

- Bring a large pot of salted water to a boil. In large bowl, combine ranch dressing, Italian dressing, mayonnaise, basil, and cheese; mix well.

- Seed and chop the bell peppers; add to dressing mixture. Pick over crabmeat, if real, or flake, if using surimi.

- Cook the tortellini according to package directions until al dente. Place peas in colander; drain pasta over peas.

- Add to mixture in bowl and stir to coat. Serve immediately, or cover and chill for 2–3 hours before serving.

Orange Chicken Pasta Salad

Combine ½ cup mayonnaise, ½ cup orange yogurt, ¼ cup orange juice, 1 teaspoon dried thyme, and 1 tablespoon Dijon mustard. Stir in 12 ounces rotini, cooked, 2 cups cubed cooked chicken, 15-ounce can drained mandarin oranges, 2 cups red grapes, and ½ cup walnut pieces. Mix well, chill, and stir before serving.

Pasta Veggie Salad

Combine ½ cup olive oil, ⅓ cup apple cider vinegar, ¼ cup Dijon mustard, 1 teaspoon dried oregano, and ⅓ cup Parmesan cheese. Add 12 ounces cooked gemelli pasta, 1 each chopped red, yellow, and orange bell pepper, 1 chopped red onion, 2 cups frozen baby peas, 1 cup diced cheddar cheese, and 2 cups grape tomatoes. Mix, chill, and serve.

Mix Dressing

Finish Salad

- If may look like there's a lot of dressing, but there's a lot of food for that dressing to coat. The hot pasta will absorb it.

- If you'd like, make more dressing and refrigerate it along with the salad.

- If the salad is dry, you can stir in more dressing, or serve it on the side for guests.

- There are other salad dressing combinations that would be delicious in this recipe, like French and blue cheese, or Caesar and ranch.

- Surimi is an artificial crab that is made from real fish. It's colored and shaped to look like crab legs.

- To stretch this salad, serve it on mixed salad greens. That also adds color, flavor, and nutrition.

- You can use real crabmeat if you'd like. Jumbo lump crabmeat is the best. Back fin and claw meat is less expensive.

- Fresh crabmeat needs to be picked over. Remove any bits of cartilage and shell with your fingers.

CHICKEN SALAD

Classic chicken salad is packed full of chicken and fruit.

Chicken salad, that beloved staple of women's lunches in the twentieth century, is easy to make and can be made with most fruits and vegetables.

Tender, perfectly cooked chicken is the secret to this salad. Poached chicken or chicken baked in parchment paper is your best bet. These cooking types result in very moist and tender chicken. You can also marinate the cooked, cubed chicken in a liquid before it's added to the rest of the salad.

The chicken will absorb some of the liquid and its flavor. Use the same liquid you're going to use to make the salad dressing.

Chicken salads can be made with fruit, with a sweet dressing, or with vegetables, with a savory dressing. *Yield: 8 servings*

Ingredients

3 cups chopped cooked chicken

¼ cup orange juice

½ cup low-fat sour cream

½ cup low-fat mayonnaise

½ teaspoon curry powder

Salt and pepper to taste

2 cups red grapes

1 cup green grapes

2 nectarines, chopped

½ cup chopped dried apricots

½ cup heavy whipping cream

Creamy Fruit Chicken Salad

- In medium bowl, combine chicken with orange juice; stir and refrigerate for 10 minutes.

- In large bowl, combine sour cream, mayonnaise, curry powder, salt, and pepper and beat until smooth with wire whisk. Stir in chicken and orange juice.

- Add grapes, nectarines, and chopped dried apricots; stir gently to coat. Cover and chill for 1–2 hours.

- In small bowl, beat cream until stiff peaks form. Fold into salad, then serve.

Parchment Paper Baked Chicken
Place chicken breasts on sheets of parchment paper, 1 breast per sheet. Sprinkle with dried herbs to flavor the chicken, then top each with a thin slice of lemon or orange. Fold the parchment paper around the chicken and place on cookie sheets. Bake at 375 degrees F for 20–25 minutes until temperature registers 160 degrees F.

Parmesan Chicken Salad
Combine ½ cup mayonnaise, ½ cup plain yogurt, ¼ cup milk, ⅓ cup grated Parmesan cheese, and 1 teaspoon dried basil. Add 3 cups cubed cooked chicken breast, 1 cup chopped celery, 2 cups grape tomatoes, ⅓ cup chopped green onion, and 1 cup chopped mushrooms. Stir, chill, and serve on lettuce leaves.

Poach Chicken Breasts

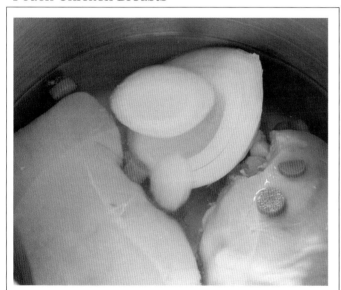

Fold Whipped Cream into Salad

- To poach chicken breasts, place them in cold water to cover, with a halved onion and chopped carrot.

- Bring to a simmer; reduce heat to low until liquid barely moves. Poach for 10–15 minutes until internal temperature reaches 160 degrees F.

- Let the mixture cool at room temperature for 20–30 minutes, then refrigerate the chicken in the liquid.

- The chicken can be cubed or shredded and used immediately, or frozen up to 3 months.

- Just a tiny bit of curry powder doesn't make the salad taste of curry, but enhances the sweet and tart flavors of the fruits.

- You can substitute 1 cup low-fat or nonfat frozen whipped topping, thawed, for the whipped cream, but the salad will be sweeter.

- Fold the cream in just before serving so the dressing remains fluffy and light.

- You can use other fruits if you'd like. Jarred mango, chopped peaches, or blueberries would be good.

DELI BEEF SALAD

Deli roast beef, in a spicy dressing with thin noodles, makes an exotic main dish salad

Beef salads are probably the least common cold main dish salads. Beef usually isn't served cold, but it can be delicious with the right dressing and accompanying ingredients.

You can cook the meat and add it to the salad, or use leftover or deli cooked meat. If you're using sliced steak, be sure to cook it to medium or medium well. If you use well-done steak, it will be chewy in these salads.

For the dressing, use your imagination! Think about flavors you like to serve with steak or hamburgers. A dressing made from steak sauce and yogurt would be delicious, as would one made from mustard, relish, and mayonnaise.

Enjoy these easy beef salad recipes. *Yield: 6 servings*

Ingredients

3 tablespoons low-sodium soy sauce

1 tablespoon fish sauce

3 tablespoons lime juice

1 teaspoon grated lime zest

2 tablespoons honey

⅓ cup peanut butter

⅛ teaspoon cayenne pepper

1 pound thinly sliced deli beef

4 cups chopped napa cabbage

1 (8-ounce) can baby corn, drained

¼ cup chopped cilantro

Thai Beef Salad

- In large bowl, combine soy sauce, fish sauce, lime juice, lime zest, and honey.

- Stir in peanut butter and cayenne pepper and beat with wire whisk until smooth. Dressing can be made ahead of time.

- Cut the beef into thin strips and toss with peanut butter mixture.

- Place cabbage on serving plate and top with baby ears of corn. Spoon beef mixture on top and sprinkle with cilantro. Serve immediately.

Beef and Potato Salad

In 2 tablespoons butter, sauté 1 pound thinly sliced beef sirloin steak; remove. Cook 1 chopped onion, 2 cloves minced garlic, 4 cups frozen hash brown potatoes. Combine ½ cup plain yogurt, ½ cup mayonnaise, ¼ cup brown mustard, 2 tablespoons horseradish, and ¼ cup beef broth. Add beef, sautéed vegetables, 2 cups grape tomatoes, and 2 cups mushrooms; mix.

Taco Salad

In bowl, combine 1 pound cubed deli roast beef, 16-ounce jar salsa, 2 cups corn, 2 minced jalapeño peppers, 1 tablespoon chili powder, 1 chopped red onion, 1 yellow bell pepper, and 2 cups chopped tomatoes; mix. Serve on torn lettuce; top with 2 cups crushed tortilla chips and 2 cups shredded cheddar cheese.

Slice Beef into Strips

- The beef is important in this salad, so make sure that the deli slices the beef about ⅓ inch thick.

- If the beef is cut thinner than that, it will tend to fall apart when mixed in the salad.

- You can also cube the beef. To use leftovers, save a grilled steak, or use some cooked roast beef.

- The beef will absorb some moisture from the dressing. You could toss the beef with the dressing ahead of time; store in fridge.

Mix the Sauce

- Fish sauce, also called nuoc mam, is an intensely flavored Asian sauce that adds a rich depth of flavor.

- The dressing won't taste fishy. You can substitute teriyaki or hoisin sauce for the fish sauce if you'd like.

- For an easier dressing, combine a Thai peanut sauce with some lime juice and chopped green onion.

- The sauce can be made ahead of time and stored, covered, in the refrigerator until you're ready to use it.

MAIN COURSE SALADS

BEAN SALAD

Legumes are combined in a spicy salsa dressing for a super quick salad perfect for summer

Bean salads are so easy to make because you can start with drained canned or frozen beans.

Everybody knows about the standard three-bean or four-bean salad, made of kidney, garbanzo, and green beans marinated in a sweet and sour dressing. But bean salads go beyond that traditional recipe.

You can combine legumes with pasta, with meats like chicken or shrimp, and with just about any vegetable in the produce department. And the dressings can range from sweet and sour to savory or spicy.

If you think of beans as pasta or grains, you'll see a lot of salad possibilities open up. *Yield: 6 servings*

Ingredients

¼ cup peanut oil

¼ cup sugar

⅓ cup taco sauce

¼ cup red wine vinegar

1 (15-ounce) can yellow wax beans

1 (15-ounce) can kidney beans

1 (15-ounce) can garbanzo beans

1 red onion, chopped

2 minced jalapeño peppers

Mexican Three-Bean Salad

- In large bowl, combine oil, sugar, taco sauce, and vinegar and mix well. Let stand for 10 minutes, then whisk again.

- Be sure that the sugar is dissolved before adding the vegetables.

- Drain all the canned beans and rinse thoroughly; drain again. Add to sauce along with the onion and jalapeños.

- Cover and refrigerate for 3–4 hours to blend flavors before serving. Add other chopped vegetables or meats to salad for variation.

Southwest Bean Salad
In bowl, combine ⅓ cup each olive oil, lime juice, and chopped cilantro with ½ teaspoon salt, ⅛ teaspoon cayenne pepper, 2 minced cloves garlic, 2 minced jalapeño peppers, and 2 teaspoons chili powder. Add 15-ounce cans kidney, black, and pinto beans, drained, along with 1 chopped red onion, 2 cups thawed frozen corn, and 2 red bell peppers.

Black Bean Chicken Salad
Combine ½ cup yogurt, ½ cup mayonnaise, ½ cup salsa, ¼ cup chopped cilantro, salt, pepper, and ¼ cup chicken broth. Add 3 cups cubed cooked chicken, 2 (15-ounce) cans drained black beans, 1 chopped red onion, 8-ounce can drained sliced mushrooms, and 2 cups chopped tomato. Mix and chill, then stir and serve.

Drain and Rinse Beans

Toss Salad

- Canned beans are so easy to use, but they can be very high in sodium. Look for low-sodium products.

- Always drain, rinse, then drain beans again. This will help reduce the sodium content somewhat.

- For no sodium, cook your own dried beans. Place beans in a pot, cover with water, and boil hard for 2 minutes. Let stand 1 hour.

- Drain, cover with water again, and cook 2–3 hours until beans are tender. The beans can be frozen.

- The beans are fairly tender, so use care when tossing with other ingredients. Use a spoon with a large bowl.

- To save more time, use a prepared salad dressing. Zesty Italian, a creamy blue cheese dressing, or creamy Parmesan would be good.

- Add meats like cubed cooked chicken, cooked shrimp or scallops, or grilled salmon to the salad.

- Toss the salad again before serving. Since these ingredients don't absorb dressing, it will drain to the bottom of the bowl.

MAIN COURSE SALADS

GRAIN SALADS

Tabbouleh, made from cracked wheat and quinoa, is an inexpensive and healthy base for summer salads

Cooked grains are some of the healthiest foods you can eat. They include wheat, cracked wheat, barley, corn, brown and wild rice, quinoa, and farro.

All of these foods are very easy to cook. They just simmer in water, broth, or other liquid for a few minutes until tender. They are all fairly mild, too, so can be used with many differ-

ent kinds of foods. Within the category of grains, there are quick cooking options. Cracked wheat cooks more quickly than wheat berries, and you can use instant wild and brown rice. Whatever grain you choose, make sure it's cooked properly and is still slightly chewy.

These salads are just as versatile as the others. *Yield: 6 servings*

Ingredients

½ cup quinoa

½ cup cracked wheat

2 cups vegetable broth

½ teaspoon cumin

2 teaspoons chili powder

¼ cup olive oil

¼ cup lemon juice

Salt and pepper to taste

¼ teaspoon red pepper flakes

1 cup chopped celery

2 tomatoes, seeded and chopped

2 cups frozen edamame, thawed

½ cup chopped cilantro

Spicy Veggie Tabbouleh

- Cook quinoa and cracked wheat according to package directions, using vegetable broth instead of water.

- Meanwhile, in large bowl combine cumin, chili powder, oil, lemon juice, salt, pepper, and red pepper flakes.

- Add the cooked quinoa and cracked wheat and toss gently to coat.

- Prepare vegetables and stir into salad. Sprinkle with cilantro. Cover and chill for 2–3 hours before serving.

Barley Black Bean Salad

Cook 1 cup pearl barley as directed on package. Meanwhile, combine ¼ cup each olive oil, Dijon mustard, chopped parsley, 2 tablespoons lemon juice, salt, and pepper. Stir in hot cooked barley, 2 15-ounce cans drained black beans, 1 each red, yellow, and green bell pepper, and 1 cup sliced mushrooms. Mix well, cover, and chill.

Tex-Mex Wild Rice Salad

Cook 1 cup wild rice according to package directions. Combine ½ cup mayonnaise, ½ cup salsa, ⅓ cup sour cream, 1 minced jalapeño pepper, and ½ cup chopped red onion. Add 1 pound cooked medium shrimp, 1 cup diced Pepper Jack cheese, 15-ounce can drained baby corn, and 2 cups frozen thawed edamame. Mix and chill; stir before serving.

Cook Quinoa and Cracked Wheat

- Quinoa is an ancient grain that provides complete protein: that is, all of the essential amino acids the body needs.

- It's a round grain that has a nutty flavor and tender texture. Be sure to rinse it before cooking because it has a bitter coating.

- The quinoa will expand to 4 times its volume after cooking, so plan amounts accordingly.

- Cracked wheat usually just has to be soaked in hot or boiling water until tender; follow package directions.

Add Vegetables

- Tabbouleh is usually made from just cracked wheat. Adding another grain enhances flavor, nutrition, and interest. Wild rice or barley would also be good.

- Classic vegetables used in tabbouleh are cucumbers, tomatoes, and green onions.

- Edamame, or soybeans, is another unusual tabbouleh ingredient. The nutty taste and slightly crunchy texture are delicious.

- You could use black beans, cannellini beans, or great northern beans instead of the edamame.

MAIN COURSE SALADS

177

TUNA OR SALMON SALAD

Tuna salad is updated with fresh fruits in an easy and delicious main dish salad

Tuna salad is a staple of box lunches, while salmon salad is a little more upscale. Either one of these fatty fish is delicious in main dish salads.

These rich-tasting fish combine well with fruits and vegetables, so you can go sweet or savory with the dressings and other ingredients.

You can use canned tuna or salmon, or look for the fairly new pouch varieties. The pouch salmon doesn't have bones, and is packed in very little liquid.

For the freshest tasting salads, cook tuna or salmon yourself. Grill or broil tuna or salmon steaks for 10–12 minutes, let cool, then flake and use. *Yield: 6 servings*

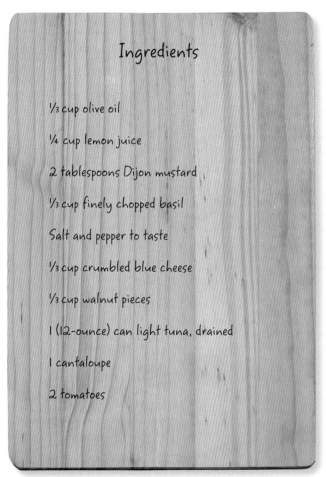

Ingredients

⅓ cup olive oil

¼ cup lemon juice

2 tablespoons Dijon mustard

⅓ cup finely chopped basil

Salt and pepper to taste

⅓ cup crumbled blue cheese

⅓ cup walnut pieces

1 (12-ounce) can light tuna, drained

1 cantaloupe

2 tomatoes

Cantaloupe Tomato Tuna Salad

- In large bowl, combine olive oil, lemon juice, mustard, basil, salt, and pepper and mix well.

- Blend in blue cheese and walnuts. Flake tuna and stir into dressing; set aside.

- Cut cantaloupe in half and scoop out seeds. Using a melon baller, make as many melon balls as possible.

- Cut tomatoes into 8 wedges and cut each wedge in half. Add cantaloupe and tomato to salad; stir gently. Serve immediately or chill for 2–3 hours.

You have several choices when buying canned salmon and tuna. Sockeye salmon is red salmon, which is the best qualify of canned fish, and it's the most expensive with the richest flavor. Pink salmon is less expensive and will work just fine in burger recipes. Chunk light tuna has the lowest mercury level of all canned tuna. Also look for tuna labeled "dolphin safe" for lowest mercury levels.

• • • • RECIPE VARIATION • • • •

Salmon Pepper Salad: Brush 1 salmon steak with 1 tablespoon olive oil. Grill over direct medium heat for 10–12 minutes until done. Cool. Combine 1 cup creamy Italian salad dressing, ¼ cup sour cream, ¼ cup grated Parmesan, salt, and pepper. Add salmon along with 1 each red, green, and yellow bell pepper and ⅓ cup chopped green onion. Stir, chill, then serve.

Prepare Cantaloupe and Tuna

- A melon balling tool is a good choice for most quick and easy kitchens.

- Not only will it make perfect balls from melons, cantaloupe, butter, and ice cream, it can be used to seed apples and pears.

- Canned tuna flakes easily. Be sure to drain it well. Light chunk tuna has the least amount of mercury.

- If you're using your own cooked tuna, work it with your fingers and it will flake naturally.

Blend Salad

- Don't overmix salads that use canned meats; the meat will fall into tiny pieces and won't be apparent in the salad.

- Cantaloupe and tomato may sound like a strange combination, but it's really delicious.

- Both "fruits" are sweet and juicy, and the slight tartness of the tomato complements the super-sweet melon.

- Stir this salad again before serving. The ingredients don't absorb the dressing, so it needs to be recombined before you eat it.

TOFU STIR-FRY

Tofu and noodles are stir-fried with vegetables in this hearty and healthy main dish

Tofu, that much-disparaged meat substitute, can be delicious when properly prepared. It's very good for you, so making it taste great is the way to get your family to love it.

There are several different types of tofu. Soft or silken tofu is used for puddings and dressings. The type of tofu you want for stir-frying is firm or extra-firm.

For best results, drain the tofu before you add it to the marinade. Place on a plate and top with another, resting a can on top to weight it down. Let drain for fifteen to twenty minutes, then use as directed in recipe. The tofu will absorb flavors from the marinade. Then add your own flavors and favorite ingredients to create a delicious tofu dish. *Yield: 6 servings*

Ingredients

2 tablespoons low-sodium soy sauce

¼ cup teriyaki sauce

2 tablespoons rice wine vinegar

1 cup vegetable broth

1 (14-ounce) package extra-firm tofu, drained

12 ounces spaghetti pasta

2 tablespoons peanut oil

1 onion, chopped

1 (16-ounce) package frozen stir-fry vegetables

½ cup water

2 tablespoons cornstarch

Tofu Lo Mein

- In large bowl, combine soy sauce, teriyaki sauce, vinegar, and vegetable broth.

- Cut drained tofu into 1-inch pieces. Marinate in soy sauce mixture for 10 minutes. Bring a large pot of water to a boil. Cook pasta in boiling water according to package directions.

- Heat oil in wok or large skillet over medium-high heat. Add onion and vegetables; stir-fry for 5–6 minutes. Drain tofu, reserving marinade, and stir-fry for 2 minutes.

- Add water and cornstarch to marinade and add to wok with drained spaghetti. Stir-fry for 2–3 minutes until hot.

~ VARIATIONS ~

Garlic Tofu Stir-Fry

Prepare 14-ounce package firm tofu. Combine 3 tablespoons soy sauce, ¼ cup cider vinegar, and ⅓ cup vegetable broth; marinate tofu 15 minutes. Drain; add 1 tablespoon cornstarch to marinade. Stir-fry 1 cup each sliced carrots, cauliflower florets, and chopped onion with 5 cloves garlic in 1 tablespoon oil. Add tofu; stir-fry 3 minutes. Add marinade; stir-fry until thickened.

Mushroom Tofu Stir-Fry

Prepare 14-ounce package firm tofu. Mix ¼ cup oyster-flavored mushroom sauce, 1 teaspoon chili paste, ½ cup vegetable broth, and 2 tablespoons soy sauce. Marinate tofu 10 minutes. Drain; add 1 tablespoon cornstarch to marinade. Stir-fry 1 cup each sliced cremini, button, and portobello mushrooms, 1 red bell pepper, and 1 cup green beans. Add tofu, stir-fry, add marinade; stir-fry until thickened.

Marinate Tofu

- Firm and extra-firm tofu are solid enough to stir-fry and grill. Real labels carefully to make sure that's what you're buying.

- When you press out the excess liquid, these forms of tofu take on the texture of meat.

- Cut tofu using a sharp knife. Be sure the cubes are all about the same size so they heat evenly.

- Any Asian marinade can be used in place of the homemade version. Use your favorite in this easy recipe.

Stir-Fry Vegetables

- The vegetables take longer to cook to a crisp-tender state than the tofu does to heat up, so add them first.

- Taste some of the vegetables when you think they're done. The color will intensify as they cook.

- When they are easy to bite into but still have some texture, they're done.

- The vegetables continue to cook when the tofu is added and when the sauce cooks, so be sure to take that into account.

RISOTTO

Classic risotto is updated with soybeans and roasted garlic for a delicious meal

Risotto is an elegant classic Italian dish that seems complicated and difficult. Not only is it easy to make, but it can be prepared, start to finish, in just thirty minutes.

The keys to risotto are to use Arborio, or short-grain rice, and to stir almost constantly with a metal spoon. Arborio rice has lots of starch, and stirring constantly makes the rice release that starch, which creates the creamy sauce.

If you want this to be a vegan dish, you can omit the butter that's stirred in at the end. Add a tablespoon or 2 of olive oil instead, along with some vegan cheese.

You can add any vegetable you'd like to risotto, and flavor it with your favorite herbs and spices. Have fun! *Yield: 4 servings*

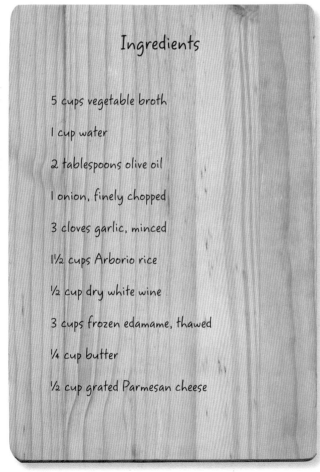

Ingredients

5 cups vegetable broth

1 cup water

2 tablespoons olive oil

1 onion, finely chopped

3 cloves garlic, minced

1½ cups Arborio rice

½ cup dry white wine

3 cups frozen edamame, thawed

¼ cup butter

½ cup grated Parmesan cheese

Garlic and Edamame Risotto

- In medium saucepan, combine vegetable broth and water; heat over low heat.

- In large saucepan, heat oil over medium heat. Add onion and garlic; cook and stir for 6 minutes.

- Add rice; cook and stir for 3–4 minutes. Add wine; cook and stir until absorbed. Gradually add the hot broth mixture, ½ cup at a time, stirring constantly.

- After 20 minutes, the rice should be al dente and the sauce creamy. Stir in edamame, butter, and cheese; cover; cook 3–4 minutes, then stir and serve.

Arborio rice is an Italian short-grain rice. That means the rice has a lot of amylopectin, a type of starch that has lots of branches. Those branches trap and hold moisture, which makes the rice stickier when it's cooked. The rice releases that starch when it cooks, making the sauce creamy.

• • • • RECIPE VARIATION • • • •

Asparagus Risotto: Heat 6 cups vegetable broth in saucepan. Cook 1 chopped onion, 2 cloves garlic, and 1½ cups arborio rice in 2 tablespoons olive oil. Gradually add broth, stirring constantly, ½ cup at a time. When ¾ of the broth has been added, stir in 2 cups asparagus pieces. Keep cooking. When done, stir in ½ cup Parmesan cheese.

Cook Onion, Garlic, and Rice

- The onion and garlic flavor the oil, which in turn flavors the rice, so the whole dish tastes good.

- Be sure that the onion and garlic, and any other root vegetables you add, are thoroughly cooked before you add the rice.

- The oil you choose for the risotto can be mild, or highly flavored to add more flavor to the finished dish.

- Sauté the rice in the oil to start the cooking process and add a nutty flavor.

Stir Risotto

- If there's one secret to risotto, it's to stir the rice almost constantly with a metal spoon.

- The physical manipulation of the rice helps break down its cells, which lets the starch release into the cooking liquid.

- Add the broth ½ cup at a time, which is about a ladleful. Then cook and stir until the liquid is absorbed.

- This method of adding the liquid also helps break down the rice, so the sauce is nice and creamy.

MICROWAVE BEANS AND RICE

Beans and rice, a classic New Orleans dish, is updated in the microwave oven

Beans and rice has kind of a low-country flair about it. Yet it's been nourishing populations for generations. And it's delicious, as well as being so good for you.

Beans, or legumes like kidney beans, black beans, pinto beans, and cannellini beans, don't provide complete protein. You need to add grains or vegetables so your body gets all the amino acids it needs. That's where the rice comes in. Rice provides the missing amino acids so the whole dish is hearty and nutritious.

The combination of flavors and textures is delicious, too; beans are the perfect foil to tender rice. Flavor this dish with everything from hot peppers to cheese. *Yield: 6 servings*

Ingredients

- 2 tablespoons olive oil
- 1 onion, chopped
- 4 cloves garlic, minced
- 3 cups vegetable broth
- ½ cup water
- 1½ cups medium-grain rice
- 2 (15-ounce) cans kidney beans
- 1 cup chopped celery
- 1 red bell pepper, chopped
- ½ teaspoon dried oregano leaves
- ⅓ cup chopped fresh cilantro
- ¼ teaspoon Tabasco sauce
- Salt and pepper to taste

New Orleans Red Beans and Rice

- In microwave-safe casserole, combine olive oil, onion, and garlic. Microwave on high for 3–4 minutes until tender.

- Stir in vegetable broth and water along with rice. Cover and microwave on high for 14–18 minutes until rice is almost tender.

- Drain beans and rinse; drain again. Stir into rice mixture along with remaining ingredients.

- Microwave, uncovered, on high for 2–3 minutes, stirring once, until rice is tender and mixture is hot. Let stand for 5 minutes, then serve.

~ VARIATIONS ~

Black Beans and Rice
Cook onion and garlic in oil in microwave as directed. Add 1 cup uncooked long-grain white rice and 3 cups vegetable broth. Cover and microwave on high for 15 minutes. Stir in 2 (15-ounce cans) rinsed and drained black beans, ⅓ cup seafood cocktail sauce; microwave for 3 minutes. Stir in 1 cup grated Gouda cheese; let stand, stir; serve.

Spicy Beans and Rice
Cook onion and 2 minced jalapeños as directed. Add 1 cup uncooked long-grain white rice and 3 cups vegetable broth. Cover; microwave on high 15 minutes. Add 2 cups sausage crumble substitute, 2 (15-ounce) cans pinto beans, 1 tablespoon chili powder, and 14-ounce can diced tomatoes. Microwave 3–5 minutes. Stir in ⅓ cup chopped cilantro; serve.

Microwave Onion and Garlic

- The microwave cooks onions and garlic very evenly and quickly. If you want to add other root vegetables, do it now.

- Stir the vegetable mixture well so the edges don't overbrown or burn and the food cooks through.

- If your microwave is over 1,000 watts, stir the rice mixture once during the cooking time.

- Be careful; the microwave dish will be hot. Always use hot pads when you remove the dish, and watch out for steam.

Add Red Beans

- You can really only use canned beans in the microwave oven. Dried beans won't absorb the water evenly.

- Be sure to drain, rinse, and drain the beans very well. The sweet liquid they are packed in isn't very desirable.

- The dish has to stand for at least 5 minutes, but no longer than 15–20, after it finishes cooking.

- The rice will absorb the last bit of moisture, and the flavors will blend during this standing time.

GRILLED VEGETABLES WITH TOFU

A dry rub is usually used on the grill, and adds superb flavor to mild tofu and veggies

Yes, you can grill tofu. Extra-firm tofu can be grilled directly on the grill rack. You may want to grill softer tofu on a grill mat, so it doesn't break on the grill and fall into the fire.

Vegetables develop a wonderful extra dimension of flavor when they're grilled. Root vegetables develop a lot of sugar, and the caramelization from the heat adds complex tastes.

To get grill marks on the tofu and vegetables, when you place them on the grill, leave them alone for a few minutes. Pick one up with some tongs; if it releases easily, turn it over and leave it alone again.

Have fun grilling tofu with these easy recipes. *Yield: 6 servings*

Ingredients

1 pound extra-firm tofu, drained

2 tablespoons olive oil

1 teaspoon ground ginger

1 teaspoon salt

1 tablespoon sugar

½ teaspoon ground cloves

1 teaspoon anise seeds

½ teaspoon pepper

2 green bell peppers, sliced

2 onions, sliced

2 yellow summer squash, sliced

2 cups baby carrots

½ cup teriyaki sauce

Asian Rubbed Tofu and Veggies

- Drain tofu by weighting with a plate for 20 minutes, then cut into 1-inch slices. Brush with olive oil.

- In medium bowl, combine ginger, salt, sugar, cloves, anise, and pepper; sprinkle $^2/_3$ over tofu and rub in.

- Toss vegetables with remaining ⅓ of the dry rub and place in grilling basket.

- Grill tofu over medium direct heat, turning once, until browned, about 4–5 minutes. Grill vegetables in basket at same time. Toss with teriyaki sauce and serve.

~ VARIATIONS ~

Tofu Veggie Kabobs

Drain and press 1 pound extra-firm tofu. Marinate it for 15 minutes in ⅓ cup zesty Italian salad dressing. Skewer on metal kabobs along with red onion wedges, 2 bell peppers cut into strips, and 2 cups whole cremini mushrooms. Grill over direct medium heat, brushing with more salad dressing, 5–7 minutes. Serve immediately.

Grilled Tex-Mex Tofu

Drain and press 1 pound extra-firm tofu. Rub with 1 tablespoon chili powder, 1 teaspoon dried oregano, 1 teaspoon cumin, and ¼ teaspoon cayenne pepper. Cut into 1-inch slices. Grill along with 3 bell peppers, cut into strips, and 4 ears of corn, cut into 3-inch pieces. Brush all with 1 cup salsa while grilling.

Put Dry Rub on Tofu

- Tofu is a flavor sponge; it will absorb the flavors you cook it with. Build layers of flavor with a rub and a marinade.

- So think about your favorite grilled flavors and add them to the recipe.

- A dry rub will add more intense flavors than a marinade. Make sure you rub it in evenly.

- There are many dry rubs you can purchase already completed. Keep one on hand for impromptu grilling.

Grill Tofu and Vegetables

- To give tofu a meatier texture, freeze it and defrost it before flavoring with a dry rub or marinade and grilling.

- Tofu, even when cut into larger slices, grills quickly. You can grill it just until warm, or let the edges get crisp.

- The vegetables can also be threaded on skewers instead of being in the grill basket.

- This recipe can be grilled ahead of time and served at room temperature if you'd like. There aren't any perishable ingredients.

MICROWAVE RISOTTO

The microwave cooks risotto quickly and easily, with a lot less work than stovetop methods

You can make risotto in the microwave oven. Because most microwaves have a turntable, the mixture is moving as it cooks.

If your microwave does not have a turntable, stir the risotto several times while it's cooking so the grains of rice are agitated a bit.

Traditional risotto usually starts with a ladle full of white wine for flavor. The wine is quickly absorbed and adds a lot of flavor to the dish. The alcohol will not cook off, so take that into consideration. Flavored vinegars are a good substitute for the wine.

Have fun making your own microwave risotto. Try Tex-Mex flavors, Greek risotto, or an Italian version. *Yield: 4 servings*

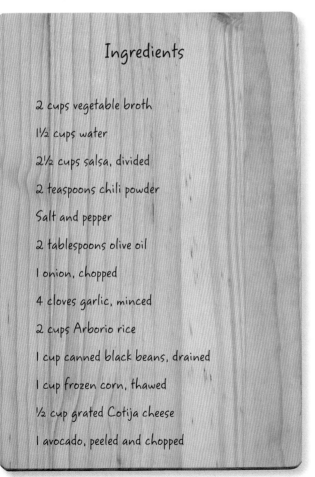

Ingredients

2 cups vegetable broth

1½ cups water

2½ cups salsa, divided

2 teaspoons chili powder

Salt and pepper

2 tablespoons olive oil

1 onion, chopped

4 cloves garlic, minced

2 cups Arborio rice

1 cup canned black beans, drained

1 cup frozen corn, thawed

½ cup grated Cotija cheese

1 avocado, peeled and chopped

Tex-Mex Risotto

- In 1½ quart dish, combine broth, water, ½ cup salsa, chili powder, salt, and pepper. Microwave on high 3–4 minutes until simmering.

- Combine olive oil, onion, and garlic in 3-quart dish. Microwave on high for 2 minutes. Add rice; microwave for 1 minute.

- Add broth mixture. Cover and microwave on 50 percent power 10 minutes.

- Stir in remaining ingredients except cheese and avocado; cover and cook on 50 percent power for 7–8 minutes. Stir in cheese and avocado; cover; let stand for 4 minutes. Stir and serve.

~ VARIATIONS ~

Classic Italian Risotto
Microwave 1 chopped onion and 3 cloves garlic in 2 tablespoons oil. Stir in 2 cups Arborio rice; microwave 2 minutes longer. Add ½ cup white wine and 3½ cups warmed vegetable broth; cover; microwave 10 minutes until rice is tender. Stir in ⅓ cup grated Parmesan cheese and 2 tablespoons cream. Cover; let stand 5 minutes. Stir and serve.

French Risotto
Microwave 1 chopped onion and 4 cloves garlic in 2 tablespoons oil. Add 2 cups Arborio rice; microwave for 2 minutes. Add 1 cup white wine, 1 teaspoon dried herbes de Provence, 3 cups vegetable broth. Microwave 10–12 minutes until tender. Stir in ½ cup Parmesan cheese, 2 tablespoons fresh thyme, 3 tablespoons butter. Stir and serve.

Add Rice

- Microwave the rice for a bit before adding the broth so it absorbs some of the onion and garlic flavor.

- Because the spices and salsa are added with the broth, the rice will absorb their flavors and so will the sauce.

- Use the technique of adding spices to the liquid no matter what type or flavor of risotto you are making.

- Some spices, like curry powder, benefit from this much cooking time because the flavors develop.

Stir Risotto

- The key to risotto is tasting the rice. Take some out, blow on it because it's hot, and taste it.

- The rice should be tender, with a slight firmness in the center. This is al dente, which means "to the tooth."

- The avocado is added at the very end, when cooking is done, because it turns bitter when heated.

- Form leftover chilled risotto into balls, roll in bread-crumbs, and fry for a nice appetizer.

SLOW-COOKER VEGETARIAN SOUP

Textured vegetable protein looks and tastes like ground beef, but is much healthier

The slow cooker is a perfect vehicle for making soups, especially vegetarian soups. All you have to do is add the food, turn it on, and come back hours later to a perfectly cooked soup.

Root vegetables cook particularly well in the slow cooker. Because they are so dense, they are usually placed in the bottom of the appliance, where they are close to the heat

and covered with liquid. In a soup, the root vegetables can be stirred together with all the other ingredients and they will become nice and tender.

Variations on slow cooker soups are very easy. Be sure to write down your wonderful changes to these basic recipes.
Yield: 6 servings

Ingredients

2 (15-ounce) cans kidney beans, rinsed

1 (12-ounce) package meatless crumbles

1 onion, chopped

2 cups baby carrots, chopped

2 jalapeño peppers, minced

3 cups tomato juice

1 cup water

2 (14.5-ounce) cans diced tomatoes, undrained

1 tablespoon chili powder

¼ cup tomato paste

Vegetarian Slow Cooker Chili

- Be sure that the kidney beans are drained, rinsed, then drained again.

- Combine all ingredients in 4-quart slow cooker and stir well.

- Cover and cook on low for 7–8 hours, or on high for 3–4 hours, until chili is blended and hot.

- You can thicken the chili by mixing 2 tablespoons cornstarch with ½ cup water. Add to the slow cooker; cook on high for 20 minutes until thick.

For best results, make sure that the slow cooker is one-half to two-thirds full. Any less food, and it will overcook and burn in the allotted time. Any more, and the food will be under cooked. Soup recipes are very forgiving, so reduce or increase ingredient amounts.

Slow Cooker Lentil Soup: Combine 2 cups lentils, 5 cups water, 6 cups vegetable broth, 1 cup salsa, 1 chopped onion, 4 cloves garlic, 3 chopped carrots, 3 peeled and diced potatoes, 1 teaspoon salt, 1 teaspoon dried basil leaves, and 28-ounce can stewed tomatoes in a 5-quart slow cooker. Cover; cook on low 8–9 hours.

Layer Ingredients in Slow Cooker

- Soups cooked in the slow cooker are very flavorful because no evaporation takes place during the cooking process.

- Volatile flavor compounds are kept in the appliance with the food, so add spices and herbs judiciously.

- Also, since there is no evaporation, don't fill the slow cooker with liquid. The vegetables will give off liquid as they cook.

- Vary your chili by using different types of beans, other salsas, and vegetables like peppers and mushrooms.

Add Cornstarch to Chili

- Cornstarch is the best quick thickener for soups cooked in the slow cooker; flour takes longer to thicken.

- Be sure that the cornstarch is thoroughly dissolved in a small amount of liquid before you add it to the soup.

- If the cornstarch isn't dissolved, the soup will have lumps, which is not desirable.

- Cook for 20–30 minutes on high to activate the cornstarch. Add other tender ingredients like peas at this time, too.

VEGETABLE STIR-FRY

Classic vegetable stir-fry is flavored with ginger and hoisin sauce in this easy recipe

Vegetarian main dishes are healthy, colorful, and delicious. Remember the complete proteins that your body needs? You don't need to eat them all at one sitting. Complete proteins can be spread over the day's meals. And that means you can eat a straight vegetable meal with no problem.

Vegetables stir-fry so beautifully. The quick cooking method

preserves color, texture, and vitamins and minerals. And it's easy to add flavor to these simple stir-fry recipes. Fresh herbs, spices, and condiments like soy sauce, mustard, hoisin sauce, and teriyaki sauce can all be found in vegetarian versions.

Have fun making your own vegetarian vegetable stir-fry recipes. *Yield: 4 servings*

Ingredients

1 tablespoon cornstarch

½ cup vegetable broth

2 tablespoons low-sodium soy sauce

2 tablespoons peanut oil

1 onion, chopped

3 cloves garlic, minced

1 tablespoon minced gingerroot

1 cup baby carrots, sliced lengthwise

1 cup snow peas

2 cups sliced mushrooms

Ginger Stir-Fried Vegetables

- In small bowl, combine cornstarch, vegetable broth, and soy sauce; mix and set aside.

- In large skillet or wok, heat peanut oil over medium-high heat. Add onion, garlic, ginger, and carrots.

- Stir-fry for 4–6 minutes until vegetables are crisp-tender. Add snow peas and mushrooms.

- Stir-fry for 2–4 minutes longer until all vegetables are crisp-tender. Stir soy sauce mixture and add to skillet; stir-fry for 2–3 minutes until sauce bubbles.

• • • • RECIPE VARIATION • • • •

Sesame Vegetable Stir-Fry: Combine ½ cup vegetable broth, 1 tablespoon cornstarch, 2 teaspoons sesame oil. Stir-fry 1 pound green beans, 1 chopped onion, 2 minced garlic cloves, and 1 cup sliced carrots in 1 tablespoon oil until crisp-tender. Add 1 cup grape tomatoes and broth mixture; stir-fry until thickened. Top with 2 tablespoons toasted sesame seeds.

Prepare Gingerroot

- Fresh gingerroot looks like a complicated creature from space, but it's easy to prepare.

- First cut off a piece about an inch long; this will provide you with about a tablespoon of grated or minced ginger.

- Then use a swivel-bladed vegetable peeler or sharp paring knife to remove the rough skin and expose the juicy flesh.

- Then mince the ginger or grate it. Add the ginger to the pan along with any juices produced.

Stir-Fry Vegetables

- Vegetables like onion and garlic, which take time to mellow, and carrots and potatoes, which are hard, are added to the skillet first.

- More tender vegetables, like mushrooms, bell peppers, and tomatoes, are added last.

- You'll know the vegetables are done when they are crisp-tender and their color is very bright.

- That means that when you bite into one, it yields in your mouth but there's still a bit of crunch in the center.

RICE AND TOFU STIR-FRY

Firm tofu is an excellent stir-fry ingredient; paired with rice and veggies, it's delicious

Tofu in a stir-fry really does act like a meat substitute. Its slightly chewy texture, with crisp edges from the heat, is similar to meat, and the tofu can absorb any flavor you add to the dish.

Always use cold rice when stir-frying. The starch in the rice has had time to reform while it chills, making the rice firm enough to stand up to the rigors of stir-frying. The grains will be separate and have good texture.

Classic stir-fried rice is made with soy sauce; vegetables like onions, garlic, grated carrots, and peas; and an egg or two. You can add tofu to any stir-fried rice recipe to increase the protein content. *Yield: 6 servings*

Ingredients

1 pound extra-firm tofu, drained

3 tablespoons oyster-flavored mushroom sauce

2 tablespoons low-sodium soy sauce

1½ cups vegetable broth

1 tablespoon cornstarch

⅛ teaspoon pepper

2 tablespoons peanut oil

2 cups broccoli florets

2 cups sliced mushrooms

3 cups cold cooked rice

Savory Rice and Tofu Stir-Fry

- Drain and press tofu and cut into 1-inch cubes. In small bowl, combine mushroom sauce, soy sauce, broth, cornstarch, and pepper; pour over tofu.

- In large skillet or wok, heat peanut oil over medium-high heat. Add broccoli; stir-fry for 4 minutes.

- Add mushrooms; stir-fry for 3–4 minutes longer until crisp-tender. Add rice; stir-fry for 2–3 minutes.

- Drain tofu; add to skillet; stir-fry for 2–3 minutes. Stir sauce and add to skillet; stir-fry for 2–3 minutes until bubbly.

Stir-Fried Rice with Tofu

Prepare ½ pound firm tofu. Cut into ½-inch cubes; toss with 2 tablespoons soy sauce. Stir-fry 1 chopped onion and 2 cloves minced garlic in 2 tablespoons oil. Add 1 cup grated carrots and tofu; stir-fry 3 minutes. Add 3 cups cold cooked rice; stir-fry 3 minutes. Beat 2 eggs with 1 tablespoon soy sauce and 1 teaspoon sesame oil; add to skillet. Stir-fry; serve.

Peanut Rice with Tofu

Prepare ½ pound firm tofu. Cut into ½-inch cubes; toss with 1 teaspoon ground ginger. Stir-fry 1 chopped onion in 2 tablespoons oil. Add 1 chopped green bell pepper and tofu; stir-fry 3 minutes. Add 3 cups cold cooked brown rice; stir-fry 3 minutes. Add ½ cup peanut sauce and ½ cup chopped peanuts; stir-fry and serve.

Prepare Sauce

- Oyster sauce really is made from oysters. It's a thick, highly concentrated sauce used in small quantities in stir-fry recipes.

- For vegetarians, use oyster-flavored mushroom sauce that has the same taste and properties. Look for it in the health food aisle.

- You could substitute hoisin sauce for the oyster sauce; the dish will be less savory and sweeter.

- Don't marinate the tofu longer than 10–15 minutes. Just let it stand while you prepare the other ingredients.

Stir-Fry

- Use only firm or extra-firm tofu in stir-fry recipes, and be sure to drain and press it before use.

- Make sure that the rice is very cold before you add it to the skillet. Warm rice will just clump together and be sticky.

- Long-grain white or brown rice is a better choice for stir-frying than medium- or short-grain rice.

- The long-grain rice stays separate, while the shorter grain rice tends to clump together.

VEGETABLE AND BEAN PACKETS

Beans and vegetables are a hearty and filling combination for one-dish meal packets

You don't need meat to make a hearty one-dish meal! A mixture of vegetables and beans is filling and delicious. These vegetable packets are great for entertaining, too. You can make them ahead of time and store them in the fridge, then bake when you're ready to eat.

These packets can also be cooked on the grill. The smoky fla-

vor added by the grill enhances the vegetables and beans. If you poke some holes in the bottom of the foil packet for recipes without sauce, that smoky flavor will permeate the food.

If you're entertaining a crowd, there's sure to be a vegetarian or two. If you're caught unaware, pull out this easy and delicious recipe. *Yield: 4 servings*

Ingredients

I tablespoon olive oil

I onion, chopped

3 cloves garlic, minced

I (16-ounce) package frozen broccoli and cauliflower mixture, thawed

2 (15-ounce) cans cannellini beans

¼ cup vegetable broth

½ cup crumbled feta cheese

Feta, Bean, and Veggie Packets

- Preheat oven to 425 degrees F. Tear off 4 18-inch x 12-inch sheets of heavy duty foil, or 4 sheets of parchment paper.

- Combine olive oil with onion and garlic in small bowl; toss to coat. Divide among foil pieces.

- Top with drained vegetables, and rinsed and drained cannellini beans.

- Drizzle each with vegetable broth and top with feta cheese. Fold foil over or crimp parchment paper. Place on cookie sheets; bake for 15–20 minutes until hot.

Potato Bean Packets

On 4 12-inch x 18-inch sheets of foil, divide 6 diced small red potatoes, 2 cups grated carrots, 15-ounce can drained black beans, 1 chopped onion, 4 cloves minced garlic, and 2 cups cut green beans. Combine 3 tablespoons mustard with 1 tablespoon olive oil and 1 teaspoon dried Italian seasoning; spoon over vegetables. Fold and grill for 18–22 minutes.

Peas and Corn with Beans

On 4 12-inch x 18-inch sheets of foil, divide 2 cups frozen baby peas, 3 cups frozen corn kernels, 2 cups frozen edamame, 1 chopped onion, 3 cloves minced garlic, and 15-ounce can drained kidney beans. Drizzle with ½ cup zesty Italian salad dressing. Fold and bake at 425 degrees F for 20 minutes.

Layer Ingredients on Foil

Add Cheese

- Always drain thawed vegetables; too much water from the veggies will ruin the recipe.

- Thaw frozen vegetables by letting them stand in the refrigerator overnight. Or you can thaw under cool running water.

- Make sure you always drain canned beans, rinse the beans thoroughly, and drain again before using in recipes.

- You can drizzle a little bit of flavored vinegar or flavored oil on the vegetables before you close the packets.

- If you're serving strict vegetarians or vegans, just don't add the cheese. Top the vegetables with salsa or chili powder.

- If you grill the packets, move them around several times on the grill, using a large spatula.

- Be careful when you un-wrap the packets, because a lot of steam will billow out, and steam can burn.

- The foil itself will quickly lose heat, but the food inside the packets is very hot.

MICROWAVE STUFFED POTATOES

Stuffed potatoes are an excellent choice for a vegetarian dinner; they can be flavored many ways

The microwave is an excellent appliance for cooking potatoes. They don't need much preparation, and the end result is a steamed potato with fluffy flesh.

In the microwave, timing depends on how much food you put in it, especially when cooking dense foods like potatoes and other root vegetables. Add two to three minutes for each extra potato. Standing time after cooking is particularly important with potatoes. Because they are so dense, it takes time for the heat to travel through the potato and cook it evenly.

Stuffing ingredients are easily cooked in the microwave, and the finished potato heats in minutes. *Yield: 8 servings*

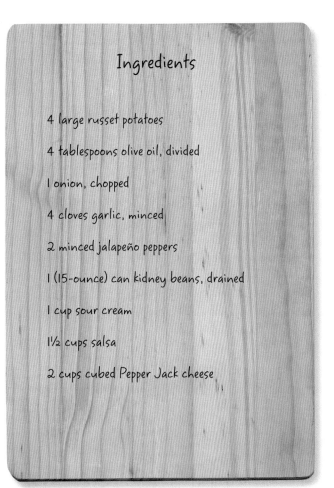

Ingredients

4 large russet potatoes

4 tablespoons olive oil, divided

1 onion, chopped

4 cloves garlic, minced

2 minced jalapeño peppers

1 (15-ounce) can kidney beans, drained

1 cup sour cream

1½ cups salsa

2 cups cubed Pepper Jack cheese

Tex-Mex Stuffed Potatoes

- Scrub potatoes; prick with fork. Rub with 1 tablespoon olive oil. Microwave on high for 10–14 minutes, turning over once, until tender.

- Remove potatoes; let stand 10 minutes. Cut in half and scoop out flesh; place in bowl. Beat in 2 tablespoons olive oil.

- Combine 1 tablespoon olive oil, onion, garlic, and jalapeño peppers in microwave-safe dish. Microwave on high for 3–4 minutes.

- Add beans, sour cream, salsa, and cheese, then beat into potato flesh. Stuff skins. Microwave on high for 6–8 minutes until hot.

~ VARIATIONS ~

Buffalo Stuffed Potatoes

Scrub 4 large potatoes and rub with olive oil. Microwave on high for 10–14 minutes; let stand for 10 minutes. Cut potatoes in half; place flesh in bowl. Beat in ¼ cup butter, 1 cup sour cream, ⅓ cup Louisiana-style hot sauce, 1 teaspoon Tabasco sauce, and 1 cup crumbled blue cheese. Stuff shells; microwave as directed until hot.

Cheddar Stuffed Potatoes

Scrub 4 large potatoes and rub with olive oil. Microwave on high for 10–14 minutes; let stand for 10 minutes. Cut potatoes in half; place flesh in bowl. Beat in ¼ cup butter, 1 cup prepared onion dip, 2 cups shredded cheddar cheese, and ⅓ cup chopped green onion. Stuff shells and microwave as directed until hot.

Prepare Filling

- The microwave is a good choice for cooking foods like onions, garlic, and jalapeño peppers.

- The heat will break down some of the strongest compounds in those foods and bring out the sweetness.

- Be sure to add the kidney beans, sour cream, and salsa to the hot onion mixture first, then add the cheese so it doesn't melt.

- You can make the filling mixture while the potatoes are cooking the first time in the microwave oven.

Hollow Out Potatoes, Mix Filling

- The potatoes have to stand on a solid surface for 10 minutes after they finish cooking, so the heat distributes and the flesh is evenly cooked.

- When you scoop the flesh from the skins, be sure to leave about ¼ inch of flesh for a sturdy container.

- The potato filling will have a better texture if you first add fat to the hot flesh, then everything else.

- The fat coats the potato starch, separating it and preventing it from becoming gluey.

STEAMED VEGETABLES WITH RICE

Bamboo steaming baskets make a beautiful dinner

Steaming is one of the healthiest and easiest ways to cook vegetables, especially a large quantity. You can use one large steamer basket, or, for a prettier presentation, fill several bamboo baskets and layer them over simmering water.

The rice should be cooked before you steam the vegetables, so it's ready and waiting for them. A rice cooker is a great way to cook the grains to perfection, and takes some pressure off you. Vegetables that steam well include mushrooms, onions, garlic, asparagus, green beans, bell peppers, broccoli, snow peas, sugar snap peas, thinly sliced carrots, peas, zucchini, and summer squash.

Steam a combination of your favorite vegetables for an easy and fresh-tasting dinner. *Yield: 6 servings*

Ingredients

2 cups brown rice

4 cups vegetable stock

2 tablespoons low-sodium soy sauce

1 pound fresh asparagus

1 pound cremini mushrooms, sliced

1 red onion, chopped

¼ cup teriyaki sauce

2 tablespoons water

¼ cup toasted sesame seeds

Steamed Asparagus with Brown Rice

- In large saucepan, combine rice, stock, and soy sauce. Bring to a simmer, then cover, reduce heat, and simmer for 35–40 minutes until rice is cooked.

- When rice is halfway done, prepare asparagus by snapping off ends. Cut into 2-inch lengths.

- Combine with mushrooms and onion in steamer basket. Set over simmering water; steam for 6–10 minutes until tender.

- When rice is done, fluff with fork and stir in steamed vegetables along with teriyaki sauce, water, and sesame seeds.

~ VARIATIONS ~

Asian Steamed Broccoli with Rice

Cook 1½ cups brown rice in 3 cups vegetable stock. Cut 1½ pounds fresh broccoli into florets and chop 1 onion. Place in steamer baskets along with 2 cups chopped broccoli rabe. Combine 2 tablespoons each olive oil, soy sauce, 2 cloves minced garlic, and ⅛ teaspoon cayenne pepper; drizzle over broccoli. Steam for 10–14 minutes; serve with rice.

Steamed Squash with Rice

Cook 1½ cups brown rice in 3 cups vegetable stock. Cut 2 medium zucchini and 2 yellow summer squash into ⅓-inch slices and place in steamer. Add 1 chopped red onion, 2 cloves minced garlic, and 2 red bell peppers, julienned. Drizzle with 2 tablespoons olive oil, salt, and pepper. Steam for 7–10 minutes; serve with rice.

Prepare Vegetables

- If you bend asparagus toward the end of the stalk, it will naturally break where the stalk becomes tough.

- Discard the tough ends or save them and freeze to use when making vegetable broth.

- Always choose vegetables that have approximately the same cooking time when steaming. Or remove veggies from the basket when they're done.

- Since vegetables cook at different rates, cook the harder vegetables before adding the tender veggies so they are all crisp-tender.

Finish Dish

- If you're steaming a large amount of vegetables, place them in separate bundles in the steamer so you can remove as they cook.

- For a beautiful presentation, you can mix the rice with the steamed vegetables.

- Then place in individual bamboo steamer baskets and stack over hot water until it's time to serve.

- If you have leftover rice, you have another meal! Stir-fry the rice with some garlic and add frozen peas and a beaten egg or two.

201

PASTA WITH VEGETABLES

A classic meatless vegetable pasta sauce is hearty and delicious

Vegetables add great color, texture, and flavor to pasta. You don't even need the cheese! You can toss plain sautéed or steamed vegetables with pasta, or simply add more vegetables to a traditional pasta sauce.

You can use traditional pasta sauce vegetables, which include tomatoes, mushrooms, onions, and garlic, or add unusual vegetables to shake up the meal.

Unusual spaghetti sauce add-ins include green beans, as-paragus, soybeans, kidney and black beans, zucchini, and carrots. All of these foods will really increase the fiber and nutritional content of the meal.

If you don't want to add cheese to top these mixtures, sauté some whole wheat breadcrumbs in olive oil until crisp, then use that. Yum. *Yield: 6 servings*

Ingredients

3 tablespoons olive oil

I onion, chopped

4 cloves garlic, minced

2 (14.5-ounce) cans diced tomatoes with Italian seasoning, undrained

I cup chopped Roma tomatoes

2 teaspoons sugar

½ cup dry white wine

I teaspoon dried basil leaves

½ teaspoon crushed red pepper flakes

I pound spaghetti pasta

½ cup grated Romano cheese

Pasta Pomodoro

- Bring a large pot of salted water to a boil. Meanwhile, in large saucepan, heat olive oil over medium heat.

- Add onion and garlic; cook and stir until tender, about 5–6 minutes. Remove pan from heat and add canned tomatoes.

- Return pan to heat and add fresh tomatoes, sugar, wine, basil, and red pepper flakes. Bring to a simmer; simmer for 8–10 minutes.

- Cook pasta according to package directions until al dente. Drain and add to sauce; simmer for 1–2 minutes, sprinkle with cheese.

Heavy-on-the-Veggies Pasta

Boil a pot of water. Sauté 1 chopped onion, 2 cloves garlic, 1 cup grated carrots, and 1 pound asparagus pieces in 2 tablespoons olive oil. Sprinkle with salt, pepper, and thyme. Cook 12 ounces pasta; drain. Reserve ½ cup cooking water. Add pasta, water, and 1 cup chopped tomatoes to onions; cook and stir. Sprinkle with cheese; serve.

Veggie Garbanzo Bean Pasta

Boil a pot of water. Sauté 1 chopped onion, 4 cloves garlic, and 1 cup grated carrots in 2 tablespoons olive oil. Add 16-ounce jar pasta sauce, 1 chopped yellow summer squash, 2 cups sliced mushrooms, 15-ounce can drained garbanzo beans, 1 teaspoon Italian seasoning; simmer. Cook 12 ounces pasta, drain, add to sauce with salt and pepper.

Chop Vegetables

- Fresh chopped tomatoes in a sauce, even when you're using canned tomato products, adds great flavor.

- The sugar helps to counter the tomato's acidity. Only add a teaspoon or two. You won't taste the sugar in the finished sauce.

- Any finely chopped vegetables, even carrots or other root vegetables, are delicious in this sauce.

- Add a few tablespoons of salt to the water you use to cook the pasta so it's well flavored.

Top Spaghetti with Sauce

- Pomodoro sauce is usually served with angel hair pasta. That pasta can be difficult to cook correctly because it cooks so fast.

- Spaghetti or linguine pastas are both perfectly acceptable alternatives for this flavorful sauce. Or use shorter pastas like penne.

- You can substitute fresh basil leaves for the dried if you have them on hand. Use 1–2 tablespoons minced fresh basil.

- And experiment with different cheeses to top the recipe. Try grated Havarti, Gouda, Asiago, or Swiss.

PANTRY PIZZAS

Refried beans are the secret ingredient for these rich pizzas

Pizzas are one of the best and simplest quick and easy recipes. Once you have the crust down, top your pizza with anything you'd like, from sautéed vegetables to grilled meats to black beans and cheese.

With your well-stocked pantry, you will be able to make pizzas with a crust and some simple ingredients. Some of the best pizza ingredients include refried beans, tomato sauce, mustard, and legumes like black or pinto beans.

Even the cheese can be from the pantry! The pregrated Parmesan cheese in the green can is supposed to be stored at room temperature.

So look through your pantry, use your imagination, and have fun creating pizzas practically out of thin air! *Yield: 6 servings*

Ingredients

2 tablespoons olive oil

1 onion, chopped

1 (6-ounce) can tomato paste

½ cup water

1 cup salsa

1 (15-ounce) can refried beans

1 (15-ounce) can pinto beans

2 large premade seasoned pizza crusts

2 cups shredded cheddar cheese

1 cup shredded Pepper Jack cheese

Refried Bean Pizza

- Preheat oven to 400 degrees F. In large saucepan, heat olive oil over medium heat. Add onion; cook and stir for 5 minutes.

- Add tomato paste; let paste brown in spots without burning. Add water; scrape pan to loosen drippings.

- Add salsa, refried beans, and drained pinto beans to skillet; heat through.

- Place crusts on cookie sheet. Spread with bean mixture, and sprinkle with cheeses. Bake for 25–30 minutes until cheese is melted and brown.

Bean and Veggie Pizza

Preheat oven to 400 degrees F. In bowl, combine 15-ounce can drained black beans, 15-ounce can drained corn, 1 cup tomato sauce, 4-ounce jar drained mushrooms, ½ cup chopped red onion, 1 teaspoon dried oregano, 2 tablespoons mustard, ½ cup Parmesan cheese. Spread on one large prebaked focaccia. Bake for 20–25 minutes until pizza is hot.

Italian Flag Pizza

Preheat oven to 400 degrees F. Drain 14-ounce can diced tomatoes. Combine with 1 cup taco sauce, ¼ cup tomato paste, 1 tablespoon bottled garlic, 1 teaspoon dried basil, salt, and pepper. Spread on prebaked pizza crust. Drain 15-ounce can spinach very well; drop over sauce. Top with 1 cup grated Parmesan. Bake for 20–25 minutes until hot.

Mix Sauce

- You can find refried beans made with pinto beans or made with black beans; it's your choice.

- The beans are very thick, so they should be mixed with some kind of sauce before spreading on the crust.

- Some canned vegetables that would be good in this pizza sauce include canned corn, green beans, and mushrooms.

- Be sure that the sauce isn't too wet; it should be thicker than pancake batter. If it's too wet, heat it until it's thicker.

Finish Dish

- To prebake the crust, roll it out on a greased cookie sheet sprinkled with cornmeal.

- The crust should be about ¼ inch thick. Bake at 400 degrees F for 10 minutes. Remove and top.

- Cheese is really the finishing touch on most pizzas. You can use cheeses from the fridge or from the pantry.

- Cheese is a good indicator of pizza doneness. When the cheese is melted and browning in spots, the pizza is done.

REFRIGERATOR PIZZAS

As long as you have a crust, you can make pizza using items in your refrigerator

Your refrigerator is a rich source of pizza toppings. A pizza is a great way to use up leftovers, whether those leftovers are sliced hard boiled eggs, grilled steak, cooked beans, or chopped tomatoes.

If you top a pizza with foods that are already cooked, it shouldn't bake or grill very long, because you're only reheat-ing the food. In that case, the pizza crust should be prebaked so it will become crisp in the same time.

If you top a pizza with uncooked foods, like chopped bell peppers or mushrooms, it should bake or grill for a longer time period. And you can start with an unbaked crust. Enjoy making pizzas seasoned with imagination. *Yield: 6 servings*

Ingredients

I cup ricotta cheese

I cup diced mozzarella cheese

I egg

I teaspoon dried Italian seasoning

⅛ teaspoon pepper

⅓ cup chopped flat leaf parsley

I baked pizza crust

I cup sliced kalamata olives

¼ cup chopped sun-dried tomatoes in oil

½ cup crumbled blue cheese

Blue Cheese Olive Pizzas

- Preheat oven to 400 de-grees F. In bowl, combine ricotta, mozzarella, egg, Italian seasoning, pepper, and parsley.

- Spread onto a prebaked pizza crust. Top with olives, drained tomatoes, and blue cheese.

- Bake for 20–30 minutes until cheese melts and browns. Let cool for 5 min-utes, then cut into quarters to serve.

- You can top the pizza with fresh tomatoes or salsa at this point for a contrast.

Pizza Crust

Mix 2 cups flour, ½ cup whole wheat flour, and ½ cup cornmeal. Dissolve 2 packages yeast in 1¼ cups warm water; add to flour with 2 tablespoons olive oil and 1 teaspoon salt. Mix, then knead. Let rise for 45 minutes; roll into 2 crusts. Bake at 400 degrees F for 10 minutes, then top and bake. Freeze before topping to store.

Scrambled Egg Pizzas

Roll out thawed puff pastry square to 12 inches x 12 inches. Place on cookie sheet; bake at 400 degrees F for 15 minutes. Beat 6 eggs with ⅓ cup milk, 1 teaspoon salt, ⅛ teaspoon pepper. Scramble in 2 tablespoons butter. Spread on crust. Top with 4-ounce can drained mushrooms and 1 cup each shredded Havarti and cheddar cheeses. Bake for 15–18 minutes.

Prebake the Crust

Mix Filling, Top Pizza

- Prebaked crusts stay crisper and hold up better with heavy toppings. You can prebake crusts in advance.

- If you're using focaccia bread (known by the brand name Boboli) for the crust, it doesn't have to be prebaked.

- Crusts should be prebaked until they are firm to the touch. Don't bake them until they are brown.

- Freeze prebaked crusts by wrapping in freezer wrap after they cool. Label and freeze up to 3 months. To use, just top and bake.

- The topping on a pizza can be anything from a basic tomato sauce to a blend of cheeses to scrambled eggs and bacon.

- There should be some cheese on a pizza, simply because it helps hold everything together.

- Other choices for crust include flour or corn tortillas, pita breads, French bread (either sliced or halved), and refrigerated dough.

- Don't top pizzas ahead of time. The topping will soak into the crust and it will all fall apart.

GRILLED PIZZA

Pizza on the grill has a special smoky flavor you just can't get in the oven

Grilled pizza is a relatively new phenomenon. Restaurants discovered it in the 1990s, and it didn't take home cooks long to catch on.

Pizza cooked on the grill has a fabulous smoky flavor. The crust is super crisp and chewy, and the cheese melts to creamy, bubbly perfection. What's not to like?

When you grill dough, there are a few rules to follow. First, make sure that the grill is preheated and that the grate is clean. Oil the grate and oil the crust.

Flip the crust onto the grate from a cookie sheet. As the crust grills, move it around as soon as it's firm, so it cooks evenly.

Have fun creating gourmet pizzas at home. *Yield: 6 servings*

Ingredients

½ pound Italian sausages

1 red bell pepper, sliced

1 green bell pepper, sliced

1 onion, sliced

1 cup pizza sauce

2 tablespoons Dijon mustard

1 prebaked pizza crust

1½ cups shredded mozzarella cheese

Grilled Sausage Pizza

- Preheat grill. Scrape grill; rub with oil. Brush sausages, peppers, and onions with oil.

- Grill sausages directly on grill. Place peppers and onions in grill basket and grill. When sausages are done and vegetables are crisp-tender, remove.

- Slice sausages into ½-inch slices; chop peppers and onion. Combine pizza sauce and mustard.

- Spread sauce mixture on crust. Top with sausages, peppers, onion, and cheese. Return to grill. Grill pizza, covered, rotating pizza occasionally, 6–9 minutes.

If you are going to grill pizzas a lot, you should consider purchasing special equipment. You may want a pizza stone, which is a stoneware round that heats up on the grill. You just add the pizza and it cooks to perfection. You'll definitely need a pizza peel or large spatula to manipulate the pizza on the grill.

• • • • RECIPE VARIATION • • • •

Red Pepper Mozzarella Pizza: Preheat grill. Roll dough to 12-inch circle; brush with olive oil. Cook 1 chopped onion and 3 cloves garlic in 2 tablespoons olive oil. Add 1 chopped red bell pepper, 1 cup chopped tomatoes, 2 tablespoons fresh chopped basil, salt, and pepper. Grill dough; flip. Spread onion mixture on, then 2 cups shredded mozzarella cheese. Grill for 8–10 minutes.

Grill Pizza Dough

Finish Pizza

- Focaccia crust doesn't have to be grilled before it's topped.

- Start with that type of crust for your first attempt so you don't have to flip it.

- When using dough, it may take a bit of practice to get the crust evenly on the grate. Even if it isn't perfect, it will still taste good.

- When the crust is brown and crisp underneath, it's time to flip. Use a pizza peel or large spatulas to flip it onto a cookie sheet.

- If you work fast, you can flip the crust directly back onto the grill and top it. But that's hot work!

- Once the pizza has been flipped, quickly top it with your chosen ingredients.

- Then slide it back onto the grill using the cookie sheet, or grab your pizza peel or large spatulas.

- At this point, cover the grill and cook the pizza until the cheese is melted and browned. Then slide it onto the cookie sheet, cut, and serve.

GRILLED SANDWICHES

Everything is grilled in this sandwich: the vegetables, the spread, and the bread

Grilled sandwiches can go beyond grilled cheese or a tuna melt, although those can be delicious if done well. Think about a grilled vegetable sandwich, or a Cobb salad in a sandwich, or luscious sliced steak grilled with melted Havarti cheese.

You can grill sandwiches on a plain old saucepan, or you can use a fancy sandwich press. In between, there's a stovetop griddle and the dual contact grill. All you really need is a pan, a cover, and a spatula.

The fillings for grilled sandwiches always have to be cooked ahead of time, or be ready to eat as-is. Grill the meat, vegetables, or fruits before you assemble the sandwich, finish on the grill, and enjoy. *Yield: 6 servings*

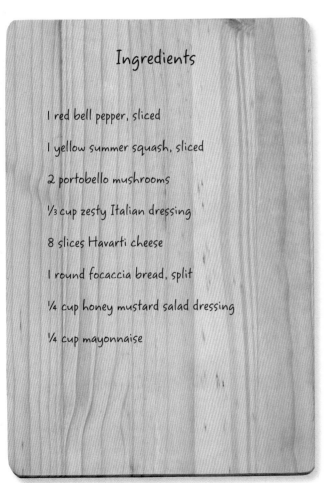

Ingredients

I red bell pepper, sliced

I yellow summer squash, sliced

2 portobello mushrooms

⅓ cup zesty Italian dressing

8 slices Havarti cheese

I round focaccia bread, split

¼ cup honey mustard salad dressing

¼ cup mayonnaise

Grilled Veggie Sandwich

- Combine sliced bell peppers and sliced squash with whole mushrooms and Italian dressing.

- Heat dual contact grill. Grill vegetables in batches until crisp-tender. Let the portobello mushrooms cool for 5 minutes, then slice.

- Spread bottom of focaccia bread with mustard and top with mayonnaise. Place half of cheese, then vegetables, on bottom.

- Top vegetables with more cheese and top of focaccia. Cut into 4 wedges. Grill the sandwiches on the dual contact grill until bread is crisp.

Updated Grilled Cheese Sandwich

Spread 1 side of 8 slices whole wheat bread with 3 table-spoons softened butter. Place bread, buttered side down, on work surface. Divide 4 slices American cheese, 4 large slices tomato, 12 fresh basil leaves, and 4 slices Swiss cheese on half the slices. Combine into sandwiches. Grill, turning once, for 5–7 minutes until cheese melts.

Grilled Brie Cranberry Sandwich

Combine ½ cup whole-berry cranberry sauce with ⅓ cup dried cranberries. Slice 8 ounces of Brie cheese into thin slices. Make sandwiches with 10 French bread slices, the cranberry mixture, cheese, and fresh basil leaves. Spread softened butter on outsides of sandwiches; grill 5–7 minutes.

Grill Vegetables

Grill Sandwiches

- Vegetables grill beautifully on either a dual contact grill, a panini maker, or an electric griddle.

- Cut bell peppers and mushrooms into strips, and onions, zucchini, and summer squash into slices, so they fit on the grill.

- The vegetables will grill for about 2–4 minutes on a 2-sided grill; double that time on a plain grill where they are turned.

- Brush the vegetables with olive oil, salad dressing, or a combination of herbs, oil, and seasonings.

- When you're grilling most foods, you don't press down or the juices will be pressed out.

- Grilled sandwiches are different. Press down with the spatula or the top of the panini grill to melt the cheese and crisp the bread.

- For a makeshift panini grill, cover a clean brick completely with several layers of foil; use that to weight the sandwiches as they cook on a griddle.

- The sandwiches are done when the bread is crisp and brown, and the cheese is completely melted.

DELUXE WRAPS

These healthy and low-fat wraps taste super rich, and they're quick to make

Wrap sandwiches are made by literally wrapping food in a thin bread. Tortillas, whether corn or flour, are usually used, but you can use softened cracker bread or pita breads.

Wraps are served cold or at room temperature. They're not typically cooked before serving, although you can heat them in the microwave oven if you'd like.

These wraps are a great way to use up leftovers. In fact, make them with "planovers." When you're grilling a steak, chicken, or salmon, make one extra and refrigerate it. When it's sliced, it's the perfect filling for a deluxe wrap sandwich with a spread and some veggies. Invent your own deluxe wrap sandwich using your favorite ingredients. *Yield: 6 servings*

Ingredients

2 cups sliced cooked chicken breast

2 tablespoons lime juice

1 teaspoon grated lime zest

1 tablespoon chili powder

½ cup low-fat sour cream

1 (4-ounce) can diced green chiles, drained

6 10-inch flour tortillas

1 yellow bell pepper, thinly sliced

1 cup green salsa

1 cup shredded Co-Jack cheese

Chicken Enchilada Wraps

- In medium bowl, combine chicken strips with lime juice and lime zest; toss and let stand for 5 minutes.

- In small bowl, combine chili powder, sour cream, and chiles and mix. Soften tortillas by wrapping in paper towel; microwave on 50 percent for 1–2 minutes.

- Place tortillas on work surface. Spread with the sour cream mixture and top with sliced chicken mixture and bell peppers.

- Top evenly with salsa and shredded cheese. Fold up bottom of tortilla one turn, fold in sides and serve.

Chutney Ham Wrap

Soften 4 10-inch flour tortillas in the microwave oven. Spread each with a tablespoon of softened cream cheese, then top each with 2 tablespoons mango chutney. Add 1 thin slice boiled ham to each tortilla, then 2 slices Havarti cheese. Roll up, folding in sides. Serve immediately.

Cobb Salad Wraps

Soften 4 10-inch flour tortillas in the microwave oven. Spread each with 2 tablespoons sour cream. Top with 2 tablespoons French salad dressing, chopped red onion, crisply cooked bacon, sliced cooked chicken breast, chopped tomatoes, chopped avocado, and crumbled blue cheese. Wrap up, then wrap in microwave-safe paper towel. Microwave on 50 percent power for 3–5 minutes until cheese melts and sandwiches are hot.

Prepare Chicken & Vegetables

Soften Tortillas

- For wrap sandwiches, slice meats and vegetables fairly thin so they are easy to bite into. You can also chop or dice filling ingredients.

- All wrap sandwiches should have some creamy or cheesy mixture to add moisture to the meats and vegetables.

- Good creamy mixtures include flavored sour cream, softened cream cheese, and creamy salad dressings.

- Tender vegetables can be used as is, but others, like asparagus, carrots, and broccoli, should be cooked first.

- Make sure that you use microwave-safe paper towels for wrapping the tortillas for warming.

- If the tortillas are very dry, sprinkle them with a bit of water before microwaving.

- Not all tortillas will have to be softened. Roll one up; if it rolls without cracking, it's soft enough. Add the filling and wrap it up.

- As soon as the tortillas are softened, use them. They will become hard fairly quickly since the microwave dries them out.

A LA KING SANDWICHES

Puff pastry is the elegant base for these open-faced sandwiches

A la king is an old fashioned type of sandwich recipe that can be updated in many different ways. The basic a la king sandwich is comprised of meat in a creamy sauce, served over some type of bread.

Everyone has had chicken or turkey a la king, served over biscuits, English muffins, or toast points. One of the best ways to update the sandwich is to use more interesting breads as the base.

Puff pastry is one choice. It turns the a la king sandwich into a gourmet treat. And it's easy to use.

You can also change up the creamy meat sauce by adding a lot more vegetables or fruits. Enjoy these easy and elegant sandwiches. *Yield: 6 servings*

Ingredients

2 tablespoons olive oil

1 onion, chopped

1 green bell pepper, chopped

1 cup shredded carrots

3 tablespoons flour

Salt and pepper to taste

1 teaspoon dried thyme leaves

1 cup chicken broth

1 cup milk

2 cups shredded cooked turkey breast

1 cup frozen baby peas, thawed

6 puff pastry shells, baked

Turkey a la King on Puff Pastry

- In large saucepan, heat olive oil over medium heat. Add onion; cook and stir for 5 minutes. Add bell pepper and carrots; cook and stir for 2 minutes.

- Sprinkle with flour, salt, pepper, and thyme; cook and stir until bubbly. Add broth and milk; cook and stir until sauce thickens.

- Stir in turkey and peas; turn heat to low and let simmer for 5–6 minutes

- Bake the puff pastry shells as directed on package. Remove middle section, place on serving platter, and pour turkey mixture over.

214

Ham a la King Sandwiches

Sauté 1 chopped onion, 2 cloves garlic, and 1 chopped yellow summer squash in 2 tablespoons butter. Add 2 tablespoons flour, salt and pepper to taste, ½ teaspoon thyme leaves. Add 1 cup milk; cook until thick. Add 2 cups cubed ham and simmer. Serve over toasted, buttered whole-wheat English muffins.

Steak a la King Sandwiches

Cut 1 leftover cooked rib eye steak into cubes. Sauté 1 chopped onion, 2 cups sliced mushrooms, and 3 cloves garlic in 2 tablespoons butter. Add 2 tablespoons flour, and salt, pepper, and marjoram to taste. Add 1 cup beef broth and ½ cup sour cream along with beef; simmer until hot. Add ½ cup shredded Gouda cheese. Serve over puff pastry shells.

Bake Puff Pastry

- Puff pastry shells are preformed. All you have to do is bake them from the frozen state.

- Then remove the little puffed cap and fill the shells. You can top the sandwich with the cap or just discard it.

- You can also make your own shells from thawed puff pastry. Sprinkle the pastry with grated cheese for flavor.

- Cut into 4-inch squares, place on cookie sheets, and bake at 400 degrees F for 15 minutes until puffed and golden brown.

Prepare Filling

- You can substitute a jar of Alfredo sauce for the flour and milk mixture if you'd like.

- Just cook the onion, bell pepper, and carrot in some olive oil; add the Alfredo sauce, turkey, and peas, and simmer.

- If you're using English muffins, first spread them with butter and toast in a toaster oven or under the broiler.

- To serve the sauce on biscuits, use refrigerated biscuit dough. Sprinkle with cheese and bake as package directs.

NO BAKE COOKIES

Caramel and chocolate are perfect partners in these quick and chewy bar cookies

No bake cookies are so easy to make and delicious. They're the perfect treat to turn to when your kitchen is being remodeled, and they're the right choice for a hot summer day.

Most of these cookie recipes do use the microwave or stovetop. They just aren't baked in the oven.

There are some tricks to making the best no bake cookies.

The most important? Be sure that the sugar is completely dissolved. If it isn't, the cookies will be grainy instead of smooth and creamy.

Once you've mastered a no bake cookie recipe, it's time to experiment. Add your favorite sweet ingredients, everything from white chocolate chips to dried fruit. *Yield: 36 servings*

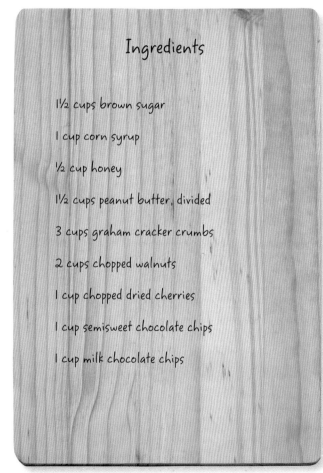

Ingredients

1½ cups brown sugar

1 cup corn syrup

½ cup honey

1½ cups peanut butter, divided

3 cups graham cracker crumbs

2 cups chopped walnuts

1 cup chopped dried cherries

1 cup semisweet chocolate chips

1 cup milk chocolate chips

Chocolate Caramel Bars

- In large saucepan, combine brown sugar, corn syrup, and honey. Bring to a boil; cover pan and boil for 1 minute.

- Uncover pan and boil, stirring frequently, for 3 minutes. Remove from heat and stir in 1¼ cups peanut butter.

- Stir in graham cracker crumbs, walnuts, and dried cherries. Press into greased 13-inch x 9-inch pan.

- In small saucepan, combine chocolate chips with remaining ¼ cup peanut butter. Melt over low heat, stirring until smooth. Pour over bars and coat; let stand until firm.

Slice and Serve No Bake Cookies

Cut 20 large marshmallows into quarters; add 20 crushed graham crackers, and ½ cup dried sweetened cranberries. Stir in 1 cup sweetened condensed milk until a dough forms. Place 1 cup finely chopped nuts on work surface; form dough into a log on the nuts and roll to coat. Wrap in waxed paper; chill for 3–4 hours. Slice to serve.

Marshmallow Peanut Butter Bars

In large bowl, combine 8 cups miniature marshmallows, ½ cup peanut butter, and ¼ cup butter. Microwave on high for 2 minutes; stir. Microwave until smooth. Stir in 5 cups rice cereal flakes, ½ cup chopped dried cherries, 1 cup chopped pecans, 1 cup miniature chocolate chips. Press into 13-inch x 9-inch pan; cool and cut into bars.

Cook Caramel Sauce

- Don't substitute honey for all of the corn syrup in the caramel sauce or the bars will be too hard.

- Cover the pan for a minute when the mixture starts to boil so steam can wash sugar crystals from the pan.

- Any sugar crystals remaining after the mixture boils will "seed" new crystals and the cookies will be grainy.

- You can use crunchy or smooth peanut butter; the choice is yours. The peanut butter makes the cookies chewy and soft.

Add Nuts and Fruits

- Have all of the ingredients prepared and waiting for you before you start to cook the caramel sauce.

- If you have to stop and prepare foods, the sauce will start to set up and it will be hard to mix in the other ingredients.

- Other ingredients that would be good in these cookies include flaked coconut, dried cranberries, and dried currants.

- Adding peanut butter to chocolate for the topping makes the frosting stay creamy and smooth.

DESSERTS

217

FRUIT SALAD

Dress up fruit salad with a white chocolate cream for an elegant last minute dessert

Fruit salad is a refreshing and healthy choice for a quick and easy dessert. You can top it with a sweet sauce if you'd like, or just drizzle with honey and add fresh herbs for an exotic taste.

And yes, herbs do combine well with fruit salads. Mint is the obvious choice, but thyme and basil bring out the sweetness of the fruits. For dessert, you want the most luscious fruits you can find. Peaches, nectarines, strawberries, blueberries, and raspberries are the obvious choices. During the winter months, make a delicious dessert salad from apples, pears, and canned exotic fruits like mangoes or kumquats.

For a finishing touch, use ice cream toppings or just a dollop of whipped cream. *Yield: 6 servings*

Ingredients

¼ cup heavy cream

1 cup white chocolate chips

½ cup ricotta cheese

1 teaspoon vanilla

2 cups sliced strawberries

2 cups raspberries

2 cups sliced peaches

2 tablespoons lemon juice

2 tablespoons honey

White Chocolate Fruit Salad

- In small microwave-safe dish, combine cream and chocolate. Microwave on 50 percent power 1–2 minutes until chocolate melts, stirring at halfway point.

- Stir mixture until smooth with wire whisk. Beat in ricotta cheese and vanilla; place in freezer 15 minutes.

- Meanwhile, prepare and combine fruits in serving bowl. In small bowl, mix lemon juice and honey until combined; drizzle over fruits.

- Remove chocolate from freezer. Beat until fluffy. Serve as a topping.

Strawberry Chocolate Salad

In serving bowl, combine 4 cups sliced strawberries, 1 cup miniature chocolate chips, and 2 cups raspberries. Drizzle with 2 tablespoons best-quality balsamic vinegar and top with 3 tablespoons chopped fresh mint. Serve immediately or cover and chill up to 3 hours.

Lemon Basil Fruit Salad

In serving bowl, combine ½ cup lemon yogurt, ¼ cup sour cream, 2 tablespoons lemon juice, 1 tablespoon orange juice, 2 tablespoons honey, 2 tablespoons minced fresh basil, 1 teaspoon grated lemon zest, and ¼ teaspoon dried basil. Add 2 cups sliced strawberries, 2 cups blueberries, 2 cups blackberries, and 15-ounce drained can mandarin oranges; toss. Chill or serve immediately.

Prepare Fruits

- Preparing fruits is easy; it just takes some practice. Never wash delicate fruits until right before you prepare them.

- Gently rinse the fruits under cold running water, then place on paper towels to dry.

- If the fruit has leaves, like strawberries, cut off the leaves and the top part of the berries and discard.

- Dip peaches in boiling water for 15 seconds. The skins will slip right off. Remove the pit and slice.

Beat White Chocolate Cream

- Ricotta cheese cuts the sweetness of white chocolate in the dessert topping while adding a creamy texture.

- In place of the ricotta, you could use mascarpone, yogurt cheese, or sour cream for a smoother texture.

- You can make the white chocolate topping ahead of time and keep it in the refrigerator.

- Don't beat the white chocolate topping until you're ready to eat. You can use an eggbeater, but a hand mixer is easier and faster.

DESSERTS

219

LAST MINUTE CHEESECAKE

Just 6 ingredients make a cheesecake filling dolloped into tiny tart shells

Cheesecake is usually a complicated recipe, involving lots of measuring, beating, and a long, delicate baking time. But there are faster ways to make a delicious, creamy cheesecake.

To make a cheesecake that doesn't require oven baking, you must use unflavored gelatin or a combination of cream cheese, sweetened condensed milk, and citrus juices.

The gelatin will firm up the sweetened cream cheese mixture in a short time, especially if you're making small cheesecakes. A few minutes in the freezer will make a soft-set cheesecake filling.

Top these cheesecakes with everything from chocolate sauce to fresh to a crumbly, buttery streusel. *Yield: 8 servings*

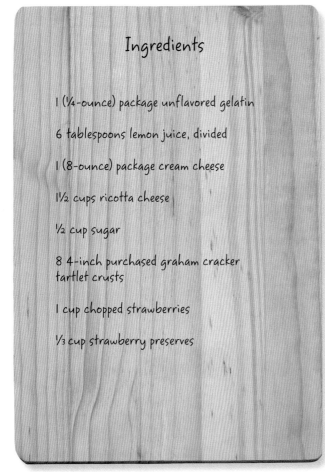

Ingredients

1 (¼-ounce) package unflavored gelatin

6 tablespoons lemon juice, divided

1 (8-ounce) package cream cheese

1½ cups ricotta cheese

½ cup sugar

8 4-inch purchased graham cracker tartlet crusts

1 cup chopped strawberries

⅓ cup strawberry preserves

Berry Swirl Cheesecake

- In small microwave-safe bowl, mix gelatin with 4 tablespoons lemon juice; mix well and set aside.

- In food processor, mix cream cheese, ricotta, sugar; process until smooth.

- Microwave gelatin mixture on high for 30 seconds; repeat until mixture is clear. Add to food processor; process until smooth.

- Dollop ricotta mixture into tartlet shells. In small bowl, combine strawberries, preserves, 2 tablespoons lemon juice; mash with fork. Drop onto cheesecakes and swirl. Cover; freeze 20–30 minutes.

Classic Lemon Cheesecake

In bowl, beat together 8-ounce package softened cream cheese with 2 tablespoons lemon juice, 1 tablespoon orange juice, and ½ cup powdered sugar until smooth. In small bowl, beat ½ cup heavy cream with 1 tablespoon powdered sugar until stiff; fold into cream cheese mixture. Divide among 4 4-inch graham cracker crusts; freeze for 20 minutes.

Quick Orange Cheesecake

In bowl, combine 8-ounce package softened cream cheese, 3-ounce package softened cream cheese, 14-ounce can sweetened condensed milk, 1 tablespoon lemon juice, and ¼ cup orange juice; beat well. Pour into 9-inch graham cracker crust and chill for 2 hours; or into 8 4-inch tartlet shells and chill for 30 minutes. Top with drained mandarin oranges and chopped mint.

Process Cheeses

- The food processor is the quickest way to blend the creamy cheesecake filling.

- You can also beat the mixture using a hand mixer. An eggbeater or wire whisk just isn't strong enough to make the mixture smooth.

- If you soften the gelatin in water instead of lemon juice, add 1 cup melted and cooled semisweet chocolate chips to the cheesecake.

- The cheesecake can be topped with raspberries, chocolate ice cream topping, or granola for crunch.

Finish Cheesecake

- To make your own graham cracker crusts, combine 2 cups crushed graham cracker crumbs with ½ cup chopped nuts and ½ cup melted butter.

- Press mixture into a 9-inch pie plate and chill. Or divide among 8 4-inch disposable pie plates and chill.

- You can make the crusts ahead of time; freeze, well wrapped, for longer storage.

- The cheesecake can be served without chilling; it will be quite soft, more like a firm pudding than a cheesecake.

DESSERTS

221

PARFAITS

Parfaits are a wonderful quick dessert that can be made ahead of time

Parfaits are an elegant dessert. They are very easy to make if you keep just a few ingredients on hand.

All you need is something fluffy, something sweet, and an ingredient like fruit, chopped candy, cookies, or cake. Fluffy ingredients include silken tofu, yogurt, whipped topping, puddings, whipped cream, ice cream, and flavored gelatins.

Pantry items for making parfaits include fruit preserves, cookie crumbs, granola, canned fruit, dried fruits, and pudding mixes. There are infinite varieties of parfaits you can make with these ingredients.

To make the prettiest parfaits, use tall, stemmed goblets, or invest in some attractive parfait glasses. *Yield: 6 servings*

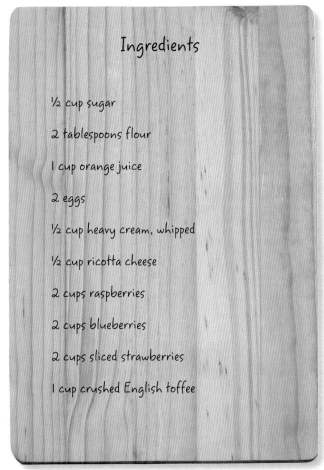

Ingredients

½ cup sugar

2 tablespoons flour

1 cup orange juice

2 eggs

½ cup heavy cream, whipped

½ cup ricotta cheese

2 cups raspberries

2 cups blueberries

2 cups sliced strawberries

1 cup crushed English toffee

Orange Berry Mousse Parfait

- In medium saucepan, mix sugar and flour. Beat in orange juice and eggs.

- Cook mixture over medium heat, stirring with wire whisk, until mixture comes to a boil and thickens.

- Chill mixture in freezer for 30 minutes, stirring occa-sionally. Beat heavy cream until stiff. Beat ricotta into orange mixture, and fold into the cream.

- Layer orange mixture and berries in 6 parfait glasses, ending with orange mixture. Sprinkle with toffee and serve immediately, or cover and chill for 2–3 hours.

Pineapple Crunch Parfaits

In bowl, combine 6-ounce can pineapple-orange juice, 1 cup sour cream, 3-ounce package French vanilla pudding mix, and 8-ounce can drained crushed pineapple. Cover and freeze for 20 minutes. Layer in parfait glasses with 1 cup granola, 2 cups peach chunks, 1 cup blueberries, and 1 cup sliced strawberries. Top with granola and serve.

Dark Chocolate and Strawberry Parfaits

In bowl, combine 8 (3.5-ounce) packages chocolate pudding with 2 tablespoons cocoa powder; mix well. Layer in 4 parfait glasses along with 2 cups sliced strawberries, 1 cup dark chocolate chips, and 1 cup thawed frozen whipped topping. Garnish with mint leaves and serve.

Fold Ricotta into Orange Cream

- It's important to bring the orange cream mixture to a full boil so it thickens properly.

- A wire whisk is the best tool to use to make sure the cream mixture is completely smooth. Work the whisk so it gets into the corners of the pan.

- Beat the ricotta into the orange cream to make sure the mixture is smooth with no lumps.

- Fold the mixture gently into the heavy cream to keep as much volume as possible.

Layer Mousse and Berries

- There are several ways to layer the orange mousse with the berries.

- You can make berries into solid layers; use one layer of strawberries, then the mousse, then one layer of blueberries, and so on.

- Or combine all the berries in a medium bowl and toss gently. Layer this mixture with the orange cream.

- Add texture and crunch to your parfaits by layering toasted nuts, crushed toffee, granola, toasted coconut, or streusel.

DESSERTS

223

MICROWAVE FRUIT TOPPINGS

Apples and pears are great partners in this caramel cinnamon sauce

Fruit toppings, cooked in the microwave or on the stove, are great last minute desserts. Not only are they good for you, but this is a great way to use seasonal produce.

Harder fruits like apples and pears are natural candidates for this type of treatment. But you can also use frozen or canned fruits; just add when the sauce is completed.

These toppings can be flavored any way you'd like. Be adventurous and add some fresh herbs like thyme, mint, rose-mary, or basil. Add fruit juices and honey, or try spices like curry powder or a bit of pepper. Some chocolate, in the form of cocoa powder or melted, is always welcome too. *Yield: 6 servings*

Ingredients

⅓ cup apple juice

½ cup brown sugar

2 tablespoons corn syrup

¼ cup heavy cream

2 tablespoons butter

2 apples, peeled, cored, and chopped

1 pear, peeled, cored, and chopped

2 tablespoons lemon juice

½ teaspoon cinnamon

4 cups ice cream

Apple Pear Fruit Topping

- In microwave-safe casserole dish, combine apple juice, brown sugar, corn syrup, cream, and butter.

- Microwave on high power for 1 minute, remove, and stir. Meanwhile, toss apples and pears with lemon juice and cinnamon.

- Stir fruit into sauce. Microwave on high power for 1 minutes, then stir. Continue microwaving for 30-second intervals until apples and pears are tender.

- Let mixture cool for 20–30 minutes, stirring occasionally. Serve over any flavor ice cream.

Citrus Compote

In microwave-safe dish, combine ½ cup orange juice, ¼ cup sugar, 1 teaspoon vanilla, and 1 tablespoon triple sec; microwave on high for 1 minute. Remove and add 15-ounce can drained mandarin oranges, 1 red grapefruit, cut into sections, and 1 teaspoon orange peel. Microwave on high for 1–2 minutes until hot, then serve.

Cinnamon Maple Apple Topping

In microwave-safe dish, combine ½ cup apple juice, ¼ cup maple syrup, 2 tablespoons brown sugar, and ½ teaspoon cinnamon; microwave on high for 1 minute. Remove and add 2 peeled and chopped Granny Smith apples. Microwave on high for 2 minutes until apples are tender.

Microwave Caramel Sauce

- The sugar must dissolve completely in the sauce before you add the fruit.

- Spoon up a little of the sauce and look at it. If you don't see grains of sugar, it's dissolved. If you do, microwave for another minute on high.

- Be very careful with this sugar syrup. It's very hot and can burn you easily. Always use hot pads when handling the dish.

- You can omit cream from the sauce, but it will harden more quickly and must be used immediately.

Microwave Fruit

- You can leave the skins on the fruit for more nutrition and fiber.

- Because the fruit is tossed with lemon juice to stop enzymatic browning, you can prepare it 30 minutes ahead.

- You can use soft fruits like nectarines, oranges, mangoes, and peaches; just microwave for a shorter time.

- What can you do with the toppings? Serve over ice cream, over plain cake, over bakery cupcakes, or over a frozen pound cake toasted on the griddle.

DESSERTS

GRILLED KABOBS
Grilling caramelizes fruit in this fun dessert

And finally, let's grill some fruit for an easy and healthy dessert. The fruits that grill best include apples, pears, pineapple, peaches, nectarines, strawberries, and oranges.

Very delicate berries like raspberries, blueberries, or blackberries don't take well to the high heat of the grill. Add those fruits after the others have grilled.

Threading the fruit pieces on skewers is the easiest way to handle them. Bamboo skewers, soaked in cold water for 30 minutes, are the best choice for this easy dessert.

If the fruits are too hard for the bamboo to puncture, first make a hole with a metal skewer, then thread the fruits.

A bit of sugar adds a caramelized crunchy crust to the grilled fruit. *Yield: 6 servings*

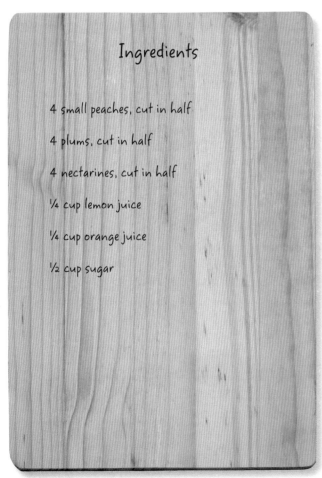

Ingredients

4 small peaches, cut in half

4 plums, cut in half

4 nectarines, cut in half

¼ cup lemon juice

¼ cup orange juice

½ cup sugar

Grilled Peach and Plum Kabobs

- Do not peel fruit. Place fruit, cut side down, in casserole dish.

- Pour lemon juice and orange juice over fruit; lift fruit so juice flows onto cut sides. Let stand for 5–10 minutes.

- Prepare and preheat grill to medium-low. Thread the fruit onto 6 metal skewers, using 4 pieces of fruit per skewer.

- Sprinkle cut sides of fruit with the sugar. Oil the grill rack, then place kabobs on grill, cut side down. Grill for 2–3 minutes, then turn and grill for 1 minute longer. Serve immediately.

You can marinate fruits in many different mixtures. Simple sugar solutions, with an acidic ingredient like orange juice, or a combination of fruit preserves with melted butter would be delicious. You can even try a dry rub with a combination of sugar and sweet and spicy spices.

• • • • RECIPE VARIATION • • • •

Grilled Banana Split: Cut 2 firm bananas into chunks. Thread on 6 bamboo skewers along with 18 large strawberries and 1 cup peach wedges. In shallow bowl, combine ½ cup pineapple juice, 2 tablespoons sugar, ½ teaspoon cinnamon, and 2 tablespoons melted butter. Roll kabobs in this mixture. Grill over direct low heat for 1–2 minutes. Serve with ice cream.

Sprinkle Fruit with Juice and Sugar

Grill Fruit Kabobs

- Lemon juice stops the fruit from turning brown because the acid denatures the enzymes in the fruit cells.

- The juice also adds a fresh, tart flavor to the fruit, and adds vitamin C.

- Sprinkling the fruit with sugar not only helps protect the fruit from the heat of the grill, it adds crunch.

- The sugar will caramelize in the heat of the grill, adding complex flavor and texture contrast to the soft fruit.

- If you're using large fruits, you can thread the fruit on 2 skewers at once. Place the skewers side by side.

- This technique will help prevent the heavier fruit from spinning as you turn the skewers.

- Watch the fruit kabobs closely on the grill, and remove them as the fruit shows grill marks.

- The fruit can burn quite easily, and the sugar coating increases that risk. Don't walk away from the grill while the fruit is grilling.

WEB SITES, TV SHOWS, & VIDEOS
Information for quick cooking

There are many places you can turn to for help and advice in the kitchen. You can find videos, recipes, and lots of tips and hints online; it's almost like having a cooking school right in your home.

Product manufacturers, books, magazines, and catalogs can also help. You'll be able to find information about products, many recipes, quick cooking tips, and where to find special ingredients and tools.

Online message boards and forums are wonderful resources as well. On popular boards, you will get an answer to your questions very quickly. Don't be afraid to ask for help!

Quick Cooking Web Sites

AllRecipes.com
allrecipes.com
- AllRecipes, which features reader-submitted recipes that are rated by members, is a reliable source of quick and easy recipes.

Family.Go
family.go.com/food/pkg-quick-easy-recipes
- This is Disney's Web site; their food section features kid-friendly recipes and ideas, along with quick dinners.

Food Network
www.foodnetwork.com/food/lf_quick_e
- Like the TV shows, the Web site for the food network is packed with information, from recipes to techniques.

Rachael Ray
www.rachaelray.com
- Rachael, one of the original quick cooks, offers many recipes and quick cooking tips

The Six O'Clock Scramble
thescramble.com
- For a $5 subscription, you'll receive a collection of quick and easy dinner menus each week along with tips and grocery list.

Taste of Home
www.tasteofhome.com/simple-delicio magazine
- This Web site features recipes submitted by readers and tested by *Taste of Home* staff. fashioned and updated recipes are reliable and quick.

Yahoo Food
food.yahoo.com/everyday/dinner/qui meals
- Yes, Yahoo has a food site! These great ideas for quick and easy meals will get you out many a tight spot.

Quick and Easy Cooking Videos

About.com Food Videos

video.about.com/food

- Dozens of sites offer hundreds of videos teaching you everything from quick cooking to making desserts and every ethnic cuisine imaginable.

Betty Crocker Videos

www.bettycrocker.com/cooking/cooking-videos

- Who's more qualified to teach you how to cook than Betty Crocker?

Food Network Easy Meals

www.foodnetwork.com/food/easymeals

- Watching videos is a wonderful way to learn how to cook, along with picking up tips to cut time in the kitchen

Free Cooking Videos

www.freecookingvideos.com

- Go back to the basics with the videos on this site; join the site and share recipes.

Great Cooking Videos

www.greatcookingvideos.com

- Hundreds of videos on topics ranging from cooking tips to supplies to Chinese and healthy cooking.

Kraft Foods Videos

www.kraftfoods.com/kf/CookingSchool/Videos/KitchenBasicsVideos.htm

- Kraft Foods can teach you how to cook, and offers great tips for saving time in the kitchen.

Video Jug

www.videojug.com

- Thousands of videos will teach you how to make food from falafel to lasagna and pesto sauce.

Quick and Easy TV Cooking Shows

Nigella Express on the Food Network

- Nigella Lawson, Britain's premier foodie, offers quick and easy meals for families, but with style.

Semi-Homemade Cooking with Sandra Lee on the Food Network

- Sandra Lee developed the concept of "30 percent" fresh food, "70 percent prepared food" for quick and easy meals.

30 Minute Meals with Rachael Ray on the Food Network

- Rachael actually prepares an entire meal, start to finish, in the time it takes you to watch the show.

Quick Fix Meals with Robin Miller on the Food Network

- Robin Miller specializes in the "planover", or cooking more food than you need at one setting to use in later meals.

BOOKS AND MAGAZINES
Hundreds of quick cooking books and magazines are here to help

Quick and Easy Cooking Books

Better Homes & Gardens. **500 Five-Ingredient Recipes.** *BH&G,* 2002
- Kitchen-tested recipes use five ingredients or less; special chapter for kid-friendly recipes.

Editors of *Cook's Illustrated.* **The Quick Recipe.** Cook's Illustrated, 2003
- Quick and easy recipes from "America's Test Kitchen" also shows the steps followed to create the recipe.

Goldfarb, Aviva. **The Six O'Clock Scramble.** St. Martin's Griffin, 2006
- Book is companion to email newsletter that offers five days of dinner menus and recipes, along with a grocery list.

Larsen, Linda. **Everything 30 Minute 5 Ingredient Meals.** Ada 2005
- Book features recipes that use five ingredients or less and can be made, start to finish, in 30 minutes.

Miller, Robin. **Quick Fix Meals.** Taunton, 2007
- Great time-saving strategies and family-friendly recipes from a tir saving expert.

Mills, Beverly, and Alicia Ross. **Desperation Dinners.** Workman P lishing, 1997
- One of the first quick cooking books, this classic offers lots of kitc tips and proven recipes.

Pillsbury. *Pillsbury 30 Minute Meals.* Wiley, 2001
- Pillsbury specializes in quick and easy recipes using their excellent products and scratch ingredients.

Ray, Rachael. *Rachael Ray's Classic 30 Minute Meals.* Lake Isle Press, 2006
- One of Rachael's many quick and easy cookbooks, this collection covers a vast array of flavors and cuisines.

Quick and Easy Magazines

Better Homes & Gardens
- Seasonal recipes, including budget friendly and quick and easy, along with kitchen makeovers and cooking tips.

Every Day with Rachael Ray
- The companion magazine to Ms. Ray's TV show offers many recipes, restaurant reviews, and wine pairings.

Family Circle
- This magazine offers lots of recipes and menus, seasonal recipes and quick cooking tips.

Good Housekeeping
- This venerable magazine focuses on taking care of your home. Kitchen tips and recipes featured in every issue.

Simple and Delicious
- This magazine, from *Taste of Home,* has a collection of quick and easy recipes submitted by readers.

Woman's Day
- Magazine has many quick and simple recipes in each issue, along with cooking lessons and tips.

EQUIPMENT RESOURCES
Find equipment through these resources to stock your kitchen

Catalogs for Kitchen Equipment

Brookstone
- If you need an electric apple peeler or an electronic kitchen gadget, Brookstone has lots of new ideas.

Brylane Home
- Catalog has lots of kitchen equipment, including specialty tools, utensils, and dishware.

Frontgate
- This catalog has top of the line tools and equipment, especially for outdoor kitchens.

Solutions
- Lots of new equipment and tools to make cooking quick and easy.

Sur la Table
- Catalog offers lots of kitchen equipment along with dishes, serving utensils, and flatware.

Williams-Sonoma
- Top of the line equipment, along with cookbooks and many appliances, tools, and accessories.

Web Sites for Kitchen Equipment

Chefscatalog.com
- Web site offers cookware, tools, and appliances like griddles, sma ovens, and coffeepots.

Chefsresource.com
- Cutlery, flatware, gadgets, tools, knives, and brands like Cuisinart featured.

Cooking.com
- Kitchen fixtures, large appliance, cutlery, cookbooks, and tools ca be found at this site.

METRIC CONVERSION TABLES

Approximate U.S. Metric Equivalents

Liquid Ingredients

U.S. MEASURES	METRIC	U.S. MEASURES	METRIC
¼ TSP.	1.23 ML	2 TBSP.	29.57 ML
½ TSP.	2.36 ML	3 TBSP.	44.36 ML
¾ TSP.	3.70 ML	¼ CUP	59.15 ML
1 TSP.	4.93 ML	½ CUP	118.30 ML
1¼ TSP.	6.16 ML	1 CUP	236.59 ML
1½ TSP.	7.39 ML	2 CUPS OR 1 PT.	473.18 ML
1¾ TSP.	8.63 ML	3 CUPS	709.77 ML
2 TSP.	9.86 ML	4 CUPS OR 1 QT.	946.36 ML
1 TBSP.	14.79 ML	4 QTS. OR 1 GAL.	3.79 LT

Dry Ingredients

U.S. MEASURES		METRIC	U.S. MEASURES	METRIC
17⅗ OZ.	1 LIVRE	500 G	2 OZ.	60 (56.6) G
16 OZ.	1 LB.	454 G	1¾ OZ.	50 G
8⅞ OZ.		250 G	1 OZ.	30 (28.3) G
5¼ OZ.		150 G	⅞ OZ.	25 G
4½ OZ.		125 G	¾ OZ.	21 (21.3) G
4 OZ.		115 (113.2) G	½ OZ.	15 (14.2) G
3½ OZ.		100 G	¼ OZ.	7 (7.1) G
3 OZ.		85 (84.9) G	⅛ OZ.	3½ (3.5) G
2⅘ OZ.		80 G	1/16 OZ.	2 (1.8) G

FIND INGREDIENTS

There are many resources for ingredients other than the grocery store

Catalogs and Online Resources

Amazon Grocery

www.agrocerydelivery.com

- Amazon.com has a grocery delivery service. Offers general foods and hard to find items.

The Baker's Catalog

- From King Arthur's Flour, this catalog offers cooking equipment and baking ingredients, including specialty flours and flavorings.

Peapod

www.peapod.com

- Online grocery store serving some areas of the United States

Safeway.com

- Grocery chain offers delivery of food items, as well as recipes and tips for healthy living.

Schwans

- Home delivery service for groceries, serving parts of the United States.

Farmers' Markets

Farmer's Market

www.farmersmarketla.com

- Los Angeles Farmer's Market Web site; the original farmer's market.

Farmer's Market Search

apps.ams.usda.gov/FarmersMarkets

- USDA site lets you search for a farmer's market by state, city, county, and zip code, as well as methods of payment.

National Directory of Farmer's Markets

farmersmarket.com

- Site has index of U.S. Farmer's Markets listed by state.

HOTLINES & MANUFACTURERS
Find help with cooking problems and equipment manufacturers

Hotlines

Butterball Turkey Holiday Line
1-800-323-4848
- Hotline available year round; answers questions about turkey cooking and prepration.

Empire Kosher Poultry Hotline
1-800-367-4734
- Year-round hotline answers questions about poultry.

Perdue
1-800-473-7383
- Year-round hotline helps with cooking questions, especially poultry products.

Reynolds Turkey Tips
1-800-745-4000
- Year-round hotline answers consumer questions about turkey preparation; free recipes.

USDA Meat and Poultry Hotline
1-800-535-4555
- Year-round line offers information about food safety, answers consumer questions about meat preparation.

Manufacturers

Black and Decker
www.bdappliancestore.com

- These sturdy appliances, from can openers to mixers and toaster ovens, are perfect for any kitchen.

GE Appliances

www.geappliances.com

- Outfit your entire kitchen with GE appliances. Online service and customer support.

George Foreman Grills

www.georgeforemancooking.com

- Maker of the dual contact indoor grill, griddles, lots of cookbooks, and customer support.

KitchenAid

www.kitchenaid.com

- Manufacturer of mixers, dishwashers, fixtures, and countertop appliances.

Rival

www.rivalproducts.com

- Manufacturer of the original Crock-Pot, with product information, recipes, and an on-line store.

Thermador

www.thermador.com

- Manufacturer specializes in professional-grade appliances and cookware, from built-in coffee machines to dishwashers and cooktops.

Whirlpool Appliances

www.whirlpool.com

- Company can completely outfit your kitchen, from ranges to wine coolers.

Zojirushi

www.zojirushi.com

- Rice cooker manufacturer, with service, support, and how to use appliances.

GLOSSARY
Learn the language first

RESOURCES

Al dente: Italian phrase meaning "to the tooth" describes doneness of pasta.

Baste: To brush cooking food with a liquid, keep it moist as it roasts or bakes.

Beat: Manipulating food with a spoon, mixer, or whisk to combine.

Blanch: To briefly cook food, primarily vegetables or fruits, to remove skin or fix color.

Broil: To cook food close to the heat source, quickly.

Brown: Cooking step that caramelizes food and adds color and flavor before cooking through.

Coat: To cover food in another ingredient, as to coat chicken breasts with bread crumbs.

Chop: To cut food into small pieces, using a chef's knife or a food processor.

Deglaze: Adding a liquid to a pan used to sauté meats; this removes drippings and brown bits to create a sauce.

Dice: To cut food into small, even portions, usually about ¼" square.

Dry Rub: Spices and herbs rubbed into meats or vegetables to marinate and add flavor.

Flake: To break into small pieces; canned meats are usually flaked.

Fold: Combining two soft or liquid mixtures together, using an over-and-under method of mixing.

Grate: A grater or microplane is used to remove small pieces or shreds of skin or food.

Grill: To cook over coals or charcoal, or over high heat.

Marinate: Letting meats or vegetables stand in a mixture of an acid and oil, to add flavor and tenderize.

Melt: To turn a solid into a liquid, by the addition of heat.

Microwave: An appliance that cooks food through electro-magnetic waves, which causes molecules to vibrate, creating heat.

Pan-Fry: To cook quickly in a shallow pan, in a small amount of fat over relatively high heat.

Shred: To use a grater, mandoline, or food processor to create small strips of food.

Simmer: A state of liquid cooking, where the liquid is just below boil.

Slow Cooker: An appliance that cooks food by surrounding it with low, steady heat.

Steam: To cook food by immersing it in steam. Food is set over boiling liquid.

Stir-Fry: To quickly cook food by manipulating it with a spoon or spatula, in a wok or pan, over high heat.

Toss: To combine food using two spoons or a spoon and a fork until mixed.

Whisk: Both a tool, which is made of loops of steel, and a method, which combines food until smooth.

INDEX

INDEX